LEVITICUS

ABINGDON OLD TESTAMENT COMMENTARIES

ABINGDON OLD TESTAMENT COMMENTARIES

LEVITICUS

TIMOTHY M. WILLIS

Abingdon Press
Nashville

ABINGDON OLD TESTAMENT COMMENTARIES
LEVITICUS

Copyright © 2009 by Abingdon Press

This book is printed on acid-free paper.

Library of Congress Cataloging-in-Publication Data

Willis, Timothy M.
    Leviticus / Timothy M. Willis.
       p.   cm.—(Abingdon Old Testament commentaries)
    Includes bibliographical references.
    ISBN 978-1-4267-0017-0 (binding: pbk./trade : alk. paper)
    1. Bible. O.T. Leviticus—Commentaries.   I. Title.

    BS1255.53.W55 2009
    222'.1307—dc22

                                2008044711

Ancient language fonts were developed in the public domain for scholars who comprise the Society of Biblical Literature, including SPTiberian for Hebrew, SPIonic for Greek, and SPAtlantis for transliteration.

09 10 11 12 13 14 15 16 17 18—10 9 8 7 6 5 4 3 2 1
MANUFACTURED IN THE UNITED STATES OF AMERICA

CONTENTS

CONTENTS

CONTENTS

CONTENTS

CONTENTS

CONTENTS

CONTENTS

FOREWORD

The *Abingdon Old Testament Commentaries* are offered to the reader in hopes that they will aid in the study of Scripture and provoke a deeper understanding of the Bible in all of its many facets. The texts of the Old Testament come out of a time, a language, and sociohistorical and religious circumstances far different from the present. Yet Jewish and Christian communities have held to them as a sacred canon, significant for faith and life in each new time. Only as one engages these books in depth and with all the critical and intellectual faculties available to us can the contemporary communities of faith and other interested readers continue to find them meaningful and instructive.

These volumes are designed and written to provide compact, critical commentaries on the books of the Old Testament for the use of theological students and pastors. It is hoped that they may be of service also to upper-level college or university students and to those responsible for teaching in congregational settings. In addition to providing basic information and insights into the Old Testament writings, these commentaries exemplify the tasks and procedures of careful interpretation.

The writers of the commentaries in this series come from a broad range of ecclesiastical affiliations, confessional stances, and educational backgrounds. They have experience as teachers and, in some instances, as pastors and preachers. In most cases, the authors are persons who have done significant research on the book that is their assignment. They take full account of the most important current scholarship and secondary literature, while not attempting to summarize that literature or to engage in technical academic debate. The fundamental concern of each volume is analysis and discussion of the literary, sociohistorical, theological, and ethical dimensions of the biblical texts themselves.

The New Revised Standard Version of the Bible is the principal translation of reference for the series, though authors may draw upon other interpretations in their discussion. Each writer is attentive to the original Hebrew text in preparing the commentary. But the authors do not presuppose any knowledge of the biblical languages on the part of the reader. When some awareness of a grammatical, syntactical, or philological issue is necessary for an adequate understanding of a particular text, the issue is explained simply and concisely.

Each volume consists of four parts. An *introduction* looks at the book as a whole to identify *key issues* in the book, its *literary genre* and *structure,* the *occasion and situational context* of the book (including both social and historical contexts), and the *theological and ethical* significance of the book.

The *commentary* proper organizes the text by literary units and, insofar as is possible, divides the comment into three parts. The *literary analysis* serves to introduce the passage with particular attention to identification of the genre of speech or literature and the structure or outline of the literary unit under discussion. Here also, the author takes up significant stylistic features to help the reader understand the mode of communication and its impact on comprehension and reception of the text. The largest part of the comment is usually found in the *exegetical analysis,* which considers the leading concepts of the unit, the language of expression, and problematical words, phrases, and ideas in order to get at the aim or intent of the literary unit, as far as that can be uncovered. Attention is given here to particular historical and social situations of the writer(s) and reader(s) where they are discernible and relevant as well as to wider cultural (including religious) contexts. The analysis does not proceed phrase by phrase or verse by verse but deals with the various particulars in a way that keeps in view the overall structure and central focus of the passage and its relationship to the general line of thought or rhetorical argument of the book as a whole. The final section, *theological and ethical analysis,* seeks to identify and clarify the theological and ethical matters with which the unit deals or to which it points. Though not aimed primarily at contemporary issues of faith and life, this section should provide readers a basis for reflection on them.

Each volume also contains a select bibliography of works cited in the commentary as well as major commentaries and other important works available in English.

The fundamental aim of this series will have been attained if readers are assisted not only to understand more about the origins, character, and meaning of the Old Testament writings but also to enter into their own informed and critical engagement with the texts themselves.

Patrick D. Miller
General Editor

INTRODUCTION

M odern people love a good romance. They love stories that show how couples meet and fall in love. A good plot involves some significant conflict or obstacle that the couple must overcome to be together, such as differences in ethnic or socioeconomic backgrounds, parents or friends who object to the relationship, relationships with someone else, or conflicting career goals. The story concludes as they resolve the conflict and "true love" wins out, so that they can "live happily ever after." Of course, most of the "ever after" part of life consists of more mundane activities, but this part of life never makes it into the stories. This is the part of life that consists of long hours spent working in an office, the daily ordeal of getting stuck in traffic, the almost mindless repetition of maintaining the house, dealing with car repairs, cooking meals (and cleaning up afterward), doing laundry, and taking care of dozens of other routine tasks. This part of life barely receives mention in the stories, but it poses its own challenges to a loving relationship. The challenge for the couple is to cultivate an ongoing commitment to keep the love that brought them together vibrant and healthy over many years.

The Old Testament deals with the whole story. It tells about a love story between the Lord and the people of Israel. An exciting and marvelous part of that story takes place in the book of Exodus, as the Lord rescues the people from Egypt and then enters into a covenant relationship (marriage) with them. But the story does not end there. The story of the relationship continues into the "ever after" phase, the phase of routine and repetition and the need to work consistently at maintaining the relationship. The book of Leviticus deals with the "ever after" phase of a relationship.

It is about routine tasks, such as maintaining the house (the sanctuary) and doing the laundry (purification laws). It is about how the people are going to cultivate their commitment to their relationship with the Lord in their daily interactions (rituals) and in special "anniversaries" (regular holy festivals). As in any couple's relationship, some of these activities are designed to turn their thoughts back to the more "romantic" times, moments when their love for each other overcame the obstacles and conflicts that threatened to pull them apart. So Leviticus is not about significant high points and low points in Israel's relationship with the Lord; instead, it is about the everyday business of living in that relationship over many, many years.

LEVITICUS THE BOOK

The book of Leviticus is not about Levites. The name comes from the Greek title, *Leuitikon,* a Hellenistic designation for things having to do with "priests." The Hebrew title, *Wayyiqra',* is merely the first word of the text ("and he summoned"). There is some question, however, regarding the appropriateness of designating Leviticus as a "book." It is difficult, in some sense, to explain how this work stands on its own. Leviticus must have Exodus preceding it to provide a historical context, and it must have more books after it to bring that history to the social context that Leviticus envisions. There is very little narrative within its pages, only a few chapters at one point (Lev 8–10) and a few verses at another (24:10-12). The great majority of it consists of a series of "speeches" made by the Lord to Moses (and Aaron), which he is then to pass on to the priests or the people.

The speeches of Leviticus hold together almost like a long aside between Exodus and Numbers. The book of Exodus concludes with the construction of the Tabernacle, which is to be the Lord's tent for dwelling among the Israelites. The final paragraph of that book speaks of how the people would move themselves and the Tabernacle in order to be with the Lord as the Lord's glory moves from place to place through the wilderness. The book of Numbers continues this train of thought by listing the various tribal groups of Israel and how they are organized for traveling through the wilderness, with the Tabernacle at the center (but also cf. Exod 40:34-38; Num 9:15-23). The book of Leviticus falls between these two texts about movement through the wilderness, focusing on what the people were to do while they were stationary. It is from this vantage point that one can justify the isolation of Leviticus as a separate "book." It is not an insertion or intrusion, but it does constitute a long pause in the narrative flow of the Pentateuch.

The book presents its message in two primary sections. The first is about life in and around the Lord's home ("the tent of meeting," chaps. 1–16), and the second is about life on the property attached to this dwelling (the land, chaps. 17–27). The minimal narrative framework of the divine speeches reflects the context of the Sinai encampment, but the perspective of the speeches eventually takes the reader beyond the immediate context of Sinai to the future context of life in the land of Israel.

LITERARY GENRE, STYLE, AND STRUCTURE

Most of the book is presented in the form of speeches that the Lord addresses to Moses (and Aaron, in chaps. 11–15), which he is to convey to "the people of Israel" and, in some cases, to "Aaron and his sons." Only chapters 8–10 truly break from this pattern; the other short narrative functions primarily as the introduction to a speech on the law of retaliation (24:10-12, 13-22). Similar narrative headings and summaries clearly demarcate the majority of speeches. It is fairly easy to group these speeches into blocks of material, based on contents, common vocabulary, and style. The following represents a general outline derived from these combined features:

Leviticus 1–16—Establishing, Maintaining, and Renewing
  Cultic Purity
  Chapters 1–5—Procedures for primary offerings and sacrifices
  Chapters 6–7—Allotments from each offering
  Chapters 8–10—Account of the ordination of the first priests

Chapters 11–15—Purity standards for food and hygiene

Chapter 16—Renewal of a pure cult after defilement

Leviticus 17–27—Holiness in the Land

Chapter 17—Proper honor for the blood of living things

Chapters 18–20—Interpersonal ethics and morals

Chapters 21–22—Holiness of priests and offerings

Chapters 23–26—Life that conforms to the Lord's holy design (sabbath)

Chapter 27—Fulfillment of vows

Most of the speeches consist of "case law," built on the general structure of extended "When/If... then..." statements. Several speeches include secondary cases that consider variations on the primary case ("But if... then..."). There are only a few examples of apodictic law ("You shall [not]..."). The text addresses the words directly to the people in some laws, either individually (singular "you") or collectively (plural "you"). In other laws, it addresses the audience indirectly and hypothetically ("If anyone...").

Frequently, there is repetition of phrases and clauses within a speech or a small collection of speeches, but none of these permeates the entire book. Several of these repeated phrases occur infrequently—if at all—outside the laws of Leviticus. One stylistic feature common to many of the repeated phrases and clauses involves the use of declarative statements, usually within an introductory clause or a summary clause. For example, several of the instructions for offerings at the beginning of the book conclude with the statement, "It is... an offering by fire of pleasing odor to the LORD." Many of the laws regarding sacrificial allotments and purity begin or end with the statement, "This is the ritual of..." The diagnostic declaration, "It is (un)clean," is common in the purity laws, as is the complementary phrase, "until the evening." In more than a dozen instances, the speaker refers to a prescription as "a perpetual statute/a statute forever." Each of these phrases appears almost exclusively in Leviticus and in a few parallel passages in Exodus or Numbers. Their virtual absence outside this narrow range of books strongly suggests that they are genre specific. This appears to be "in-house language" for the priests.

Somewhat similar is the frequent use of the divine self-declaration formula in the second half of the book ("I am the LORD [your God]"). This formula stands at the opening of the Decalogue, which would easily explain its use in Leviticus and its wider distribution in the Old Testament. Still, the frequency of the formula in Lev 17–27, and the specific ways in which the writer employs it, point to a priestly milieu.

OCCASION AND SITUATIONAL CONTEXT

Chronological markers in Exod 19:1 and Num 1:1 set the assumed historical parameters for the original pronouncement of these speeches within the year that the Israelites were encamped around Mount Sinai. Internal clues within some speeches point to a later date, sometime after settlement in the land of Israel. Detailed knowledge of life in exile in chapter 26 makes a strong case for an exilic date for some portions of the book. It is more difficult to ascertain a clear picture regarding the time when the book of Leviticus was produced in its final form. The minimal narrative framework identifies most of the contents as speeches delivered to and by Moses. This reveals, at the least, the work of a final redactor/compiler other than Moses, who has brought these speeches together into their present configuration. This differentiation between speeches of Moses and a narrator that is presenting them here also opens the door to consider the possibility of multiple redaction layers within the book. Modern redaction critics typically identify two primary sources or layers here, that of the "Priestly Writer" (P) and that of the "Holiness Code" (H). Most restrict the work of H to chapters 17–26 (or 27), while they ascribe the rest of the book to P (along with portions of Genesis, and much of Exodus and Numbers).

Until recently, most redaction critics regarded H as the earlier piece, developing in the monarchic period, probably in the late 8th century or sometime in the 7th century B.C.E. On the basis of a similarity of interests in Chronicles, they argued that P redactors took H and other sources and brought them together to form the Pentateuch following the Babylonian exile. Some recent critics have challenged this reconstruction, and Leviticus has been at the center of their examinations (Knohl 1995; Milgrom 2000a, 1319–67). Two conclusions regarding the evidence have played key roles in this shifting reconstruction. One is that some of the H speeches in Leviticus are derived from laws in P sections of Exodus and Numbers (chap. 23; Num 28–29). The other is that the teachings of Ezekiel depend on the prior existence of some laws in Leviticus, particularly from H. This leads to the preliminary conclusion that H precedes Ezekiel, and then P precedes H. The presence of H language in the conclusions of chapters 11 and 16 lends support to this conclusion.

One major hurdle to such a conclusion is that it requires dating P in the monarchic period, when most scholars see strong evidence for an exilic or post-exilic P redaction of the Pentateuch. What is more, this conclusion glosses over the fact that many of these texts are anachronistic in relation to one another. For example, Moses and Aaron offer sacrifices in Exodus before the Lord gives them the instructions for those offerings in Leviticus. Parts of the Holiness Code assume knowledge of instructions that Moses does not give until late in Numbers.

The preceding considerations lead some critics to posit multiple redactions of P and H, redactions that alternate with one another chronologically. The evidence of conflicting directions of influence betrays a long history of dialogue between competing groups of priests. Other critics contend that the differences between H and P are not significant enough to warrant separating them into distinct sources. For them, differences in subject matter—rather than variant literary sources—explain the linguistic and stylistic distinctions between the Holiness Code (Lev 17–27) and the surrounding chapters of the Pentateuch.

The present commentary will note evidence of sources and redaction layers that scholars identify within a passage, and it will point to connections with other texts; but there will be nothing more than initial speculations about what the evidence proves or disproves about current theories of the overall production of Leviticus and the Pentateuch, and their relation to other parts of the Old Testament. The presentation of a full theory of the literary history of Leviticus entails assessments of texts in several other books, which go beyond the scope of the present treatment of a single book.

Theological and Ethical Significance

Leviticus brings together several important theological themes. It assumes the theological setting of a broken world on the verge of becoming whole once again. The closing chapters of Exodus set the stage, both literally and figuratively. Moses has supervised the construction of the Tabernacle (Exod 35–40), and the text reports the culmination of that process in terms that are reminiscent of the culmination of creation in Gen 2:1-3. Moses "saw" all the "work" that the craftsmen had done ("as the LORD had commanded"), and so Moses "blessed them" (Exod 39:43); and then Moses "finished the work" (40:33). The completion of the Tabernacle imitates the completion of creation; in this little part of the world, the world that the Lord originally intended is being renewed. The book of Leviticus reveals the means by which this renewed world can be maintained. This involves the offering of sacrifices (chaps. 1–7), adherence to rules of purity and holiness (chaps. 8–16 + 17–22), and the observance of the Sabbath on multiple levels (chaps. 23–27).

The text of Leviticus links these ideas directly to existing covenants. In at least one case the text points back to divine promises made to the Israelite ancestors and, perhaps, to Noah (26:42). There are many more direct references to the exodus event, which the compiler interprets on multiple levels. The exodus marks a time when the Lord delivered the people from slavery to the Egyptians, but it is more than that; it also marks a time when the Lord delivered the people from the grasp of a place characterized by death and defilement, in order to bring them to a place of life and purity, where the Lord once again dwells and walks among them.

These concepts are all part of the umbrella theme of covenant in the Pentateuch. The Sinai Covenant (of which Leviticus is a part) defines the terms for living as a holy people, but to live as a holy people is ultimately to respond appropriately to the fulfill-ment of the promises of land, offspring, and blessings made by the Lord in an earlier covenant with this people's ancestors. That covenant, in turn, was to provide a way for "all the families of the earth" to return to the original "blessed" state in which God cre-ated it (Gen 1:28–2:3; 12:2-3). The nation of Israel stands as a microcosm of the whole world, in this respect. If the people con-form their lives to the principles taught here, they will enjoy the life the Creator intended for humans to live. If they do not con-form their lives to these principles, the Lord will deny them access to life with God, just as the Lord God had denied access to the first humans (Gen 3:22-24).

One of the most basic principles in this pentateuchal conception of the world is the principle of life versus death (cf. Deut 30:11-20). The creation story established that God is the source of life, transforming a lifeless world into one teeming with living things. God's blessing on this world was that life would be fruitful and multiply. The sin of human beings introduced death into the world, and the Pentateuch portrays all of human history after that as a struggle between life and death. In this conception of things, life is more than breathing and death is more than its absence. Biblical writers refer to the juxtaposition of these states of being with a rich variety of terms, and the laws of Leviticus stand squarely in a strong stream of images that convey this juxtaposi-tion. Life exists in what is whole and clean, while death exists in what is blemished and unclean; life exists in what is righteous and holy, while death exists in what is sinful and profane. These assumptions permeate laws throughout the book. The system of offerings and sacrifices (chaps. 1–7) rests on the idea that the Lord will accept the life in the blood of certain animals to atone for the lives of humans that have been defiled by sin (17:10-12). The sim-plest rationale for the categorization of animals into "clean" and "unclean" derives from their association with life and death, respectively (chaps. 11, 15). Purification, atonement, and sanctifi-cation essentially involve a shift from the realm of death to the realm of life or, in some cases, the recognition that this shift has already happened. The transformation of one's essential state from death to life happens in some instances merely through the passage of time, but more serious matters require the performance of divinely prescribed rituals to accomplish the transformation.

It is important to recognize that it is the will of the Lord—and not the ritual acts alone—that effects the shift from death to life. The passage of time accomplishes purification because it allows the impure person to enjoy the renewal of life that is inherent to the world that God created (chap. 11). Because the Lord promoted life in each day of creation, each new day brings more life; because the Lord created all of life in a week, the passage of a week (Sabbath) accomplishes a quarantined person's transition into new life (chaps. 8–9, 12–14). It is implied that the Lord is giving new life in all these situations. Any ritual of atonement also assumes God's participation in the process. A person receives atonement because the Lord has "given" the ritual of sacrifice that function, not because the ritual in and of itself possesses a special (magical) force (17:11). Offerings and rituals effect change because God accepts them, not because they possess inherent power. And the change that they effect is to give "life" to someone (or something) that was threatened by "death" to one degree or another.

The latter half of the book develops these ideas in a slightly different direction (chaps. 18–27). Here it is the concept of holiness that predominately conveys the idea of life. Holiness is first a quality of the Lord, the Creator, and thus it is indelibly tied to the notion of life. Humans show holiness through obedience and respect for the Lord (that is, through ethical and moral living, which is adherence to the ways of God). Humans show holiness through imitation of the Lord and the past actions of the Lord on their behalf, and by conforming to the Lord's prescribed organization of time (sabbath) and space (in the land). In all this they understand themselves to be participating in the things of life and rejecting the things of death.

Finally, it would be easy to miss the theological significance of the fact that the book presents all this in the form of divine speeches, speeches communicated through Moses to the priests and the people. This has several implications. One is that there is a sense of mutual accountability among the recipients. The general population hears the instructions that are for the priests, and the priests hear the instructions that are for the general population. Each segment of society can encourage the other to remain faithful to their obligations. Another implication is the subtle message this sends about the authority of prophet-priests like Moses. That authority extends over priests and non-priests alike, and yet it is not absolute, as Aaron's response to Moses in chapter 10 demonstrates. Above all else, the divine origin of these speeches implies the ultimate need for readers to hear (obey) what is said in these pages. The book of Deuteronomy makes this more explicit with its reminder about the people's initially receptive attitude toward the Lord's laws (Deut 5:22-29). That reminder leads into the Shema, the most direct call to obedience (Deut 5:32–6:9). The same idea holds for Leviticus. These are the words of the Lord. Moses delivers them "in the name of the LORD," and so they carry divine authority. The people must "hear" these words and submit to their authority. That authority is not oriented to command and obedience alone, though; it also holds out a promise: a promise of communion with the Lord, who is the source of all life, and a promise of life itself and the continual renewal of life, which is the ultimate goal for humanity that the Lord envisions.

COMMENTARY

LEVITICUS 1–7

The first seven chapters of Leviticus hold together as a unified block, consisting of two sets of instructions. Leviticus 1:1 introduces the block, and 7:37-38 provide a corresponding conclusion. The first set of instructions concerns five primary "offerings" (1:3–6:7 [5:26]), and the second provides corresponding "rituals" (6:8 [6:1]–7:36). These generalizations mask a complicated process lying behind the production of this block.

Scholars generally hold that the first set of instructions is for the general populace, while the second set is for the priests only. This does not precisely reflect the narrative headings present in the text, however, nor the expressed intent of the laws. The narrated passages organize this block as a series of nine messages that "the LORD spoke to Moses":

1:1–3:17—Burnt Offerings, Grain Offerings, and Sacrifices of Well-being
4:1–5:13—Sin Offerings
5:14-19—Guilt Offerings for Unintentional Offenses
6:1-7 [5:20-26]—Guilt Offerings for Offenses against a Neighbor
6:8-18 [6:1-11]—Priestly "Rituals" for Burnt and Grain Offerings
6:19-23 [6:12-16]—The Anointed Priest's Grain Offering
6:24–7:21 [6:17–7:21]—Priestly "Rituals" for Sin Offerings, Guilt Offerings, and Sacrifices of Well-being

1

7:22-27—Prohibition against Eating Fat and Blood
7:28-36—Priestly Portions of a Sacrifice of Well-being

The first set of instructions consists of four messages that Moses is to communicate "to the people of Israel." These instructions relate the guidelines for presenting the five main types of offerings (1:1–6:7 [5:26]). The second set of instructions consists of five messages dealing with the consumption of the offerings (6:8 [6:1]–7:36). This set begins with the fifth message in the book. It contains two "rituals" that Moses is to pass on "to Aaron and his sons." The "rituals" concern priestly responsibilities and privileges involved in the burnt offering and the grain offering. There follows a brief message concerning a special grain offering that the high priest brings "when he is anointed." The seventh message returns to "rituals" concerning "Aaron and his sons" in the remaining offerings. Two final messages concern details about consuming the sacrifices of well-being, but Moses is to address these "to the people of Israel," as was the case in the first four messages.

Questions often arise concerning the arrangement within these two sets of instructions. The first set presents the burnt offering, the grain offering, and the sacrifice of well-being first, and then the instructions for two expiatory offerings. The arrangement of the first three offerings (which comprise one message, sharing a common narrative heading) seems to have been altered by a redactor, who apparently inserted the grain offering between the burnt offering and sacrifice of well-being. The instructions follow a slightly different order in the second set. The compiler keeps the burnt offering and grain offering together, adding a special grain offering (for one type of occasion); but then the expiatory offerings come before the sacrifice of well-being.

Complicating the broader picture is the presence of two summaries in 7:35-38. Verses 35-36 serve as a conclusion to 7:22-34 or to all of 6:8 [6:1]–7:34. This conclusion identifies what precedes it as "the portion allotted to Aaron and to his sons." This might imply the "rituals" in chapters 6–7. On the other hand, it refers to them as "offerings made by fire," a designation used primarily in the first set of instructions (chaps. 1–5). Verse 37 refers to the preceding instructions as "ritual," and the text lists them in the same order as the ritual instructions. However, verse 38 refers to what precedes as "offerings," as in the first set of instructions, and there are clear links in 7:38 back to the introduction in 1:1. The most economical explanation is that 7:35-36 originally functioned as the conclusion to 6:8 [6:1]–7:34 (or just 7:22-34), and then verses 37-38 were added to tie the second set of instructions together with the first set. This implies that the present purpose of 7:37-38 is to serve as a conclusion to all of 1:1–7:36. Curiously, this list includes an "offering of ordination" (Exod 29:22-34; Lev 8:22-36). Perhaps the instructions for that offering have been displaced. In any case, a significant consequence of this summary is that both sets of instructions now fall under the purview of the general population.

It would appear that two complementary sets of instructions regarding different aspects of the same sacrifices have been brought together in the first seven chapters. The first set prescribes cooperative acts of non-priests and priests. The second set concerns the rights of priests alone. The contents of the second set are not for the ears of the priests alone, though. The final units are addressed "to the people" and the offerings must come from them, showing that the general population is privy to all these instructions. Everyone knows what everyone else is to do.

This points to a sense of shared responsibility in Israel's cultic worship. Just as religious leaders had an obligation to instruct the nation in God's laws, so the populace had an obligation to see to it that the priests officiated with integrity. The primary responsibility is to honor the Lord in worship. The first three chapters in particular prescribe the animals that worshipers should use in sacrifice, the preparations they should make, and the procedures they should follow. By following these instructions, the people will give the Lord proper honor and respect.

LEVITICUS 1

The first chapter provides the instructions for the burnt offering. This offering comes first because it is the most common sacrifice and because of the totality of the gift to the Lord. Biblical texts prescribe or report burnt offerings for almost every type of occasion, and burnt offerings often accompany other offerings. They differ from other sacrifices in that the entire animal is destroyed in the fire. The instructions of chapter 1 have in mind voluntary, personal burnt offerings. There are numerous passages that assume the use of burnt offerings at regular, corporate gatherings, at times of repentance for sin, and at times of supplication. It would appear that these instructions (and the others in this block) are intended as examples. The underlying purpose of the burnt offering is to attract the favorable attention of the Lord (Levine 1989, 5-6).

Literary Analysis

The opening verse differs somewhat from the common narrative headings of divine speech in pentateuchal laws. It uses an additional verb ("The LORD *summoned* Moses *and spoke* to him," emphasis added) and identifies the tent of meeting as the setting for this communication. The former verb indicates a major break from the preceding block (Exod 35–40); the latter links the messages in this block to the surrounding blocks in a general way (the Lord is giving instructions). The result is an implicit reminder that these instructions constitute the first laws—temporally and in significance—given by the Lord regarding the use of the Tabernacle. The Lord promised to meet with the people at this location to deliver commands to them (Exod 25:22; 40:17-33), and these messages constitute the first of those commands.

The first message includes all of chapters 1–3. The general form of this message matches that used in much of the legislative material of the Pentateuch. A primary law is introduced by "When" (*kî*) while subsequent subordinate laws begin with "(And) if" (*wĕ'im*). There is some stylistic unevenness, however, in the overall presentation of the commands in these chapters. The initial primary command refers only to animal sacrifices (1:2b). Chapter 2, dealing with grain offerings, also begins with "When," as if starting a new primary law. On the other hand, chapter 3 begins with the subordinate introduction "(And) if," as if the instructions for sacrifices of well-being are a continuation of those for grain offerings. It would be more logical to have the sacrifices of well-being as a continuation of chapter 1; but because grain offerings most often complement burnt offerings, while sacrifices of well-being stand alone, the grain offering was placed after the whole burnt offering. Other stylistic parallels between chapters 1 and 3 reinforce the impression that the placement of chapter 2 is a secondary development.

Most of chapter 1 speaks of the one bringing the sacrifice in the third-person masculine ("When any of you [pl.] bring," v. 2). However, the final phrase of verse 2 shifts to the second-person plural ("you shall bring your offering"). This might indicate an expansion, but perhaps the multiplicity of types of animals prompts the author to shift to a plurality of actors. The primary command in 1:2 mentions only quadrupeds, yet the third form of the burnt offering involves birds (1:14-17). Many literary critics point to such inconsistencies as evidence of revisions within this block of instructions, but it might be wrong to assume that the primary command intends to be specific and comprehensive.

The formulas for secondary laws divide this chapter into three units, each prescribing one of three possible forms for a burnt offering (vv. 3-9, 10-13, 14-17). The order reflects the relative economic value of these animals in descending order (Levine 1989, 5; Jenson 1992, 176). Each unit follows a common structure. Each begins with "(And) if" and then identifies the type of animal to be sacrificed. The basic acts of the sacrifice are described next, including where the animal is to be slaughtered, how the priests are to dispose of the blood, and what they are to do with the parts that remain. Once the animal is completely prepared, it is "turn[ed] ... into smoke ... an offering by fire of pleasing odor to the LORD" (1:9, 13, 17).

Exegetical Analysis

General Heading (1:1-2)

The identification of "the tent of meeting" as the setting for these commands seems to contradict the concluding note in 7:38.

COMMENTARY

This might indicate distinct literary sources. On the other hand, the reference in 7:38 to commands given "on Mount Sinai" could also be translated "at Mount Sinai," meaning near the mountain but not necessarily on top of it (cf. Num 1:1). The term for "offering" in 1:2 is a generic term (Corban; see Mark 7:11), referring here and elsewhere to all of the sacrifices prescribed over the next seven chapters. Clay vessels from the Second Temple period bear this term, indicating that the contents were offerings (Levine 1989, 5, 201).

Burnt Offerings from the Herd (1:3-9)

The designation of "the entrance of the tent of meeting" as the location for this offering denotes the large courtyard east of the main sanctuary (v. 3). A large basin of water and the altar stood in the courtyard. More than denoting a physical location, this phrase reminds the worshipers that they are at the transition area between the divine realm and the human realm. The directive to slaughter the animal "before the LORD" serves the same function (v. 5). The sanctuary faced toward the east, giving the impression that the Lord was facing east as well. The point is to remind the worshipers that the Lord is watching their acts of worship.

The command that the worshiper place a hand on the head of the animal might serve a different purpose than that prescribed for the Day of Atonement (16:21-22). Some believe this gesture transfers sin from the human to the animal, but others assign it one of four other meanings. (1) It could be an act of "identification," showing that the worshiper is coming close to the Lord through the animal, (2) it could be a nonverbal declaration by the worshiper that he or she in particular is bringing the sacrifice, (3) it could indicate a transfer of ownership from the worshiper to the Lord, or (4) it could designate a particular animal as set aside for sacrifice alone.

There has been considerable discussion of the identification of this sacrifice as a means of atonement (v. 4). This is the only mention of atonement in the first three chapters. In the circumstances assumed here, the worshiper is not seeking forgiveness for some specific wrongdoing. Instead, she or he is motivated by the circumstances of the time to honor the Lord, and the burnt offering is a natural way of doing that. These considerations prompt some to say that atonement is a later understanding of this offering, after atonement was considered inherent to animal sacrifices (Jenson 1992, 155-56). Worshipers often brought burnt offerings in times of purification or repentance (12:6-8; Num 15:24). Perhaps this reference reflects that broader usage of this offering. It might also reflect an implicit understanding that on any occasion when a human being approaches the Lord, there is a need for acknowledging the gap that exists between the two (Levine 1989, 6-7; Knohl 1995, 151-52). The placement of the animal's blood on the altar also suggests an expiatory purpose in the sacrifice. Blood represents life (17:11, 14). The Lord is the source of life, and the sacrifice represents life that is given back to its source.

Interpreters dispute the meaning of the phrase, "an offering by fire" ('iššēh, 1:9). This Hebrew term refers most often to portions of sacrifices given solely to the Lord, but it can also include portions eaten by the priests. The term probably is a feminine noun derived from the word for "fire" ('ēš), but it seems redundant to identify a sacrifice as an offering that is burned. Some associate the term with cognate Semitic terms that mean "gift" or "food offering" (Wenham 1979, 56; Milgrom 1991, 161-62). Either derivation would fit in the present context.

It is the final phrase, however, that warrants the most explanation. The statement that a sacrifice is a "pleasing odor to the LORD" seems to accept the common ancient Near Eastern idea that gods consumed a sacrifice by breathing in its smoke. The notion that the Lord would receive physical nourishment or pleasure seems "primitive" or "pagan" to orthodox believers, and it runs contrary to other Old Testament passages (1 Sam 15:22; Ps 50:8-15; Isa 1:11-13; 40:16; Amos 5:21-24). Traditional theologians typically assume that this is an archaic expression, one that was understood in a nonliteral way for most—if not all—of Israel's religious history. The expression probably intends to communicate the Lord's approval and acceptance of the sacrifice, but nothing more. It is common in reference to the first three offerings but occurs only once in the context of sin and guilt offerings (4:31;

Jenson 1992, 156; Knohl 1995, 134-35). This supports the view that a burnt offering is primarily a sacrifice for honoring the Lord as God, rather than an appeal for forgiveness.

Burnt Offerings from the Flock (1:10-13)

The only significant difference with this second type of burnt offering is in the use of a sheep or goat rather than a bull. This difference is warranted by economic necessity. The close similarities in the descriptions of the two sacrifices suggest that the aspects mentioned in one but lacking in the other are understood to apply to both.

Burnt Offerings of Birds (1:14-17)

The ceremony for offering a bird differs in several ways from the two preceding types. The priest, not the lay worshiper, brings the bird to the altar and kills it. Perhaps this indicates not that the worshiper owned the bird, but that the priest provided it. The blood of the bird was drained directly onto the altar, probably because there was not enough to be gathered in bowls and dashed on the altar. There is no explanation for why the priest throws certain internal organs onto the ash heap rather than washing them, as he does with the other animals. Perhaps it was felt that no washing could properly cleanse these parts. In fact, there is no consensus about the identification of the second part of the bird so treated. The term can be associated with the contents of the bird's crop, or with the feathers. Finally, birds were not cut into pieces as the other animals were. The priest would wring off the head and tear the bird open, rather than cut it into pieces. These differences probably derive from the physical differences of the animals, not different literary sources.

Theological and Ethical Analysis

The instructions for the burnt offering omit any explanation of the religious or theological ideas underlying this rite. A plain reading of the text suggests that the physical state of the animal is the sole criterion for determining whether it is acceptable to the Lord.

It must be "without blemish." Two considerations indicate, however, that the spiritual/moral state of the worshiper is the ultimate criterion. First, the impression that the physical state of the animal is primary derives in part from a literal interpretation of the concluding formula, a "pleasing odor to the LORD" (vv. 9, 13, 17). This would also imply that the aroma of one type of animal is more pleasing than that of another, because different animals produce different aromas; but the text makes no distinction between the value of the aromas of these animals. Each is equally pleasing to the Lord. Second, the animal offered has no control over its state of acceptability. It is the responsibility of the person bringing the animal to ensure its worthiness. If the animal is blemished, it is rejected; but ultimately, it is the worshiper's overture to the Lord that is rejected. It is the moral/spiritual state of the worshiper's heart that ultimately affects the "aroma."

The language of "offering" probably implies similar notions. The people are to bring their "offering" (v. 2). Both words come from the same root, meaning "to draw near." The underlying notion is that a person should use special care when "coming near" someone of importance. They would exercise the greatest care, of course, when approaching the Lord, because the Lord is of greatest importance. The closest human parallel to the Lord would be a king. It is possible to manipulate a king with gifts that one "brings near" to him. Some Israelites probably assumed it was just as possible to manipulate the Lord. On the other hand, biblical writers and prophets worked to persuade them that their God is different, that the Lord "is not partial and takes no bribe" (Deut 10:17). One should not conclude that the absence of explicit commands for sincerity means that sincerity was not expected. The opposite is the case. The careful attention to physical details in these laws implicitly communicates the care with which the participants are to attend to spiritual concerns. They do not regard physical aspects as separate and distinct from spiritual aspects.

The notion of "bringing near" should alert the worshiper to the need for sincerity. The primary purpose in presenting offerings is to provide the worshiper with a way to draw near to the Lord. The worshiper desires to be near the Lord, in order to entreat or give thanks or commune with the God of the universe. This is the Lord's desire as well (Exod 29:43-46). Such communion is not naturally possible, though, because of the essential difference between a holy and divine God and unholy humans. The sincerity with which one is willing to do what the Lord demands reflects a humble attitude. It is humility to which the Lord promises to respond favorably, and a truly humble person recognizes that such a response is always an act of grace.

The grace represented in the Lord's favorable response is implied by a willingness to accept sacrifices of varying value. If the Lord were a God swayed by the material value of an offering, one offering would please the Lord more than another. This initial chapter makes it clear that all prescribed offerings are equally acceptable. The acceptance of a poor man's offering demonstrates divine grace, but no more than God demonstrates in accepting the most expensive offering.

LEVITICUS 2

Some think of the grain offering as the "poor man's substitute" for the burnt offering. This might have been its practical function at some time in Jewish history, but the instructions for the grain offering do not reflect that estimation. It is more likely that the placement of these instructions illustrates the practice of accompanying burnt offerings with grain offerings. These instructions were composed when grain offerings were one of several possible offerings, but they were moved to their present location at a time when grain offerings usually accompanied burnt offerings.

The term for "grain offering" refers generically to any sort of gift or tribute in almost three dozen passages (e.g., Gen 32:13; 33:10; Judg 3:15). Many argue that the use of the term here in a restricted sense is a late development, but that is difficult to support. One finds both the restricted sense and the general sense within the same books, and some instances of the general meaning are in late works (e.g., Judg 3:15 and 13:19; 2 Kgs 16:15 and 17:3; and Isa 1:13 and 39:1). It is safer to say this general term tended to have a specialized meaning in sacrificial contexts.

10

Literary Analysis

Syntactical features break these instructions into four or five units (vv. 1-3, 4-10, 11-12/13, 14-16). The introductions and conclusions of the first two units parallel each other, yet only the first speaks of the worshiper in the third person. Verse 1 begins, "When anyone presents a grain offering," while verse 4 begins, "When you [sing.] present a grain offering." The direct address is sustained through the rest of the chapter (plural in vv. 11-12). The first two units contain dual concluding statements. The first half of each follows the pattern of conclusions in chapter 1 (2:2, 9; cf. 1:9, 13, 17), while the second half designates the unconsumed portions as the property of the priests (vv. 3, 10). The second unit of the chapter could almost stand alone (vv. 4-10). The sequence of "When" (v. 4) followed by two instances of "if" (vv. 5, 7) demarcate three equally acceptable ways of preparing the grain offering, complementing the offering introduced by verse 1. The continuation in verses 8-10 applies to all three modes of preparation.

Verses 11-13 break from the typical pattern in significant ways. Modern translations tend to gloss over these differences. While every other sentence in the chapter begins with a conjunction, verses 11, 12, and 13 begin immediately with the object. Sharpening this distinctiveness is the repeated use of "every" (or its opposite, "none/not every") at the beginning of clauses. The addressees are plural in verses 11-12 alone, whereas there is a singular addressee elsewhere. Further, these two verses reveal what must be omitted, not what is to be included. Verse 13 contrasts to verses 11-12 by virtue of its positive stipulation for the inclusion of salt, and it reverts to the single addressee. Yet it is curious that something required for every grain offering is not mentioned before this verse. Also, this is one of only three passages in Lev 1–16 (4:22; 11:44-45) that uses the term "God," and it is the only one that uses the term without "the LORD." The final unit (vv. 14-16) is introduced by "if," which is the common way of introducing a subordinate case. This unit concludes by designating this as "an offering by fire . . . to the LORD," as one finds in 2:3 and 2:11.

These observations suggest that previously separate pieces have been used to construct the chapter. Verses 4-10 are an expanded version of verses 1-3. Verses 14-16 could have stood as corollary considerations to verses 4-10, but verses 11-12 are stylistically intrusive, and verse 13 seems disconnected from what surrounds it. It is common to attribute these differences to either multiple sources or redactions, or both.

Analysis of the contents of these units confirms these literary delineations. The first unit gives general guidelines for preparing the food, and then characterizes it as an offering for the priests and for God (vv. 1-3). The second unit elaborates on the guidelines, prescribing three acceptable means of preparing the same ingredients for a grain offering (vv. 4-10). This unit also ends with a characterization of these offerings as offerings for the priests and for the Lord. The balance of the chapter consists of subsidiary concerns. The third unit calls for the exclusion of leaven and honey (vv. 11-12), while verse 13 requires the inclusion of salt in all grain offerings. The final unit deals with the special procedures one is to use when presenting first fruits as a grain offering (vv. 14-16). This unit is a natural continuation to verses 4-10, which makes verses 11-13 seem all the more intrusive.

Exegetical Analysis

Presentation of Grain Offerings (2:1-3)

The instructions for bringing a grain offering are relatively simple, yet this simplicity masks some complex issues. This general instruction calls for three ingredients: "choice flour," olive oil, and frankincense. There is uncertainty about the procedural details in this general instruction for the grain offering. The first clause of verse 2 tells how the worshiper will bring the offering to the priests (plural). The third clause specifically identifies the priest (singular) as the one who will turn the "token portion" into smoke. The uncertainty arises over the middle clause, regarding the individual who will take "a handful" of the offering to be the "token portion." Modern translations are split on the question, with some extending the actions of the worshiper to include this one (KJV, NAS, RSV, and NJB), while others see the priest as the subject of this clause (NIV, NKJV, and NRSV). At first glance, the former seems to be the more natural conclusion. The only singular antecedent that can naturally serve as the subject of the verbs in this middle clause is the donor. On the other hand, verses 4-10 call for the worshiper to cook the offering first and bring it to the priest, but then the priest is to "remove" the "token portion" and offer it to the Lord. Subsequent references to these procedures confirm the latter reading, sometimes combining "taking a handful" (v. 2) and "remove" (v. 9) in their description (5:12; 6:15). Therefore, while it is possible that the first two units were originally independent, it is just as natural to see them serving complementary functions.

The precise significance of the "token portion" given to the Lord is uncertain (vv. 2, 9, 16). The term derives from the root for "remember," but the text does not specify who is to remember or what they are to remember. Commentators suggest it might be a reminder to the donor of the Lord's grace or majesty or acts of deliverance (Pss 71:16; 77:11), or that it might function as a reminder to the Lord of covenant obligations or the worshiper's good deeds or relative poverty (Ps 112:6; Prov 10:7). Some link it to "invoking" ["causing to remember"] the name of the Lord (Isa 48:1; Amos 6:10). The text indicates the significance of this part of the ritual by characterizing it as another "offering by fire of pleasing odor to the LORD."

The use of frankincense apparently intends to discourage the people from regarding the grain offering as "just another food" made from grain. A couple of texts link the inclusion of frankincense specifically to the notion of "remembrance" or "reminding" (Lev 24:7; Isa 66:3). Others imply a connection between frankincense and one's recognition of the awesome holiness of the Lord (Exod 30:34-38; Num 5:11-15, 23-28). "All the frankincense" of the offering is to go in this memorial portion (2:2, 16). It is possible that the prohibition against frankincense in the sin offering is tied to this as well (5:11). The "token portion" seems intended to remind all involved that this is no ordinary food. It suggests in a special way that this is something "holy." Giving a portion to the Lord and putting all the frankincense in that portion remind the worshiper and priest of that, and it shows the Lord that they remember this fact.

Verse 3 emphasizes the notion of holiness that is attached to the grain offering. Only the priests are permitted to eat of the grain offerings (David and his men being an exception; 1 Sam 21:1-7). The writer justifies this on the grounds that this offering is "most holy." This expression normally refers to the sanctuary (Ezek 43:12; 45:3; 48:12) or the furnishings within it (Exod 29:37; 30:10, 29, 36; 40:10; 1 Chr 23:13), but in Leviticus the portions of the offerings assigned solely to the priests are "most holy" (2:3, 10; 6:17, 25, 29; 7:1, 6; 10:12, 17).

Differences in Preparation (2:4-10)

Verses 4-10 serve in their present state as an alternative to verse 1b. With only minor modifications to verse 4, it would be fairly easy to reconstruct a complete instruction for grain offerings from verses 4-10 that could displace verses 1-3. Verses 4-7 expand on the procedures of verse 1, while verses 8-9 give a slightly more detailed rendition of the information in verse 2, and verse 10 is a carbon copy of verse 3. The most glaring difference is the absence of frankincense from verses 4-10. As they stand, these verses provide three equally legitimate but alternative ways for preparing a grain offering. It could be that these differences reflect distinctions in the economic status of the worshipers, but there is nothing in the text explicitly acknowledging that.

The first alternative for preparing the grain offering is to bake it in an oven. One could prepare the offering in the form of "cakes" or "wafers." The latter term comes from a root that designates something as thin, while the former is normally associated with a root meaning "pierced, perforated." Jewish tradition also indicates that "cakes" might have been "thick," contrasting them to the thinner "wafers" (Levine 1989, 11). The second option available is to prepare the offering on a "griddle" to make it crisp, something that could be broken into smaller pieces. In contrast, the third option is to cook it in a "pan," probably frying it in the oil so that it is soft.

The omission of any reference to frankincense in these verses is most curious in light of the apparent significance of this ingredient. Perhaps it is necessary to consider this in conjunction with the

fact there are several references that seem to make "grain offerings" and "frankincense" parallel but separate items (1 Chr 9:29;
Neh 13:5, 9; Isa 43:23; Jer 17:26). It could be that verses 4-10
reflect a time when the two were separate offerings, while verses
1-3 come from another time, when they are joined as one. On the
other hand, it could be that the presence of frankincense is implied
by the reference to a "token portion" (v. 9), if the presence of
frankincense implicitly designates a food item as holy.

Leaven and Honey, and Salt (2:11-13)

The disjunctive nature of the subject raised in verses 11-13
matches the shift in style. A reader might assume that what is prescribed is all that is allowed. There is no suggestion in the preceding instructions that someone might use any ingredients other
than the ones mentioned, yet the assumption here is that the people would not think it excludes their use. In fact, because the text
specifically forbids only two ingredients here, it is quite possible
that this signals the Lord's acceptance of other ingredients.

The two prohibited ingredients are leaven and "honey." The
prohibition against leaven is somewhat redundant, since the
instructions specifically call for unleavened foods in verses 4-5.
The term for "honey" denotes a broader group of foods than simple bee honey. It also includes the nectars that many fruits naturally excrete. Some scholars speculate that the paired prohibition
against leaven and honey might stem from their presence in non-
Yahwistic offerings, but more suspect instead that this reveals a
concern about fermentation. Many believe that these peoples
probably associated fermentation with life, and so the inclusion of
fermenting elements would blur the lines between life and death,
lines that are to be carefully maintained in this cultic setting. It
could be that a combination of these two considerations is at
work. Perhaps some neighboring peoples used either leavened
bread or honey, or both, in their religious practices to symbolize
the life-giving powers of their deities. If so, this prohibition would
serve to deny the claims of competing religions. Verse 12 goes on
to affirm that leaven and honey are not inherently corrupt. Other
texts call for the bringing of "first" or "choice products" to the

Lord (e.g., Exod 23:19; Num 15:20-21; Deut 26:2, 10). That would include baked goods made with leaven and honey, in an agricultural milieu. Similarly, others require that the priests receive such products as their portion (Num 18:12; Deut 18:4). These items can never rise to the level of producing "a pleasing odor," and so they are never to touch the altar.

The appended command for salt (v. 13) is most curious. First of all, it is quite emphatic. "You shall not omit from your grain offerings the salt of the covenant with your God; with all your offerings you shall offer salt." Iff this were so important, it would seem that there should have been some other mention of it; but this is the only reference to it in this chapter. There is only one other offering in the Hebrew Bible that refers to the inclusion of salt (Ezek 43:24). It is small wonder that many critics regard this as a later addition. Equally curious is the phrase, "the salt of the covenant with your God." Two passages refer to a "covenant of salt" (Num 18:19; 2 Chr 13:5). The underlying idea is that salt is a preservative, so a "covenant of salt" is long lasting. Still, this is not the same construction as in Lev 2:13. One other possible clue comes from Exod 30:35, where the Lord calls for a special mixture of incense, "seasoned with salt," reserved solely for use in the sanctuary. Perhaps Lev 2:13 is calling for something similar, something that further intends to designate the grain offerings as food prepared solely for cultic purposes.

Offerings of First Fruits (2:14-16)

The final unit offers another option for preparing a grain offering. This one substitutes "choice flour" with "coarse new grain from fresh ears, parched with fire." The requirements for oil and frankincense still remain. The precise nature of this "new grain" is unknown. The writer sets these verses in the context of incorporating "first fruits" (not the "choice products" of v. 12) into the grain offering. This suggests that this "new grain" is the only "first fruit" one might offer. Many assume that these grains are ripe but still green when harvested, and the term translated "coarse" might also imply that they are crushed. There is a prohibition against eating such grains prior to the offering of first fruits

(23:14-17), suggesting that this is some of the first prepared food available as a result of harvest.

Theological and Ethical Analysis

Once again, the text gives only the vaguest of clues about the theological ideas inherent in this offering. It is clear that the grain offering has great significance and religious value, even though the making of foods from grain is an everyday occurrence. The "recipe" for a grain offering calls for only the finest of ingredients. Other passages mention "choice flour" in connection with meals provided for royalty and special guests (Gen 18:6; 1 Kgs 4:22 [5:2 MT]; Ezek 16:13, 19); frankincense is a luxury item. Even though none of these ingredients is reserved solely for cultic use in Israelite society, this text accords a peculiarly cultic significance to the items made from them. They, like the burnt offering, produce a "pleasing odor to the LORD." Only God and consecrated priests may consume them. At the same time, certain ingredients that are quite acceptable to the Lord in other settings are strictly forbidden here.

It is also important to keep in mind that this could be a purely voluntary offering. There are occasions when the Lord requires grain offerings as part of the ritual obligations, but the occasion envisioned in this law does not presume prior wrongdoing by the worshipers or a divine command. The worshipers wish to give something to the Lord, and this law stipulates what is acceptable.

The resulting picture involves a fascinating combination of things common and things holy. Anyone at any time could prepare these particular foods for human consumption. The ingredients that the law requires might have been reserved usually as a "special treat," in some sense, but the fact remains that anyone had the means to produce such food. It is somewhat remarkable then that a relatively common item could be accorded such an exalted religious status. The rabbis find evidence for similar notions in the opening of the law. They note that the grain offering was often viewed as an acceptable substitute for the burnt offering for individuals who were so poor that they had no animal to offer (5:1-13). The worshiper here is designated "a soul" ("When *anyone* presents," 2:1, emphasis added). The rabbis say that this reflects the value that the Lord places on the worshiper. Even though the worshiper can only offer something that in some sense is commonplace, "God views his sacrifice as though he had offered his very soul" (Talmud; cited by Hertz 1936, 13). Such an interpretation betrays some Western influence regarding the meaning of soul, yet it also reflects the spirit of the law.

That "spirit" includes once again, as in the case of the burnt offering, the recognition that the ascription of "pleasing" to this offering derives primarily from the Lord's grace. The worshiper could have prepared these food items for anyone, but when he or she gives them to the Lord, the Lord graciously accepts them and they are "most holy." The variety in the mode of preparation (vv. 4-10, 13-15) further illustrates the grace involved in God's acceptance. In fact, the mode of preparation is left up to the worshiper. This suggests that the Lord permits the worshiper to decide how she or he prepares the food "best" and then offer it in that way. Such an allowance honors the varying talents of individuals. The final product is something the worshiper is proud of, yet something the individual chooses to give away for cultic use. It is this attitude—more than a particular action—that is thought to elicit the Lord's positive response.

At the same time, the law makes clear that the value humans place on something does not necessarily reflect the value that the Lord places on it. There probably were cultural reasons for excluding leaven and honey from the ingredients for this offering, but at some level, that does not matter. Humans would naturally consider leavened bread more desirable than unleavened, and bread sweetened with honey would be more attractive than "plain" bread. It would be natural to assume that the Lord would prefer what humans prefer, and so the Lord would find "pleasing" what tastes best to humans. For some reason, this is not the case. The fact that no reason is given for prohibiting these ingredients here (but not everywhere) suggests that the most compelling reason is simply that the Lord does not prefer them. God accepts them under some conditions but not here. The high status accorded to the offering indicates that it is of highest value, and the stipulations regarding ingredients reflect the need for an attitude of excellence (parallel to the demand for an animal "without blemish" for the burnt offering). The worshipers who follow these instructions show that they do them because they are what the Lord wants.

These observations open the door to some reflection on the broader principles underlying this offering. One is that the Lord does not demand things of the people that only a few have the means to provide. They might appear menial or common, yet each can be equally acceptable to the Lord. A relatively inexpensive "cake" can be just as pleasing as the most valued animal. Making food is something anyone can do, yet the Lord—one who does not eat!—acknowledges food to be a "most holy" thing. Obviously, it is not the product by itself that pleases the Lord, nor does the mode with which it is prepared sway God. Instead, the crucial consideration seems to be the attitude with which it is done. In principle, the same could apply to the performance of any number of tasks. Just because anyone can perform a task does not mean the performance of it is of little value. In fact, this text suggests that something virtually everyone does at one time or another can be accorded the highest status by the Lord. A task performed for the Lord can be "most holy" in the Lord's eyes.

At the same time, this text shows that worshipers must consider what the Lord values rather than what humans might desire when doing something as an act of worship. Modern worshipers build sanctuaries that satisfy aesthetic sensibilities, they sing particular songs, say eloquent prayers, and stage dramatic readings designed to "enhance the worship experience." But if these worshipers are not careful, their efforts can reflect a concern to do what pleases and satisfies their own human tastes, rather than doing what is of value to the Lord. Without automatically negating the validity of those gestures, this text suggests that what the Lord deems "most holy" is not necessarily what humans would estimate to be of greatest value. The chief criterion is doing what the Lord prescribes.

All the while, surrounding these ideas is the assumption of divine grace. That the Lord would require an offering that is easy for someone to provide is a sign of grace. That the Lord would esteem something so commonplace as "most holy" is a sign of grace. This assumption is not undercut by implicit concerns about the attitude of the worshiper. Yes, the worshiper is careful to use the prescribed ingredients and devotes these items solely to cultic use; and yes, with that must come an attitude of sacrifice, of giving up something to the Lord. But accompanying these thoughts is the recognition that God is not bound to accept this offering. The Lord does so solely as an act of grace. Only a gracious God can take something so common and endow it with such great value.

LEVITICUS 3

The third type of offering is the "sacrifice of well-being." The instructions for this offering are presented within the narrative framework of the book as the concluding part of the first message delivered to Moses from the Lord. There are stylistic clues that suggest that this chapter originally continued directly from chapter 1. One can only speculate about the reason for the insertion of chapter 2. Many point to the frequent references to grain offerings as supplementary to burnt offerings. It could also be a reflection of a progression in the consumption of these offerings. The Lord is the sole "consumer" of the burnt offering, the Lord and the priests eat the grain offering, and then those bringing the animal for the sacrifice of well-being share with the Lord and the priests in eating that offering. However, there is no explicit mention of who is eating the meat of the animal until the "rituals" of 7:11-34. This omission makes clear for the reader the main intent of these opening chapters: to focus the reader's attention on the Lord's portion in these offerings.

The worshiper can offer this sacrifice, like the burnt offering, in one of three different modes. This sacrifice is different from the burnt offering in that it designates isolated parts of the animal's body that are to be "turned into smoke...[as] an offering by fire [of pleasing odor] to the LORD" (8:20-21). It also differs by making the offering of sheep or goats separate possibilities (they are combined in the case of burnt offerings); consequently, there is no provision for the use of birds. Other texts indicate that the donor and the priests will eat the remainder of the sacrificed animal, but this text only implies that by its silence about the disposal of the rest of the animal and its prohibitions against eating fat or blood.

Literary Analysis

These instructions follow the stylistic pattern used in chapter 1 for burnt offerings. They differ from the previous two sets in not having a primary law to provide a general statement about this offering. The chapter consists of a series of three prescriptions, each introduced by the conjunction "if" (3:1-5, 6-11, 12-17). This formula normally introduces supplementary or subordinate laws. From the standpoint of genre, one would conclude that the instructions for the sacrifice of well-being are supplementary to the instructions for grain offerings, which immediately precede. This is obviously not the case, though. It is more logical to view 3:1 as the continuation of chapter 1, with 1:2b serving as the introduction to both chapters 1 and 3. The syntactical pattern one finds in 3:1, 6, 12 is essentially identical to that in 1:3, 10, 14, but it differs at crucial points from the formulas in 2:4, 5, 7, 14. The worshiper is identified again by the third person throughout the chapter, whereas the worshiper is "you" (sing.) for most of chapter 2. There is, however, a minor variation regarding "if" in these instructions. The conjunction "if" at the beginning of verse 1 introduces the entire chapter, just as "when" does in 1:2 and 2:1. A second "if" in 3:1 ("if . . . an animal of the herd") has its correspondent in verse 6 ("If . . . from the flock"). Verse 6 actually introduces the two remaining units. The "if" of verse 12 has its correspondent in verse 7. Verses 7-11 and 12-16 identify legitimate alternative forms of the general category in verse 6. There is no parallel possibility for offering a dove or pigeon (1:14-17), probably because of the sparse amount of edible flesh on such birds.

There is substantial repetition and consistency among these three instructions, with over half of the first unit (vv. 1-5) repeated almost verbatim in the second and third units (vv. 6-11, 12-16). All three offerings bear the label "offering" (1:2), which the worshiper is to "offer [bring near] before the LORD." Each unit calls for using an animal without blemish, laying a hand on its head, slaughtering it at the entrance of the tent of meeting, dashing some of its blood against the altar, and specifying those parts that the priests are to "turn into smoke." Despite these similarities, there is also some variation. For example, the summary designations at the end of each unit vary by one phrase each time. The first gives the fullest rendering: "an offering by fire of pleasing odor to the LORD" (3:5; cf. 1:9, 13, 17; 2:2, 9). The designation of the sheep offering omits the middle clause (3:11; cf. 2:16), and the designation of the goat omits the third clause (3:16; however, this clause is present here in the LXX and the Samaritan Pentateuch). These variations are minor, however. The primary difference comes in the second unit, involving the location of additional fat portions in a sheep. This is probably a result of the sheep's particular anatomy.

This general consistency breaks down beginning with the final clause of verse 16 and continuing through verse 17. Following a typical summary designation, there is a note regarding the general prohibition against eating fat. The main instructions in the chapter explicitly call for the priest to set aside the fat portions of the sacrifices, so that he can "turn these into smoke" (vv. 5, 11, 16). It should be clear from this that no human should eat the fat portions, yet the text here contains a special clause to this effect. In 3:17, the mode of address unexpectedly shifts from third-person singular ("he") to second-person plural ("you," cf. 2:11-12). The end of the note in 3:17 goes a step further than the first clause (at the end of v. 16) by including the prohibition against blood (again see 7:22-27). All these factors together suggest that 3:16b-17 was not originally connected with the rest of chapter 3.

Exegetical Analysis

Sacrifices of Well-being from Cattle (3:1-5)

There is no consensus about the precise meaning of the phrase "sacrifice of well-being," which designates this third offering. Slightly less than half of the references in the Hebrew Bible to this type of offering omit the construct noun "sacrifice" (e.g., 6:12; 7:14, 33). Since "sacrifice" is often a generic term (like "offering"), there is no small speculation about how and when it came to be tied so closely to this particular type of offering. Most of the occurrences of this phrase are in Leviticus and Numbers, with only a handful elsewhere (Exod 29:28; Josh 22:23; 1 Sam 11:15; 1 Kgs 8:63; Prov 7:14). Some contend that the noun "sacrifice" refers specifically to offerings that are eaten by the worshiper, in contrast to "burnt offerings," which are burned entirely to the Lord. The main problem with this is that there are several passages that mention "burnt offering" as the object of the verb "sacrifice" (e.g., Exod 20:24).

The wide range of nuances in the root for "well-being" accounts for the variety of proposals regarding the implied intent of this offering. The most common suggestions associate it with "peace" (*šālōm*) or "well-being, health, soundness" (*šālēm*). The term might refer to the physical and mental state of an individual worshiper, the relationship among several worshipers, or the relationship between the worshiper(s) and the Lord. Some midrashic interpreters related the term to "complete," signifying that it provided for a meal shared by all (worshipers, priests, and the Lord). This offering is related to the making of a covenant in a few passages (Exod 18:12; 24:5; Josh 8:30-35), but burnt offerings are offered at the same time; so one cannot claim that the purpose of the sacrifice of well-being—and it alone—is to create or reaffirm a covenant relationship. It seems more broadly to be a celebratory event, which involves eating and recognizing the Lord's participation in human life.

It is helpful to consider the instructions for the sacrifice of well-being in comparison with the burnt offering (1:3-9). The burnt offering allows for the offering of bulls alone; the sacrifice of well-being can involve a male or a female animal. The writer never explains the reason for this difference, but either can be a "pleasing odor to the LORD." Both sets of instructions call for the worshiper to lay a hand on the head of the animal before killing it (1:4; 3:2). The burnt offering instructions seem to tie this act to atonement (1:4), but there is no such link suggested here. The instructions for the burnt offering call for the worshipers to bring the bull "to the entrance of the tent of meeting" so that it could "be slaughtered before the LORD" (1:3, 5); the instructions for the sacrifice of well-being call the worshiper to bring the sacrifice "before the LORD" and "slaughter it at the entrance of the tent of meeting" (3:1, 2). The adverbial phrases, "before the LORD" and "at the entrance of the tent of meeting," are thus shown to be interchangeable. The priests dash the blood on the sides of the altar with both offerings, and then they place the parts for burning on the altar. The obvious difference here is that the sacrifice of well-being involves burning only the fat portions surrounding certain internal organs (kidneys, liver, and tendons). This does not include the fat intertwined with the meat. Other passages suggest this specificity by referring to the "fat pieces of the offerings of well-being" (6:12 [6:5] NOAB; 1 Kgs 8:64; 2 Chr 29:35) or the "blood of his offerings of well-being" (2 Kgs 16:13). The priests then "turn these into smoke," as with the whole animal of the burnt offering (1:9). In fact, the wording of 3:5 implies that the burnt offering is still present on the altar. Verse 5b includes a slight variation on 1:8b:

> 1:8b—"on the wood that is on the fire on the altar"
> 3:5b—"on the altar, with the burnt offering that is on the wood on the fire"

In 3:5, the phrases after "on the altar" are explicatory, specifying that this is not a different altar or even at a different time. Subsequent regulations (6:8-13 [6:1-6]) show that it was common to offer burnt offerings and sacrifices of well-being together. This law probably does not intend to say that a sacrifice of well-being must always be placed on top of an active burnt offering, but merely that it is not necessary to remove the one before offering the other.

The text offers no reason for reserving the fat for the Lord. There is no support for speculation that this reflects concerns about high cholesterol or the like. In fact, one could just as easily argue that fat was a highly desirable supplement to the regular diet of the average person in that culture. In the Hebrew Bible, some writers use the term for "fat" to refer to what is best about some food (Num 18:12; Pss 81:16; 147:14). The most logical interpretation is that an Israelite would have viewed this law as reserving the most highly prized pieces of the animal for the Lord.

Sacrifices of Well-being from Sheep (3:6-11)

Like the burnt offering before it, the sacrifice of well-being can involve a sheep (or a goat; vv. 12-16) in the place of a bull, if the economic status of the worshiper warrants it. The only substantial difference is in verse 9a, which adds a detail about fat taken from the sheep's broad tail (v. 3a = v. 9a; vv. 3b-4 = vv. 9b-10). Reports of sheep with extremely large tails in these regions go back at least to the days of the Greek historian Herodotus (5th century B.C.E.). There are examples of several breeds of such sheep scattered across Asia today. In some cases, the fat of the tail serves the same function as a camel's hump. It is likely that the people highly prized this portion of the animal (1 Sam 9:24; Lev 7:3; cf. Exod 29:22; Lev 8:25; 9:19).

One other lesser difference involves the designating formula ("an offering by fire") at the end of the unit. Some variations in verses 5, 11, and 16 have already been discussed. Complicating the picture is the inclusion of the word for "food" just before this formula in verses 11 and 16. Some take this as an expanded version of the first clause, thus designating each as "a food offering by fire." Others take it as a separate clause, reading "as food, an offering by fire." This combination occurs only in these two verses and Num 28:24, which would seem to give more credence to the latter suggestion. In either case, it is unclear what the reference to this as "food" implies. Some view it as the only clue in this passage that the sacrifice of well-being was to be eaten by the worshipers; but this overlooks the obvious fact that the portions mentioned here are those given to the Lord, not to the people. This would raise again the possibility that the early Israelites shared with their neighbors the notion of a deity eating parts of a sacrifice (cf. Deut 32:38). On the other hand, these portions of the offering are no different than the burnt offering or the fat portions of a bull of a sacrifice of well-being, in that regard, so it is surprising that the writer would refer to this alone—and not to those more substantial offerings—as "food" for the Lord. No compelling solution presents itself.

Sacrifices of Well-being from Goats (3:12-16)

There are only a couple of minor differences between the bulk of these verses and those of the preceding two units. Verse 12a is an abbreviated version of verse 7a, while verses 12b-16b are virtually identical to verses 1b-5 and 7b-11 (excluding v. 9a). Verse 14a ("You shall present as your offering") is equivalent in meaning to verses 3a and 9a ("You shall offer from the sacrifice of well-being"). Other differences are negligible and are possibly the result of copyists' errors (see above on "to the LORD").

Prohibition against Fat and Blood (3:17)

The evidence for viewing the final clause of verse 16 and all of verse 17 as a secondary addition was presented above (see "Literary Analysis"). Many interpret this as a progression beyond the proscriptions of the preceding verses. Those only necessarily prohibit the eating of fat in connection with these sacrifices; these lines prohibit the eating of fat at any time (it is "a perpetual statute throughout your generations") and at any place ("in all your settlements;" cf. 7:22-25). The final clause includes a specific prohibition against consuming blood. While the earlier instructions logically imply this by calling for the dashing of the blood against the altar, here the prescription makes it explicit for the first time in Leviticus. More detailed prohibitions (and discussion) regarding this come in 7:22-27 and 17:10-16 (cf. 19:26; Gen 9:4; Deut 12:16, 23; 15:23; Acts 15:20, 29). Reconstructions of the redaction history of this prohibition in relation to the others typically locate it in post-exilic times, but the evidence for that is rather slim.

Theological and Ethical Analysis

The narrative framework combines the first three chapters into a block. These three have in common the prescribing of offerings that are either regular or voluntary. They are not prompted by sin and a need to reconcile a relationship with the Lord. If someone wishes to express their devotion to the Lord in sacrifice, here are the prescribed ways to do that. Chapter 3 is conspicuous for what it omits. By recognizing what is omitted the reader gains a clearer picture of the purpose of this chapter—in fact, of all three chapters. One of the defining characteristics of this particular offering is that the worshiper, the priest, and the Lord share in consuming it. This chapter does not mention what the priest and the worshiper consume; all the attention is on what the Lord receives. Each unit in this law details the fat portions the priest is to set aside for the Lord and "turn into smoke." Those portions will be "an offering by fire of pleasing odor to the LORD." There is no concern about what will be pleasing to the priest or to the worshiper. It is easy to understand, from this perspective, why someone would attach the general prohibitions against consuming fat and blood at the end. The people are not to consume fat and blood, not because those items are inherently dangerous to the people, but because they belong solely to the Lord.

This observation prompts another look at the first two chapters. The first obviously focuses on what the Lord is to receive, because all of a burnt offering belongs to the Lord. The second designates a "token portion" of a grain offering that belongs to the Lord, and what belongs to the priests is "what is left." The volume of the priests' portion is greater than the Lord's "token portion," but the preeminent consideration involves the Lord's portion. Even though the priests' portion is "most holy," they are receiving what amounts to "the leftovers," so to speak. This perspective could also help explain why someone might include 2:11-12. These verses focus the attention on what belongs entirely to the Lord. The people might think highly of leaven and honey as food, and the Lord will accept those as sacrificial gifts; but they are not what produce "a pleasing odor to the LORD," and so they are prohibited from his altar.

Christians in particular often ignore or dismiss the teachings about sacrifice in the Hebrew Bible. They do so theologically on the premise that the crucifixion of Christ fulfills the sacrificial requirements for forgiveness and purification (Heb 9:1–10:31; cf. Eph 5:1-2). This overlooks the offerings prescribed in Lev 1–3. These are nonexpiatory, the sorts of sacrifices to which Paul alludes when he says, "present your bodies as a living sacrifice" (Rom 12:1-2; cf. Phil 2:17; 4:18; Heb 13:16; 1 Pet 2:4-5).

Recognition that the offerings of Lev 1–3 are nonexpiatory should prompt a rethinking of some aspects of modern worship.

One aspect is the question of what constitutes "sacrifice" in modern religion. Early on in Judaism, in situations where the temple was absent or inaccessible, there was a progression from prayers or hymns accompanying offerings to the same prayers and hymns serving as replacements for those offerings. When Christianity emerged, such ideas about worship were already well established (1 Cor 10:14-22), and they carry on in Judaism and Christianity to this day. The same is true of ideas about acts of piety—"good deeds" and morality—as substitutes for sacrifices at some level, that is, one does such acts and "offers them up to God" for divine approval and "to the glory of God" (Isa 58:1-14; Jas 1:26-27). In the process, it is easy to lose sight of some fundamental ideas about sacrifice from Leviticus. Most obvious is the difficulty in identifying something that corresponds to giving all or portions of a sacrifice to the Lord. When modern believers consider the act of giving something to the Lord, it usually takes on some material form (as it did in ancient Israel). There is nothing truly equivalent, however, to the portions prescribed in Leviticus that are to be given solely to the Lord. Items and monies given to the Lord come in the form of programs and goods and services for persons in need in a community, or they are used to build and improve worship facilities or provide the salary and benefits of the clergy. But there is not a portion given solely to the Lord, like the fat portions of a sacrifice of well-being or the token portion of a grain offering.

Leviticus 1–3 focuses the attention of worshipers on what the Lord will receive in worship. Such offerings are items that the worshipers could have used for themselves or for others; instead, they are removed from the community and given solely to God, who has no physical need for them and therefore cannot really use them (Isa 1:11; Mic 6:6-8). This should cause modern worshipers to pause and reflect on what the Lord alone receives from their worship. Modern worshipers might view an offering of the sort called for in Lev 1–3 as "a waste" of what the Lord has entrusted to them. There still is a fine line between a pious gesture, such as honoring the Lord with a jar of ointment (Mark 14:3-9), and charitable contributions (Mark 7:9-13). It is common to talk about placing the Lord at the center of worship. But is there something that the Lord—and the Lord alone—receives in worship? No worshipers dispute that the Lord deserves "all glory and honor and praise" in worship. The same was true of worship in the days of ancient Israel. Yet these chapters call for giving something physical to the Lord. This raises the possibility that there might be something physical that one could offer today as well (e.g., a dance, a poem, a prayer).

Perhaps more practical, though, is the unchanging need for worshipers to evaluate the primary motivations for the forms and styles of worship that they employ. Nonexpiatory offerings challenge the notion that worship styles should be adapted to address the needs of the worshipers. They place the primary focus on what the Lord receives from worship. Forms and styles of worship play a significant role in maintaining that focus.

LEVITICUS 4:1–5:13

A different situation lies in the background of the remaining offerings. The priests present the preceding offerings on a regular basis, or whenever an individual feels an urge to bring something to the Lord. Sin and guilt offerings are prompted by some sinful act or state of impurity that puts the relationship with the Lord at risk. Such a situation precludes the individual's right to approach the Lord, and these offerings provide the means for mending the relationship.

The traditional translation for the first offering is "sin offering," but this can misrepresent the fundamental intent of the offering. This noun—in this form—never denotes sinful acts, but acts of ritual purification. Some of these regulations involve situations where persons are in a state of impurity, but not as a result of sin. A classic example is the mother who is "unclean" by virtue of childbirth (12:1-8). She must offer a burnt offering and a "sin offering" at the end of "the days of her purification." The foundational function of this ritual is to address the problem of impurity. Sin causes impurity, but it is not the only cause. Since this offering addresses the problem of impurity, several believe it is better to render its designation "purification offering" (Milgrom

1991, 253-54; but see Gilders 2004, 29-32). Although this commentary retains the translation of "sin offering" from the NRSV, the true force of the term involves purification.

Literary Analysis

There is a typical narrative heading and command to announce the following instructions. Literary indicators demarcate two major sections (4:2b-35; 5:1-13), which perhaps betray two types of sin offerings. Verse 2b relates the first general situation, "When anyone sins unintentionally." Each subordinate situation begins with the common "If/When" construction (vv. 3, 13, 22, 27, 32). These reveal five units (4:3-12, 13-21, 22-26, 27-31, 32-35). Leviticus 5:1 introduces a different circumstance, but one that still calls for a sin offering. It is commonly deemed a "graduated sin offering." It begins in the same style as 4:2; here, though, there is not just one scenario, but a series of four scenarios, linked to one another by the repetition of "or." If one were to remove "or" from verses 2-4, there would be four examples of the introductory formula common to a primary law (v. 2—"when any of you touch," etc.). A resumptive clause in verse 5 brings these together. Two examples of the formula "But if" introduce subordinate situations (vv. 7, 11). These features demarcate three units in 5:1-13 (5:1-6, 7-10, 11-13).

The concluding formulas show six units declaring that "the priest shall make atonement . . . and he/you shall be forgiven." This double notice serves as the final statement in four of the units (4:26, 31, 35; 5:10), two include an additional comment (4:20-21; 5:13), and a reference to atonement alone concludes another unit (5:6). Only the first unit omits a concluding reference to atonement and forgiveness (4:3-12), but the circumstances of that case account for the omission.

The direct discourse heading identifies the general situation as "unintentional" offenses (4:2). The literary flow implies the unintentional nature of the first case, and the text includes the term "unintentionally" at the beginning of the next three units (4:13, 22, 27). The absence of this term in the final unit implies the fact that it provides a different method for dealing with the same situation that the fourth unit addresses (4:32-35).

The instructions normally speak of worshipers in the third-person masculine singular. The only exceptions come in 4:13-15, when the whole congregation sins. It is natural to use the masculine singular in the first and third units, because they envision "the anointed priest" and "a ruler" as the offenders. The other scenarios refer to the hypothetical "anyone" or "any of you." The sequence and syntactical constructions of the instructions in chapter 4 are relatively consistent.

The introductory formula in 5:1 and the repeated use of "or when" in the following verses suggest a new primary law in 5:1-6, with subordinate cases in verses 7-13. The subordinate cases do not envision different scenarios but, like 4:32-35, provide alternate ways of dealing with the same situation. They allow for differences in economic status, yielding the label "graduated sin offering" for all of 5:1-13. Some interpreters believe the differences between these instructions and those in chapter 4 reveal two distinct sin offerings. They could also reflect the notion that the same solution (a sin offering) is appropriate for different situations. Verse 6 identifies the necessary sacrifice as a sin offering, without distinguishing it from the offering in chapter 4. The text gives no detailed instructions regarding the presentation of the sacrificial animal, as 4:27-35 provides the instructions for these particular animals. The implication is that 5:1-6 concerns sins committed by "anyone of the ordinary people" (4:27). The use of birds and grain offerings in 5:7-13 accounts for the few new details given there.

Other features persist from chapter 4 through 5:1-13. Some continue through the instructions on guilt offerings (5:14–6:7 [5:14-26]), which contain multiple primary introductory formulas (5:15; 6:1 [5:20]), and they share significant phrases with 5:1-13. This suggests an overall consistency to 4:1–6:7 [5:26]. One might attribute this consistency to a common source, a common author, a redactor, or similarity of purpose.

Exegetical Analysis

The narrative heading marks the transition from the three voluntary offerings to the first compulsory offering. It assumes the same setting as the first three chapters, with the Lord giving instructions through Moses to "the people of Israel." The first part of this message identifies the situations that warrant sin offerings as those involving "unintentional" sins (4:2). The instructions in 5:1-13 envision situations in which someone is "merely" impure. The first part arranges the offenses according to the status of the offender, moving from the anointed priest (4:3-12) to the whole congregation (4:13-21) to the prince or clan leader (4:22-26) to a common citizen (4:27-35). The second part proceeds according to the economic capabilities of those making the offering.

Heading and Introduction (4:1-2)

The introduction in verse 2 mentions only inadvertent sins, which raises questions about the extent of the sin offering's application. Numbers 15:22-31 prescribes a burnt offering, a grain offering, a drink offering, and a sin offering for unintentional sins. That text goes on to contrast unintentional sins to "high-handed" offenses. For the latter there is no means of atonement; the guilty parties are "utterly cut off." On the basis of these passages alone, many interpreters conclude that the Levitical system provides no means for forgiveness for intentional sins, only unintentional sins. It is implausible to assume that every offense that is not "unintentional" is "high-handed"; the history of Israel bears this out. There are very few examples of individuals who are "cut off" from Israel, so one would be compelled to conclude that intentional sins were extremely rare in Israel. In fact, there are numerous instances of intentional sin that do not end with "cutting off" the guilty party, and there are references to the use of sin offerings apart from cases of inadvertent sin (16:11-22; 2 Chr 20:2-25).

Some rabbinic writers interpret inadvertent sins as offenses committed by someone who did not know the law, or actions that the offender did not realize fit under the umbrella of prohibited action (Levine 1989, 19). Others argue that a "high-handed sin" is restricted to idolatry, and they interpret Num 15:22-31 as having a very narrow application. Some modern commentators assume that inadvertent sins must include "minor" infractions, but this leaves the issue only slightly less resolved. Jacob Milgrom recently resurrected another rabbinic explanation to eliminate this problem. He proposes that, if persons are guilty of intentional sins, they can "repent and confess," and that changes the status of an intentional sin into an unintentional sin. These guidelines for the sin offering would then apply (Milgrom 1991, 301-2, 373-78). This seems unbalanced. It provides for only two possible outcomes for sin: on the one hand, death or complete expulsion from the community, and on the other hand, sacrifice of a single animal. This assumes a drastic reduction in the penalty for serious crimes on the basis of a simple confession of wrongdoing. If this were the case, one would expect the biblical writers to speak more extensively about confession.

A more likely explanation is that this law does not intend to be exhaustive or comprehensive about the occasions when sin offerings are necessary. The occasions mentioned are simply exemplary. By comparison, the law for the burnt offering mentions only those occasions when an individual voluntarily presents an offering, but the majority of references to burnt offerings in the Hebrew Bible involve regular occasions on which priests presented burnt offerings for the whole nation. There is no need for a separate law for those different occasions, and it is logical to apply the same principle to the law on sin offerings. This law prescribes how to present a proper sin offering. The situation in which persons might bring such an offering is just one of many possible situations. The text does not intend to restrict its application to the occasions mentioned.

One other possible explanation is that the sin offering *by itself* constitutes the total cultic response to inadvertent sin, while intentional offenses require sin offerings in conjunction with other offerings and actions. There are several examples of the latter. The law for the Day of Atonement calls for the priest to present burnt offerings along with sin offerings (16:18, 24). There is no caveat saying that these offerings apply only to inadvertent sins; the priest and the people are cleansed of *all* their sins (16:30). Similarly, the law regarding impure discharges calls for the unclean person to sacrifice two doves or pigeons, one as a burnt offering and one as a sin offering, in order to "make atonement" (15:14-15, 29-30). This requirement is similar to that in Lev 5:7-10.

It is possible that other terms denote this process. For example, 2 Sam 11:4 reports how Bathsheba "was purifying herself after her period" (cf. Lev 5:2-3; 15:19-24). This suggests that "consecration" denotes what Lev 15:29-30 prescribes. Other passages mention "consecration" following occasions of sin (e.g., Josh 7:13; Job 1:5). It is likely that sin offerings (and others) were a part of the rituals.

Sin Offerings for the Anointed Priest (4:3-12)

The first scenario involves the "anointed priest" who commits an offense. This is an uncommon way of identifying the high priest (4:3, 5, 16; 16:32; Num 35:25). Some claim that such a designation was avoided as long as anointed kings sat on the throne, so they would not have used it before the exile. This is based on the unproved premise that only one type of official would be "anointed" at a given time (cf. 1 Chr 29:22). Other theories regarding the historical provenance of this phrase face similar problems. It occurs too rarely to draw significant conclusions about when it might have been used.

An offense committed by the high priest had serious implications for the entire nation. The text considers his case first, and it says that his sin "[brings] guilt on the people" (4:3). That, along with the specifics of the rituals, indicates that such an offense is perhaps the most serious possible. This seriousness derives from the status of the one committing it. After Moses, the high priest is the one with the greatest access to the Lord, and that places on him the greatest responsibility for honoring the Lord. He is the one on whom everyone else relies for gaining access to God; if he loses the right to serve as a mediator, the whole nation suffers the loss of contact with the Lord.

The sin offering shares several aspects with the burnt offering and sacrifice of well-being, but it also adds a few pieces to the process. One additional component for offerings involving a bull is that the priests take the unused portions to an ash heap outside the camp for burning (4:12). There are no such stipulations for sacrificing a sheep or goat. The primary difference in this offering is the way the priest handles the blood. The whole offering leads to atonement and forgiveness, but it is clear that the handling of the blood is crucial. With the previous offerings, the priest would "dash" all the animal's blood against the sides of the altar—that is, outside the entrance to the main sanctuary (1:5; 3:2). With the sin offering, the priest symbolically brings the blood closer to God, taking a portion of the blood inside the tent, and then sprinkling it "seven times before the LORD" (4:17). The text gives no explanation for this sevenfold action, but it probably implies the completeness of the act. The priest is purging the entire area of the effects of the priest's sin. The text locates this act "in front of the curtain of the sanctuary" (4:6, 17). The curtain is the divider between the main sanctuary and the inner chamber, which the priest enters only once a year (16:2, 32-34). There is some speculation about whether the priest sprinkles the blood "on the front of the curtain" rather than "in front of the curtain" (both translations are possible), but the primary intent is to imply that the sprinkling purifies the area of the main sanctuary. This might or might not include the outer surface of the curtain. Similar ideas explain the placing of some blood on the horns of the incense altar. It too is in need of purification as a result of the priest's offense. The depth of the effects of a priest's disobedience means that the offense jeopardizes the relationship between the people and their God.

The priest "pours out" the rest of the blood at the base of the altar of burnt offering, which is outside the tent. It is unclear whether this portion of the blood goes directly onto the base of the altar or onto the ground at the base. A resolution of this detail might settle some questions about the function of the act. Some insist that this reconsecrates the altar (Gorman 1990, 36-37), while others see it as an act of disposal (Wright 1987, 47-59). The act of "pouring out blood" is most common in reference to violent death or execution, so this might intend a substitutionary or representative killing of the animal in place of the worshiper. This is the only part of the blood manipulation common to all four situations in chapter 4.

The final act is to take the carcass of the bull to a "clean place" that is outside the camp and burn it entirely. Some think that the animal has taken on the impurity of the offender, and now the priest is disposing of the unclean item; otherwise, he could burn it on the altar of burnt offering. Others counter that an unclean item would defile a "clean place," so surely they would not do this if the carcass were unclean. Some add the instructions in 6:24-30 [6:17-23] to this, saying that it sanctifies whatever it touches (6:27 [6:20]). Those instructions call for the priests to eat the portions that are not the fat portions "turned to smoke" for the Lord. The third and fourth parts of chapter 4 do not include a provision about what to do with the carcass, so commentators assume the priests eat the animal's meat in those cases (as 6:26 [6:19] commands).

These considerations lead many to conclude that 4:22-26 preserves an early form of the instructions on the sin offering, while 4:3-12 and 4:13-21 reflect subsequent developments to deal with exceptions. The reason for the exception in verses 11-12 might be that the priest must lose all benefits that would come from possession of the bull (cf. 7:8). On the other hand, the following occasion also calls for the destruction of the bull's carcass outside the camp. In that light, some conclude that the law is composed to dispel any notion that the Lord would benefit from sin, and so this offering cannot even be presented like a burnt offering (Hartley 1992, 61). On the other hand, the Lord "benefits" from this offering just as much as he does from a sacrifice of well-being.

Most commentators assume that the special circumstances involving the sin of a priest explain the absence of references to atonement and forgiveness in this section. It is thought to be inappropriate for a priest to make atonement for himself or to declare himself forgiven (but see 16:11-14). It is possible that some clauses were dropped in the process of redaction or transmission. The atonement clause would come between verses 10 and 11 (cf. 4:20-21, 26, 31, 35). Most commentators believe, however, that the omission of an atonement clause is intentional.

Sin Offerings for the Congregation (4:13-21)

The final clause of verses 13-21 identifies this as "the sin offering for the assembly" (*haqqāhēl*, v. 21). Much of this matches the anointed priest's offering. If the group "errs unintentionally," they offer a bull, the elders (as representatives) lay their hands on its head, and the bull is killed; the priest sprinkles its blood in the sanctuary, places it on the horns of the interior altar, and pours it at the base of the exterior altar; the priest then turns the fat to smoke for the Lord, and burns the rest of the carcass outside the camp. Even though the description of the final two acts is substantially abbreviated (vv. 19-20a, 21), it is clear the writer is referring to the same actions as in verses 8-12. The question about why the priest burns the bull outside the camp remains.

The primary differences from the first unit pertain to the identity of the offenders and the circumstances of their offense. At first glance, the terms "congregation" (*'ēdāh*) and "assembly" (*qāhēl*) appear to be interchangeable; but there might be reason to see a distinction between them. The "congregation" sins, but the "assembly" is unaware of it (v. 13). The "assembly" brings the bull for offering, but the "elders of the congregation" lay their hands on its head (vv. 14-15). Some propose that "congregation" refers to the whole nation (v. 13), while "assembly" refers to the national leaders only. In this interpretation, "assembly" and "elders of the congregation" are synonymous (Hertz 1936, 27; Harrison 1980, 64). The problem with this is that the note at the end identifies this as a "sin offering for the assembly" (v. 21). Others reverse these, identifying the "congregation" with the leaders and the "assembly" with the whole nation (Wenham 1979, 98-99; Hartley 1992, 62). This implies that the leaders are guilty of sin, yet the general population provides the animal for sacrifice. Noth resolves this redactionally, with "assembly" as the earlier term that is being replaced by "congregation." Milgrom proposes the reverse sequence (Noth 1965, 40; Milgrom 1991, 242-43). There are instances elsewhere in which both identify the whole nation or a group of its representative leaders; so, perhaps they are synonyms and the writer uses both simply to provide stylistic variety.

The more curious aspect of the setting is the initial ignorance about and later exposure of the sin. The congregation sins, yet the sin "escapes the notice of the assembly" and only later "becomes known." In the meantime, the congregation's action "incur[s] guilt" (v. 13). "Guilt" can be understood in the sense of legal culpability or in the sense of personal remorse. Most commentators consider the guilt a natural consequence of the sinful action (culpability), with recognition of the wrong resulting later (v. 14). N. Kiuchi brings these together, proposing that culpability automatically produces remorse, and that remorse/guilt causes the sin to become known (Kiuchi 1987, 31-34; Hartley 1992, 62). This still leaves unanswered questions about how a sin can escape notice in the first place.

Another approach is to reexamine the meanings of "escapes the notice" and "becomes known." Both are passive forms. It is typical to associate the first word with "hide" and say that the sin is "hidden" or unknown, while the second word reports that what was hidden has now "become known." However, the causative form of the first word often means "to ignore" (Lev 20:4; 1 Sam 12:3; Job 42:3; Isa 1:15; Ezek 22:26). It is possible that the sin here is ignored or considered insignificant, so that the sense of "become known" is more akin to "be acknowledged (for what it is)." In this light, this is a case of people engaging in particular activities that they originally justify or rationalize but later acknowledge as sin. This explains how the whole group can violate one of the Lord's prohibitions "unintentionally."

The other significant difference between this unit and the first is the atonement and forgiveness clause in verse 20b. The clause is very formulaic. The explicit identification of "the priest" is unnecessary, but this matches the wording in parallel verses (4:26, 31, 35; 5:10, 13). This brief clause gets to the heart of the meaning and function of the sin offering. This offering has the effect it does because the Lord says it does. One might wish to attribute this to "primitive" notions about the magical powers of blood, except that a simple offering made of fine grain can have the same effect (5:11-13). For reasons that the text does not explore, the Lord designates these offerings as efficacious (see 17:11).

Reflection on the oft-repeated affirmation of the clause "and he/they will be forgiven" reveals the crucial aspect of divine prerogative. The passive verb leaves the subject of forgiveness—the one who forgives—unnamed. The obvious implication is that this is the Lord, but there is no explication of why the Lord renders such a decision or how the writer can be so certain that the Lord will do so. The certainty must come from the belief that the Lord has promised to forgive. On the other hand, the text states repeatedly who—and what—is affected by the sin offering. This ritual provides atonement for the individual(s) bringing the offering, as well as for the sanctuary and its furnishings (16:15-19, 33). Milgrom champions the view that this offering purifies only the sanctuary and its furnishings (the "sancta"). He proposes that "impurity was a physical substance, an aerial miasma that possessed magnetic attraction for the realm of the sacred" (Milgrom 1991, 257). The thought is that the impurity is a "physical substance" that leaves the person and attaches itself to the sanctuary and sancta. The sin offering purifies those things alone. The offenders are not purified in this act because the contamination has already left them; apparent references to the atoning of persons actually refer to atoning for the contamination that they brought to the sanctuary. Milgrom supports his proposal by pointing out that the priest applies the blood—a "ritual detergent"—only to the altar and other parts of the sanctuary (Milgrom 1991, 256). If one wished to purify the worshipers, the priest would "wash" them in some similar way.

Milgrom's primary arguments arise from Lev 16, so it will be more appropriate to address them more fully there. For now, it is sufficient to recognize that he overstates the case for such a narrow interpretation of the function of the sin offering. Milgrom's view separates atonement and forgiveness; atonement is for the sanctuary, forgiveness is for the offender. Yet this law repeatedly links atonement and forgiveness (4:26, 35; Hayes 1998, 5-15). Forgiveness involves the worshiper, and it is only logical to assume that the offering somehow affects forgiveness; it is most likely that atonement involves the worshiper in similar fashion. The recognition that the sin offering brings cleansing to the sanctuary exposes the fact that a person's sin is thought to have an effect beyond the person. Even an inadvertent sin alters the basic relationship between the Lord and Israel by desecrating the Lord's dwelling place. The law communicates the means for addressing this situation.

This highlights the need to scrutinize the meaning of "atone." At some level, atonement has the effect of healing a broken relationship, of making two hostile parties "at one" with each other; but that is not the whole picture. The root meaning of "atone" might involve the notion of "cover" (based on Arabic cognates). This would account for interpretations of atonement as "propitiation." The offering "appeases" the Lord's righteous anger. This understanding is insufficient, though. Mesopotamian cognates point to the meaning "rub off" (Levine 1989, 23). In other words, the offering does not simply cover over an offense; it erases it. This is closer to "expiation," the notion that an offering "makes complete satisfaction for" an offense (Brichto 1976, 29). In order for the offering to accomplish this, its effect must entail both the offender and the sanctuary, because the offense affects both. The offense "stains" the offender and it "stains" the sanctuary. The sin offering removes the "stain" from both (see 17:11).

Sin Offerings for a Ruler (4:22-26)

The third scenario involves the unintentional sin of a "ruler." This term is common in the latter half of Ezekiel to designate a royal figure in the post-exilic community, but it commonly denotes a traditional clan leader in other texts (e.g., Num 7). Either meaning (royal leader or clan leader) is possible in Lev 4:22, although the latter is slightly more likely. The level of defilement is less for this ruler than for the priest, suggesting perhaps that the ruler has a more limited sphere of influence. It is also possible that the priest's cultic status makes his offenses more serious than a king's offenses.

The ritual procedures for a ruler's sin offering closely parallel the procedures for the anointed priest and the procedures for the whole congregation. Two differences reflect the lesser cultic status of the ruler. The first is the use of a male goat rather than a bull. This parallels the distinctions among burnt offerings and sacrifices of well-being. The second is manifested in the location of the blood-manipulation portion of the procedures. The priest does not enter the main sanctuary with the blood, in this case. Instead, he remains at the entrance, where the altar of burnt offering stands. There is no sprinkling with the blood, and the placing of the blood on the horns of the altar shifts from the interior altar of incense to the exterior altar of burnt offering. A ruler cannot approach as close to the Lord, and so the effects of a ruler's sin do not penetrate as deeply as the priest's into the sacred area.

Sin Offerings for a Common Person (4:27-31, 32-35)

The fourth scenario envisions an offense by "ordinary people." There has been some disagreement whether this phrase denotes "landed aristocrats" or "commoners." These opposing possibilities arise from other books of the Hebrew Bible, in which the phrase can distinguish tribal groups from the royal establishment, or it can denote the native inhabitants of a land. Interpretation of the phrase in the context of Lev 4 goes hand in hand with one's interpretation of "ruler." If "ruler" denotes a royal figure, this could be a member of the landed aristocracy or a commoner; if "ruler" denotes a clan leader, this phrase almost certainly denotes a commoner. In either case, the cultic status of such an individual is lower than that of a ruler. This person brings a female goat or sheep (4:27-31, 32-35), while a ruler has to bring a more valuable male. The procedures for this offering match those for the ruler's offering (4:22-26). The description of the burning of the fat for the Lord varies slightly from that in 4:26. In 4:31 the writer adds the depiction of it as "a pleasing odor to the LORD," and in 4:35 it is included among "the offerings by fire to the LORD." These descriptors derive from those associated with the sacrifice of well-being (3:5, 11, 16).

Sin Offerings for Sins of Omission (5:1-6)

The subsequent four situations no longer involve inadvertent sins, but it is difficult to provide a single label that describes what they have in common. The primary questions concern the first verse. The offender is "subject to punishment," but those in verses 2-4 are "guilty." The latter speak of the offender being "unaware" of the sin, and the final two mention that the person must "come to know it." The first case involves someone who knows the offense but does not testify to it. What loosely ties these verses together is the verb "sin" (ḥāṭāʾ, vv. 1 and 5). The confession comes "when you realize your guilt." The common thread running through all four situations is that this is a sort of secondary sin. An initial sin was committed, but now someone has sinned by not speaking up about the first offense. In the first case, the subject has not spoken about someone else's sin; in the remaining cases, it is one's own sin.

What is uncertain is why the individual has not yet spoken about the offense. In the first case, the person is a witness; he or she has either "seen" or "learned of" the offense. There is a "public adjuration" [a curse]. This could mean someone uttered a curse and needed to be exposed for his or her impiety; it could mean that a victim uttered a curse, calling down the Lord's wrath on the perpetrator and—by extension—any who knew of the crime; or it could be that community leaders have imposed a curse on any who refrain from helping to rectify the offense. A failure to "speak up" makes one complicit in the sin. A precise interpretation of the remaining situations hinges on the meaning of the phrase, "and is unaware of it" (cf. "escapes the notice," 4:13). Interpreters disagree over whether the person knew from the beginning that she or he was in a guilty state but either ignored it or "forgot" it, or if the person was genuinely ignorant of personal guilt until someone pointed it out to her or him or her or his conscience alerted her or him (Hartley 1992, 67-68). The latter is less plausible in the final case because it seems unlikely someone could utter a rash oath and not recognize it as such. It is more plausible that there are individuals who have been ignoring a problem, either deliberately or by carelessness (Kiuchi 1987, 27-30).

The challenge presented by this law is to address the problem "when you come to know it" (v. 4). The person is "subject to punishment" and "guilty" (and therefore unclean), whether or not she or he is aware of it. It is the contamination itself—not a cognitive awareness of it—that makes one unclean. Uncleanness places the entire cultic community at risk, because the Lord will pull away when impurity is present. The writer demonstrates this by bringing these scenarios together in verse 5, where he uses the ending of verses 2-4 as the beginning of verse 5. The guilty party must "realize your guilt" (v. 5; cf. "guilty" in vv. 2-4). This evokes a two-part response. First, "you shall confess the sin." The Hebrew word for "confess" here derives from the term for "know." The offender is to "make known" or "acknowledge" his or her offense. The second part of the response is to bring the sin offering. In this case, the offering functions as a "penalty" paid to make reparation for the offense. The term is translated "guilt offering" in other contexts, where it denotes a reparation for an offense (5:14–6:7 [5:26]). The value of this penalty is the same as the least valuable sin offering in chapter 4. Allowing items of lesser value in the following verses might mean that those offenses are of less significance than the unintentional sins of chapter 4. Alternatively, perhaps because all are sin offerings, whenever there was a need for a sin offering then the offenders would bring what they could afford from the possibilities being given.

The Options for Offering Birds (5:7-10) or Grain (5:11-13)

The law now turns to options available to the poorer members of the society. Such a person cannot afford to pay the usual penalty. This suggests that the rationale for variations in the earlier requirements is based in part on the financial capabilities of the persons involved. It implicitly reiterates that the standard for determining a sacrifice's value is in the attitude of the giver rather than the identity of the gift. The goal is to cultivate repentance in the heart of the offender, not to punish by causing financial ruin.

The first option involves two birds (cf. 1:10-17). One serves specifically as the sin offering and one as a burnt offering. These instructions prescribe only the presentation of the bird for the sin offering; for the other bird, the statute refers the reader to "the regulation" of the burnt offering (i.e., 1:14-17). In these instructions, the sole concern is with the blood; there is no instruction for the disposal of the rest of the bird. The blood is sprinkled on the side of the altar and "drained" at the base of the altar (1:15; 4:22-35).

The combination of offerings is significant. This might imply that it was normal to present burnt offerings in conjunction with sin offerings, even though the preceding instructions do not mention this fact (12:8; 14:21-22). There are dozens of references to occasions when sin offerings were made, and only one—apart from 5:6—does not mention burnt offerings at the same time (Ezek 44:27). Those passages tend to mention the sin offering first, followed by the burnt offering. The sin offering apparently restores a broken relationship between the Lord and humans, while the burnt offering celebrates the renewal of that relationship. This part of the passage does not mention the offering of a burnt offering with the sin offering, but the following paragraph implies that it is assumed.

The final alternative involves a modified grain offering. The use of oil or incense is strictly forbidden (5:11). Some suggest that the austerity of such an offering assumes that the Lord would not find it enticing, yet it is graciously accepted. It might also reflect the association between incense and holiness, showing that incense is to be used only after consecration has been accomplished. The priest sets aside a "memorial portion" (2:2, 9), which he offers to the Lord in the same way he offers the fatty portions of the animals. The note at the end of verse 13 about the priest's portion seems out of place stylistically (2:3, 10); it might represent a secondary expansion (cf. 6:14-18 [6:7-11]).

The absence of blood from this final alternative raises fundamental questions about the sin offering. The manipulation of blood seems to be what distinguishes the sin offering from the others, so it is surprising to discover that the priest could make atonement for someone without blood. This passage supports those who deny the belief in a magical component to blood. Instead, it shows that the blood is symbolic, and it once again places the means of forgiveness and atonement squarely on the Lord. Several suggest a connection between this type of offering and a Mesopotamian purgation ritual involving flour (Milgrom 1991, 306-7; Budd 1996, 97-98). That ritual calls for rubbing flour on the guilty party, however, so an absolute parallel is difficult to prove.

Theological and Ethical Analysis

The instructions for the sin offering reveal much about the Israelite understanding of sin and forgiveness. The sin offering constitutes what is at the core of much biblical ritual: reconciliation with the Lord. The sin in the garden disrupted the relationship between the Lord and humanity, and ritual constitutes the human side of the process of reconciliation. The divine side—acceptance of the ritual and its concomitant forgiveness—remains beyond human control.

Sin offerings show the seriousness of sin. Sinful actions that are unintentional or seemingly insignificant still require reconciliatory ritual. Prophetic writings often stress the importance of the human heart, criticizing their listeners for carrying out the Lord's laws externally, but negating their actions with the attitude of their hearts. The laws do not deny that the heart is important, but they demonstrate that good intentions alone do not make something right. If individuals touch an unclean object—even if they are unaware that they have done so—they are unclean. If they engage in an activity and assume that the Lord permits it, but then the sinfulness of the activity "becomes known," they are not excused on the grounds of prior ignorance. Times of reform in Israel's history represent possible examples of this. Somehow, over time, the people became convinced that certain behaviors and practices were not forbidden. Then someone "made known" to them the true nature of those actions and called for repentance.

A broad definition of sin underlies these laws. The term for "sin offering" denotes the ritual by which the state of impurity is removed or negated. One typically enters into that state as a result of sinful actions, but that is not the only way. Any time the sin offering is required—even for inadvertent physical contact or the birth of a child—the person is in a state of impurity. Impurity threatens the "life" of that person and others around that person. The extent of the impurity is determined in part by the status of the offender within the believing community. The principle seems to be that the "guilt" extends to all for whom the person is ritually responsible. Whether this is mitigated by the teachings of Jeremiah (31:27-30) and Ezekiel (18:1-32; cf. Deut 24:16) would require additional study. In any case, the requirements for sin offerings assume that any sinful state contaminates the sanctuary. The magnitude of this contamination and its effects are difficult to fathom, and its implications are not developed in this text. But it is clear that the Lord is personally offended by the presence of sin. It is a "stain" on the Lord's holy person and the Lord's holy dwelling; it is no trivial matter.

By exposing sin as a contaminant, Lev 5 infers the need to expose and confront sin. It is important for individuals to "speak up" (5:1) when they know of wrongdoing. A failure to do so leaves the entire community in danger of divine disapproval. This is often a difficult course to negotiate. The proper motivation should be a desire to do what is best for the community; but other, less pure motivations often come into play. The text promotes a proper motivation by offering no reward for accusations. The law focuses on the dangers posed to everyone, and it appeals to loyalty to the group as the motivation for bringing an offering (cf. Matt 18:15-17).

The primary physical purificant is the blood of the sacrificial animal. The laws of the sin offering supply no explanation for why this is so (cf. 17:11). The ritual practices of other ancient Near Eastern peoples do not provide any real insights on this question. In fact, contrary to popular assumptions, many of those peoples did not associate blood and ritual purification (McCarthy 1969, 166-76). This makes the Israelite practice all the more intriguing. Blood is said to provide atonement and forgiveness. From a scientific perspective, this makes little sense. Milgrom describes the function of the blood as a "detergent," but there is no chemical reaction at work that separates sin from the person or the sanctuary. The implied explanation is that blood has its effect because the Lord decrees that it does.

One recognizes this by stepping back and looking at this passage in its entirety. The fundamental assumption is that blood is necessary for atonement and forgiveness (cf. Heb 9:22). The animal must be without blemish, only the priest can handle the blood, and he must apply it in certain ways and in certain places that are different from all other offerings. But what blood is required? There is nothing unique about bull's blood, because the blood of sheep or goats or pigeons purifies just as well. Still, the priest must manipulate the blood in a specific way. Then there is the exception that allows for the use of the simplest of breads, without any blood (5:11-13). This would seem to undermine this principle entirely, but what it really does is establish a more fundamental principle: a sin offering is effective to the extent that the Lord is willing to accept it. The Lord assigns a value to an offering based on the circumstances in which it is given. There is a didactic aspect to this, because the priest and worshipers would recognize the need to go further into the sanctuary as a sign of the greater seriousness of some offenses. Still, at some level, the laws recognize that the most valuable of human offerings is not really sufficient in and of itself to produce atonement and forgiveness; the Lord must accept it. The prophetic doctrine of the insufficiency of sacrifice affirms these ideas (1 Sam 15:22-23; Isa 1:11-15).

As with the burnt offering, the value of the sacrificial animal reflects the relative economic status of the worshiper. The offending party is giving up something of value for the purpose of reconciliation with the Lord; it symbolizes the value the person places on having a right relationship with the Lord. There is a sense of balance in this. Although a (relatively) significant amount is required, it is never to the extent of depriving the person of the Lord's blessings. If a sacrifice would result in long-term financial hardship, a lesser offering is allowed. This too assumes the Lord's desire for reconciliation, in spite of the offense. By way of contrast, one can consider the consequences of the "high-handed" sin (Num 15:22-31). That law calls for "cutting off" the offending party, effectively depriving them of the Lord's blessings.

By any measure, the value the Lord assigns to the sacrifice far exceeds the monetary value of the offering. It is likely that the animal serves as a substitute or representative for the person(s) bringing it. Theologically speaking, the "price" for the offense might actually be greater than the life of the offender. Yet, ultimately, the

COMMENTARY

Lord accepts something that is of lesser value than the offender's life, namely, the life of an animal that belongs to the offender. The magnitude of this acceptance is particularly obvious in the case of national sin (4:13-21), where a single animal provides atonement for an entire nation. The Lord's willingness to accept something less than what is warranted clearly conveys a gracious and merciful attitude.

The realization that the sin offering is expiatory deepens this sense of divine grace and mercy. Older interpretations of the meaning of atone tend to associate it with propitiation, concluding that the sacrifice appeased the Lord's wrath but did not remove the sin. The idea of atonement as "covering" works well with this understanding. The Lord no longer "sees" the sin, so the anger dissipates. More recent work reveals that the meaning of "rub off" is inherent in the Hebrew term. The sin offering does not simply appease the Lord's anger; it rubs the sin out of existence. There is no attempt to explain how this is made real; the implication is that it is real because the Lord graciously declares it to be real.

These conclusions raise questions for Christian interpreters regarding the relationship between the sin offerings and New Testament teachings on the sacrificial meaning of Jesus' crucifixion, particularly in Heb 8–10. Some contend that the Hebrews writer claims the offerings of Leviticus did nothing more than show what was possible, effectively demoralizing the people by reminding them that their sins needed to be removed but had not been. This denies the efficacy of sin offerings. Some conclude that sacrifices provided propitiation only, appeasing the Lord but not eradicating the sin. Some assert that sin offerings provided propitiation, while the complete removal of sins (expiation) comes only in the crucifixion of Christ. The present work adopts the interpretation that, in Hebrews, the claim is being made that Christ's sacrifice provides expiation to a greater extent. The sin offerings prescribed in Leviticus brought expiation, but only for sins that had already been committed; therefore, the priests had to present the offerings over and over again. The claim of Hebrews is that the crucifixion of Christ eliminates the need for any further sin offerings. The crucifixion brings expiation, just as sin offerings did, but the expiation of the crucifixion extends to all sins yet to be committed. Thus it is a sacrifice offered "once for all," in contrast to sin offerings that the priests were to make repeatedly (Heb 7:27; 9:12, 26; 10:2, 10).

Lurking at the edge of this entire discussion is the issue of forgiveness for intentional sins. Many interpreters conclude that sin offerings applied only to the types of sins explicitly mentioned in these laws. On this basis, there is no offering that deals with intentional sins, except perhaps the Yom Kippur offerings (chap. 16). It is far from certain, however, that the laws of sin offerings are exhaustive. The laws regarding other offerings are not exhaustive in their consideration of possible occasions for those offerings, so it is logical to assume that the writer did not intend to restrict the use of sin offerings to the occasions spelled out in Lev 4–5. It is clear from Num 15:22-31 that some offenses are beyond atonement, but the demarcation of that distinction is unclear.

LEVITICUS 5:14–6:7

(Note: The numbering of Lev 6:1-7 is different in the Hebrew text [6:1-7 ET = 5:20-26 MT], affecting the numbering of all of chapter 6. In the following discussions, the numbering of the Hebrew text is given in brackets where it differs from the English.)

The final type of offering prescribed is the guilt offering, sometimes called the reparation offering (ʾāšam). Some interpreters regard it as a subset or outgrowth of the sin offering. Almost all the texts mentioning guilt offerings are within literary strata considered to be late, and the development of such a variant would not be out of the question. Some passages call for guilt offerings to provide purification (14:10-32; 19:20-22; Num 6:9-12). In the present text, there is some overlap in the terminology used regarding these two offerings. Moreover, the details of the sacrificial ritual are not given in the case of the guilt offering. Leviticus 7:1-7 shows that the ritual for the guilt offering is essentially the same as the sin offering ritual. Nevertheless, there are some significant differences. The most distinctive difference is the concern here with the monetary value of the offering. It carries a sort of "compensation for damages" component, which one does not find with the sin offering. The guilt offering deals with "trespasses" (see 6:2 [5:25]), suggesting it addresses a different concern than the sin offering. Also, several texts mention the two offerings as separate components of a single event (Num 18:9; Ezek 40:38-42; 42:13; 44:29; 46:20). Thus, these two offerings accomplish similar (or complementary) goals, but they are separate offerings. A philosophical rationale for this offering is lacking in the text, so explanations of its specific purpose are speculative, to some degree.

Literary Analysis

The literary style of these regulations is mostly consistent with the regulations immediately preceding them. The text refers to worshipers in the third-person masculine singular, as in chapters 1, 3, and 4. (Note: The NRSV regularly translates Hebrew third-person masculine singular forms with English second-person forms, in order to reflect more accurately the gender-neutral perspective that the laws intend.) The verbs commonly appear in the form of a simple conjunction ("and") + perfect, although occasionally the direct object comes first, followed by the imperfect (5:16; 6:6 [5:25]). Contrary to the previous laws, there are two narrative headings for different circumstances (5:14; 6:1 [5:20]), yet there is only one offering. The divine speech that follows the introduction normally begins with a directive to "speak" or "command" the Lord's words to a third party (1:2; 4:2; 6:9, 25; 7:23, 29). The law for the guilt offering omits such a directive (cf. 13:1-2; 14:33-34; 23:26-27). The direct address begins by identifying the situation for the offering. There are three introductory formulas: "When any of you commit a trespass" (5:15), "If any of you sin" (5:17), and "When any of you sin and commit a trespass" (6:2 [5:21]). These suggest a tripartite structure (5:15-16, 17-19; 6:2-7 [5:20-26]). Surprisingly, each unit begins with the formulation normally reserved for a primary law ("When"), rather than transitioning with "and if" for subordinate cases. In fact, the second unit begins with a conflated reading that includes "if" and "when" (the LXX omits "if"). These features suggest that the present text consists of previously independent pieces that someone has redacted together. Many argue that the first and third units originally stood together, while the middle unit was inserted last; but the evidence for this is not ironclad.

Each unit includes a statement about atonement and forgiveness (5:16, 18; 6:7 [5:26]), as with the sin offering. The clauses following the forgiveness notice could be original to the instructions or secondary. There is a general stylistic parallel between the circumstance section of the final unit and the corresponding portion of the preceding law concerning unwitting offenses (6:2-3 [5:21-22] and 5:1-4). Both give a series of scenarios linked by "or," rather than envision a single scenario that would warrant this offering. It is likely the instructions for these two offerings were paired together from an early stage in their development.

Exegetical Analysis

Guilt Offerings for Unintentional Offenses against Holy Things (5:14-16)

The first presumed occasion is that someone has committed a "trespass...unintentionally," and that the infraction involves "the holy things of the LORD" (5:15). The phrase translated "unintentionally" is the same one used in 4:2, 22, and 27. It is difficult to link this with "trespass," however, because "trespass" usually connotes an intentional offense (e.g., Josh 7:1; 1 Chr 5:25; Ezek 20:27; 2 Chr 26:16, 18; 29:6, 19; Ezra 9:2, 4; 10:2, 6, 10). In Lev 5:14-16, "infidelity" or "breach of covenant" is closer to the center of the term's meaning (Num 5:12, 27). But how can one be guilty of an unintentional infidelity? Perhaps the use of "trespass" reflects the significance of the "holy things of the LORD." They would be items or places specially devoted to the worship of the Lord. Perhaps this law envisions cases of mixing Yahwistic and non-Yahwistic worship, especially the use of tabernacle/temple items in rituals that mimic foreign practices. Such mixing might develop gradually, almost imperceptibly. Another possibility involves the priestly portions of offerings (Num 5:5-10; 18:8-32), which implies that a worshiper might inadvertently withhold or damage a portion set aside for priests (chap. 22). The present law is vague enough to obscure what offenses it intends.

The specification of a ram as the sacrifice raises its own questions (v. 15). The text mentions no other animal, which is curious in light of the variety one finds with the sin offering and the burnt offering. One would not expect every Israelite to have a ram, so this could be prohibitive to some. On the other hand, a ram is not the most expensive animal, so it would not be a great burden to wealthy landowners. Some commentators suggest that only the wealthy are expected to commit this offense. However, based on previous examples, it is difficult to imagine that there could be a "one price fits all" perspective for such cases. In fact, subsequent references to guilt offerings call for other animals (e.g., 14:12, 24-25), suggesting once again that these laws are exemplary rather than exhaustive.

There is also uncertainty regarding the ram's financial value in verse 15 (cf. 27:25; Num 18:16). The worshiper adds one-fifth of the ram's value or the damaged item's value as a payment to the priest. An abbreviated version of this in 5:18 and 6:6 [5:25] produces a different connotation. Many interpreters regard the reference to "a ram . . . or its equivalent" as allowing the worshiper to substitute for the ram with money. A few believe that the offender could give the priest the money for a ram (plus 20 percent), and the priest would then acquire the ram and offer it. But the phrase "or its equivalent" is problematic (5:18; 6:6 [5:25]). The Hebrew text does not include "or." The term for "equivalent" usually conveys the sense of "assessment, assessed value." The law might call for the worshiper to bring a ram for sacrifice, the priest assesses its monetary value, and then the worshiper gives one-fifth of that value as a penalty to the priest, while the animal is offered up in sacrifice. Or it could be that the one-fifth penalty is determined from the value of the item that has been damaged by the offender.

The reference to a "sanctuary shekel" is generally thought to indicate a silver standard that was heavier than other silver standards, but the exact weight is unknown. The connection with the sanctuary strongly suggests that the priests are responsible for maintaining this standard. The addition of one-fifth of the assessed value in the restitution reflects a low rate (cf. Exod 22:7-9).

The possibility of substituting money for the ram seems to run contrary to the significance placed on blood for atonement in the purification law (but see 5:11-13). Some eliminate the problem by finding an implied requirement for an additional sin offering in the reference to atonement. They deduce from this that these are situations that demand two offerings; however, the reading in 5:16, 18, and 6:7 [5:26] is the same as in 4:20, 26, 31, and 35, which refer to a single offering. Assuming an additional offering in chapter 5 implies an additional offering throughout chapter 4. It is simpler to recognize that atonement is achieved through the guilt offering involving a ram in chapter 5, with a supplementary monetary penalty assessed in certain situations.

Guilt Offerings for Unwitting Offenses (5:17-19)

The second unit differs from the first primarily in the circumstances that call for a guilt offering. The wording of the circumstances shares some aspects with the circumstantial clauses in 4:2 and 5:1-4. The effect is to collapse or combine sins that are unintentional and sins that are unwitting. There is no mention of the addition of one-fifth of the value of the ram. The supplemental fee might be implied, or it might be intentionally omitted because this is a less serious offense. Some argue that 5:17-19 refers to cultic infractions, representing a time when cultic infractions and moral infractions were distinct (cf. 19:20-22); but again the language is too vague for one to be certain. The law implies that one should not take chances when it comes to sin. Even persons who are unaware of their sin should take responsibility for the offense.

Guilt Offerings for Offenses against a Neighbor (6:1-7 [5:20-26])

A separate narrative heading in 6:1 would seem to indicate a shift to a markedly different law, but that is not necessarily the case. There is a lengthy circumstantial section comprising verses 2-4, but the main body of the law in verses 5-7 [24-26] closely parallels the earlier prescriptions for guilt offerings. The text identifies the sins in 6:1-7 [5:20-26] unit as "trespasses," as in 5:15. These infractions are committed against one's "neighbor." (The Hebrew term here is rare, limited to Leviticus and Zech 13:7.) Some harmonize the two messages by asserting that sins against one's neighbor must have been regarded as sins against the holiness of the Lord. Others highlight the dual reference to "swearing falsely" (vv. 3, 5). Such an oath, they say, implicates the Lord as a "corroborating witness." The purpose in swearing the oath is to assert one's innocence, but in this case it is assumed that one is guilty of the offense. The guilty party uses the Lord's name to cover the sin, and that defames the Lord's holy reputation. The person has, in effect, sinned against "the holy things of the LORD" (5:15). It is unclear, though, what necessitates the guilt offering, whether (a) the offense against the neighbor and the false oath are separate offenses, each requiring a guilt offering, (b) it is the combination of offenses that necessitates the guilt offering, or (c) the guilt offering is made to atone only for the act of swearing falsely, because that alone implicates the Lord. There is a case in Lev 19:20-22 calling for a guilt offering, but it does not mention a direct offense against the Lord. That would support the first alternative. At the same time, it prompts one to wonder why the law in 6:1-7 [5:20-26] makes swearing falsely so prominent. Perhaps the problem comes from assuming that 6:1-7 [5:20-26] is an exhaustive law, when the writer only intends it to be an exemplary law.

Differences in recent English translations reveal another uncertainty. The NRSV places the transition from circumstance to resolution in the middle of verse 5. This gives the impression that the guilty party wants to return what was taken but cannot, so restitution is made by means of the guilt offering. Other translations place the shift from circumstance to resolution in verse 4. The offender has wronged a neighbor and then lied about it, so the offender returns or reimburses what was taken to the wronged party and makes restitution. These instructions could imply a dual payment, involving both the return of the stolen item with its 20 percent penalty and the offering of a ram as a guilt offering. The dual payment could correspond to a dual offense, one against one's neighbor and the other against the Lord (in swearing falsely).

Theological and Ethical Analysis

It is difficult to establish the distinctions between the guilt offering and the preceding sin offering. This difficulty includes distinctions regarding the purposes of offerings. The message of the guilt offering is that an offender must recognize when an offense causes material damage to the victim's property, and that, as the cause of that damage, the offender is responsible for making compensation. This material damage is in addition to any "personal" damage against the Lord. The compensation for the material damage goes beyond the real value of the damaged item, including a 20 percent penalty. The text does not give a rationale for the penalty, but it likely was a belief that the victim deserved compensation for the temporary loss of the use of the item or that the victim suffered some other "intangible" damage.

The underlying principle is that an offense can cause several types of damage, and the offender is responsible for trying to address all dimensions of the offense. The offender's relationship with the Lord is disrupted, and an animal sacrifice repairs that disruption. Whenever physical damage to property is involved, the offender is responsible for repairing that damage. This law attaches a monetary penalty for less well-defined aspects of the offense, a certain intangible component to the damages. In this, the offender is made aware of the full extent of the offense, and the importance of mending what has been damaged. The demands entailed in this process of restitution are not burdensome on the offender, indicating that the goal of this process is reconciliation. It is important to repair physical or material damages, but that is only one part of the process of repairing the relationship. An overly burdensome punishment inhibits the reconciliation that it should be promoting.

LEVITICUS 6:8–7:38

Leviticus 6:8 [6:1]–7:38 consists of instructions for Aaron and his sons concerning the offerings treated in 1:2–6:7 [5:26]. The order is almost the same, except that the sacrifice of well-being is treated last. The text does not explain this change of order. The general opinion among interpreters is that the first block groups voluntary offerings together and then follows with required offerings, while this second block arranges the offerings according to their relative degree of holiness. The primary indication of holiness is in the identification of the "consumers" of each offering. The burnt offering is the most holy offering, because the Lord consumes it. Priests and then lay worshipers share in increasing degrees in the consumption of the remaining offerings. Leviticus 7:7-10 recapitulates the regulations for the first four offerings, highlighting the portions that the priests were to take for themselves. The sacrifice of well-being, which comes last, is the only offering from which the lay worshipers eat.

Literary Analysis

The contents and style remain relatively consistent from 6:8 [6:1] through 7:10. Beginning with 7:11, more complicated issues emerge. Therefore, it will be helpful to treat 7:11-34 separately.

Leviticus 6:8 [6:1]–7:10 contains three narrative headings (6:8, 19, 24 [6:1, 12, 17]) for five units of instruction (6:8-13, 14-18, 19-23, 24-30 [6:1-6, 7-11, 12-16, 17-23]; 7:1-10). One heads the first and second units, one heads the third, and one heads the fourth and fifth. It is likely that these headings expose redaction activity. Omitting the narrative introductions, there is stylistic uniformity in the first, second, fourth, and fifth units. All four units begin with the same phrase (6:9, 14, 25 [6:2, 7, 18]; 7:1). Three of the units include an almost identical pair of clauses that speak about priestly consumption of specified portions of each offering. These clauses state that "every male among the descendants of Aaron shall eat" a portion of the offering and that "it is most holy" (6:17-18, 29 [6:10-11, 22]; 7:6). The first unit omits these clauses because the essence of the burnt offering is that all the edible portions are burned with fire ("consumed" by the Lord). In the second and fourth units, there is one additional comment after this pair of clauses and before the next unit begins (6:18b, 30 [6:11b, 23]).

The contents of 7:1-10 show the editorial nature of these features more plainly. The introductory clause (7:1) and the pair of concluding clauses (7:6) reveal a clear connection with the framing clauses of the first, second, and fourth units; but the materials in the main body are noticeably different. The main verbs in 7:2a are plural, and the instructions for the guilt offering are similar to those for the sacrifice of well-being and the sin offering in chapters 3–4. The concern to place variant materials within the same frame as the units in 6:8-30 (excluding 6:19-23) suggests a common editor/author for all four units. Following 7:6, there is a parenthetical remark (7:7-10) that recapitulates the right of the officiating priests to claim portions of the first four offerings, but it omits any reference to the grain offering in 6:19-23 [6:12-16].

The third unit (Lev 6:19-23 [6:12-16]) stands out in this set of instructions. The narrative introduction in verse 20a differs from those around it. The second unit deals with the priestly portion of the regular grain offerings (6:14-18 [6:7-11]), but the third unit is concerned with a grain offering brought by the priests on the day of a (high?) priest's anointing. The priests take portions of the other offerings for their own use; this is the only offering from which the priests get nothing. It is logical to conclude that this reflects the separate origin of this unit. This is the only personal and voluntary offering coming specifically from priests, and it is a grain offering. It is not surprising that an editor would place this unit immediately following the instructions on priests' portions from the regular grain offerings.

The picture gets more complicated following 7:11, where attention turns to the sacrifice of well-being. It too begins with the formula, "This is the ritual"; but other typical clauses are missing, and this is the only unit that has markers for additional subdivisions. The first line identifies this unit under the general category of "sacrifice of well-being." Subsequent verses separate this into three subdivisions by use of the common construction "(but) if" (vv. 12, 16, 18). The first subdivision concerns thanksgiving offerings (vv. 12-15). It calls for the making and priestly consumption of unleavened cakes (not previously mentioned). These cakes accompany the animal sacrifice, the flesh of which the priests must eat on the day of the sacrifice. The second subdivision concerns votive or freewill offerings (vv. 16-17), allowing those to be consumed as late as the day after the sacrifice. The third subdivision is a general prohibition against eating portions of any sacrifice of well-being on the third day (v. 18), but it does not single out "every male among the priests" for this prohibition. It concludes with a formula that is more common elsewhere (5:1-4). The subject matter is similar to that in 6:8 [6:1]–7:10, but this unit diverges stylistically in significant ways from those other units. These differences arise because non-priests participate in the consumption of portions of this sacrifice, which reflects the less holy status of this offering.

Leviticus 7:19-21 does not flow smoothly from what immediately precedes. The main topic is not the sacrifice of well-being, but broader concerns about dietary uncleanness. There are several clues pointing to discontinuity between these verses and those that surround them. One can recognize this most easily by walking through the verses in reverse order. First, a narrative introduction in verse 22 indicates a new unit there. Verse 21 begins with an introductory formula that is common for primary laws ("When any one"), yet this primary law stands alone and consists of only one verse. Each of verses 19 and 20 begins with an introductory formula that never introduces a primary law (subject + relative clause), so that they stand as branches without a trunk. Meanwhile, each of verses 20 and 21 concludes with the threat "you shall be cut off from your kin." Within the first 16 chapters of Leviticus, this expression occurs only here and in the next paragraph. Thus, on form-critical grounds, verses 19-20 hold together, verse 21 stands alone, and verse 22 clearly begins a new section. In terms of subject matter, however, verses 19-21 stand together with verses 22-27 over against the preceding verses.

Verses 22-27 share some characteristics with verses 19-21, but both units seem out of place in the broader context of the sacrifice of well-being. Not only does this unit have a narrative introduction, but the Lord is now addressing the people of Israel, not just the priests (v. 23). These instructions do not bear the label "ritual," in contrast to the preceding units concerning priestly portions. In fact, there is nothing about designating portions for priestly consumption. Rather, the verses prohibit eating fat or blood at any time (cf. 3:16b-17). There is no mention of specific offerings or occasions. The subject of the verbs in verses 23-24, 26 is the second-person plural "you." In contrast, verses 25 and 27 revert to the more common "any one" as the subject (cf. vv. 20-21). The only elements that link these verses to what comes before are the subject of "eating" and the repetition of the threat, "you shall be cut off from your kin" (vv. 20, 21). There is also a loose connection between these verses and the following unit in the mention of blood and fat (v. 33). It seems, therefore, that instructions about dietary uncleanness have been inserted into instructions about consuming the sacrifice of well-being because of loose literary connections.

Verses 28-29a provide another narrative heading and direct address introduction, parallel to verses 22-23a. These verses also identify portions of offerings for priestly consumption, but the literary style is only partially consistent with what is in 6:8 [6:1]–7:10. The typical initial particle of the primary law is missing. Instead, the writer uses the participial form ["the one offering"], and the object of the verb is "offering" (as in chaps. 1–3). The latter suggests a connection with 6:19-23 [6:12-16]. The typical indefinite third-person verbs carry forward the remainder of these instructions, but they conclude with a motive clause ("For I have taken"—v. 34). This is the only instance of a motive clause in Leviticus until the end of chapter 11.

These observations leave the impression that an editor has inserted three or four paragraphs from a document on dietary restrictions into the present block of "rituals" prescribing priestly food allotments. It is possible that the narrative introductions in 7:22 and 28 serve the same functions as those proposed for 6:19 and 24 [6:12, 17]. The first might intend to point to a secondary addition, while the second shows where the main document resumes. Then again, the fact that all of 7:22-34 is addressed to the nation might signal that both are addenda.

Verses 35-36 and 37-38 appear at first glance to provide a dual summary to the first seven chapters, but the matter is more complicated than that. There are significant parallels between the two summaries. Both begin with "this is," and the second is identical to the introductions for the five main instructions in 6:8 [6:1]–7:18. Both identify these as instructions that "the LORD commanded," echoing the language of the introduction to the "rituals" in 6:9 [6:2]. Both specify the time when the Lord communicated these instructions to Moses. It is the differences in their contents that suggest different purposes and perhaps different origins. It is likely that the first summary originally stood at the end of materials having to do only with ordination (only 6:20, 22 [6:13, 15] and 7:36 mention the anointing of priests). Most of those materials apparently ended up in chapters 8 and 9, while a few pieces were redacted into this block of "rituals" (Noth 1965, 65). The second summary presently functions as a summary of chapters 1–7. Whether it always had this function is uncertain. It is the first of seven "ritual" summaries in Lev 1–15 (7:37-38; 11:46-47; 12:7b; 13:59; 14:32; 14:54-57; 15:32-33).

Exegetical Analysis

Priestly Responsibilities for Burnt Offerings (6:8-13) [6:1-6]

The "ritual" instructions for burnt offerings assume Lev 1, but they also presuppose knowledge of the daily burnt offerings in Exod 29:38-46 and Num 28:1-8. Those passages require a lamb as a burnt offering every morning and every evening (v. 13 [6]), with additional burnt offerings every Sabbath, on the first of each month, and on certain holy days. The writer addresses two concerns in verse 9 [2]: (1) the disposal of the remains of these offerings, and (2) maintaining the "perpetual" fire. Verses 10-11 [3-4] expand on the first concern, and verses 12-13 [5-6] expand on the second. Linking the two together rhetorically in verse 9 [2] is the root *yāqad*, "to burn." The term for "hearth" is derived from this root, and the corresponding verb comes at the end of the verse. The disposal of the ashes probably contributed to the maintaining of the fire.

The directive in verses 10-11 [3-4] calls for the priest to change his clothing during the disposal process. This change reflects the movement of the priest from holy space to less holy space ("outside the camp"). Linen is often worn in sacred ritual in Israel (Exod 28:42; Lev 16:4; 1 Sam 2:18). While he is near the altar, the priest wears linen; but he removes it when he goes away. The reference to a "clean place" for disposing ashes distinguishes it from "unclean" places where the people would dump their regular refuse. Even when they are no longer of use, the materials of ritual maintain a level of sanctity.

Verses 12a and 13 [5a and 6] form an inclusio regarding the maintaining of the altar fire. The sentence in between calls for adding wood only in the morning. This actually refers to replenishing the supply of wood at the altar each morning (Neh 10:34; 13:31). The main concern is with keeping the fire going all night.

The reference to "the fat pieces of the offerings of well-being" raises other questions (v. 12b [5b]). Earlier instructions direct the priests to perform this sacrifice on the altar of burnt offering, but without specifying a time (3:5). They also call for the same action with sin offerings and guilt offerings (4:10, 19, 26, 31, 35; 7:5). It might be that the fat portions of all offerings are "turned into smoke" the morning after worshipers present them, or that the priests perform such rituals only in the morning. It is also possible that the priests retained the fat portions of the sacrifice of well-being until the morning, but that they burned the fat portions of sin and guilt offerings immediately.

Priestly Portions of Grain Offerings (6:14-18) [6:7-11]

The first part of this law shows strong affinities to 2:1-3, adding that the priests present the grain offering "in front of the altar" (v. 14 [7]). This iteration elaborates on the "memorial portion" for the Lord and the remaining portion the priests eat (vv. 15-16a [8-9a]). They are to eat in "a holy place," identified as the courtyard surrounding the tabernacle (v. 16 [9]). What they eat must be unleavened (v. 17 [10]; cf. 2:11). The rest of verse 17 [10] explains the significance of the bread being unleavened. Unleavened bread is part of the Lord's special "offerings by fire" (2:3, 9, 10, 11, 16). It is "most holy," and so is comparable to the expiatory offerings (cf. 6:25, 29 [6:18, 22]; 7:1, 6). This reinforces the potential for expiation without blood (5:11-13). The priestly portion of this offering is reserved for the male priests (cf. Num 18:8-20). Within the priestly worldview, all these aspects reflect the extreme holiness associated with this offering.

The designation of this offering as a "perpetual due throughout your generations" is significant (v. 18 [11]). One finds it mentioned approximately three dozen times in the Old Testament, and almost always in Priestly legal texts. It accompanies the designation of holy days (Exod 12:14, 17, 24; Lev 16:29, 31, 34), the identification of the line of Aaron as priests (Exod 29:9; Num 18:23), and the delineation of priestly clothing (Exod 28:43), household goods (Exod 27:21; 30:21; Lev 24:3), food (Exod 30:28; Lev 7:34, 36; 10:15), and responsibilities (Num 10:8; 19:10, 21). It is used when designating items set aside for the Lord (Lev 3:17; 17:7). Such distinctions do not explicitly separate sacred and profane, but they are associated only with the sacred. The emphasis on the permanence of such mandates reflects the degree to which holiness is of concern.

This sense of holiness comes to a head in the final clause, "anything that touches them shall become holy." This phrase contrasts with Hag 2:10-14. That late prophetic text states that a holy object does not sanctify by contact, but the present text suggests that contact with the unleavened cakes ("them") does sanctify. There are some uncertainties of interpretation, though. First, the initial word of the verse refers to humans ("every male"), without inferring the sanctification of other items the offering touches (dish, cloth); but parallels to 6:27-28 [6:20-21] suggest that contact with other priestly/sanctuary objects might be precisely what the writer has in mind (Milgrom 1991, 449-53). Baruch Levine translates the phrase, "Anyone who is to touch these must be [already] in a holy state" (Levine 1989, 38). While this translation is logical, the use of a stative verb (rather than a participle) favors the former. It is surprising, however, that the writer would associate the act of sanctification with the grain offering.

The Anointed Priest's Grain Offerings (6:19-23) [6:12-16]

The "Literary Analysis" establishes the likelihood that this unit stems from a different source than the surrounding paragraphs. It assumes knowledge of chapter 2, yet it prescribes a new offering for a special occasion. Some associate it with the "offering of ordination" mentioned in 7:37-38. It does share characteristics with the ordination ceremony described in chapter 8 (8:26-28), but it only represents a small part of that ceremony. It could be that further regulations for the ordination offering have been communicated in narrative style in Lev 8–9.

The purpose of this unit is to prescribe an offering that every high priest is to offer on the occasion of his ordination (v. 22 [15]). So while the law parallels stylistically the instructions for voluntary offerings in chapters 1–3, it is actually a required offering. The priest would make the offering on the first day of the eight-day ceremony of ordination. It is unusual because the priest offers half of it in the morning and the other half in the evening. This places a bracket around the day, suggesting that the priest is offering the ordination ceremony as a gift to the Lord. The text emphasizes this aspect in verses 22-23 [15-16]. Unlike other grain offerings, this one belongs entirely to the Lord (cf. 7:7-10).

Priestly Portions of Sin Offerings (6:24-30) [6:17-23]

The regulations for the sin offering share several characteristics with those for the grain offering (6:14-18 [6:7-11]). The priests offer both "before the LORD" (6:14, 25 [6:7, 18]); in both cases, the offering is most holy; both specify which particular priests can eat of the offering, and that they eat the portion "in a holy place" (6:16, 26 [6:9, 19]); and both affirm that whatever touches it will become holy (6:18, 27 [6:11, 20]). This reveals a common understanding of the essence of the two offerings, particularly in the case of the phrase, "whatever touches its flesh shall become holy" (v. 27 [20]). The present law mandates the cleansing of any garment or dish that touches the offering. Blood on a garment must be laundered out. A clay vessel used in preparing the meat must be broken (cf. 11:33), while a thorough scrubbing and rinsing of a metal vessel is sufficient.

The reason for this concern about cleansing is not altogether clear, because of opposing translations of the phrase, "shall become holy" (v. 27 [20]; cf. v. 18 [11]). One might translate the main verb of this clause, "must [already] be holy," but then it is puzzling that there would be a requirement for the cleansing or destruction of a holy article that has come into contact with a holy offering. Some conclude that the contagion of sin has been transferred to the blood, so now the blood contaminates whatever it touches. This line of reasoning does not encompass all of verses 27-28 [20-21], though. The law implies a concern about contact with the flesh, not just with the blood, implying that both have taken on the sin that is being atoned. One could easily infer that the priests are consuming something that bears sin, but that might be the intent, because it sends the message that the sin is eradicated through the priests' actions.

Another viewpoint sees a danger in a holier object touching a less holy object. Such a view is consistent with Lev 16:23-24, where the priest's clothing acquires a quality of "superholiness" following a ritual within the inner sanctuary, or with the later doctrine that scripture documents "defile the hands" (Milgrom 1991, 1048). The principle is that something used for a holy purpose cannot be used for a less holy or common purpose, unless there is some intervening procedure of sanctification. Perhaps contact with the offering is dangerous because it is "most holy" and the touched article is merely "holy." An item might be holy, but it requires cleansing after it contacts a "superholy" offering. A similar principle is compatible with the interpretation that says the sin offering causes a touched object to "become holy." Because the offering sanctifies the other objects to a greater degree, it would be dishonoring to the offering to use those objects for any common purpose, unless there is an intervening procedure.

These laws presume that a visible, physical stain adhering to the objects used has a corresponding invisible, supra-physical stain. Just as the residue on an earthenware dish cannot be fully removed, so the supra-physical stain is irremovable. Just as a physical stain is removable from metal or cloth, so the supra-physical stain is removable. There is an inherently symbolic aspect to these acts of cleansing, and yet it is wrong to relegate it strictly to symbolism. The Israelites thought the supra-physical to be just as real as the physical. Just as a physical stain indicated the existence of a supra-physical stain, so the removal of the physical stain indicated the removal of the supra-physical.

The ultimate intent in 6:24-30 [6:17-23] is that everyone recognize the extreme sanctity of the sin offering. The priests must take the utmost care in handling the offering, even the parts they will consume. Verse 26 [19] specifies that the priest who performs the sacrifice must eat from the offering. This is not undermined by the more typical instruction in verse 29 [22] that all male priests may eat of the offering. The first instance involves a "must," and the second involves a "may." While other instructions indicate that any male priest may eat of an offering, they do not stipulate that the presiding priest must eat from it. The reference to the presiding priest suggests that he must eat a portion of the animal in every case. Some suggest that the priest's consumption of the meat indicates God's acceptance of the offering.

Another element reflecting the high esteem attached to the sin offering is in verse 30 [23], which assumes different grades of offense and offering. Some offenses require presentation of a sin offering within the sanctuary (4:3-21); the flesh of those offerings is forbidden to the priests. The instructions of 6:24-30 [6:17-23] apply to sin offerings presented outside the sanctuary, at the altar of burnt offering (4:22-35).

Priestly Portions of Guilt Offerings (7:1-10)

The "ritual of the guilt offering" mixes aspects of previous regulations. The first part deals with the guilt offering (vv. 1-6), but the remaining verses recapitulate one aspect of the first four offerings (vv. 7-10). The introductory and concluding phrases of 7:1-6 are like formulas in 6:14-18 and 24-30 [6:7-11, 17-23], but the procedures detailed in verses 1-6 are more like those in chapters 1–5, procedures that are missing from the instructions in 5:14–6:7 [5:26]. The second part identifies the priestly portion of the guilt offering (7:7-10), leading to a recapitulation of the priestly portions of other offerings.

These regulations confirm the impression of overlapping between the sin offering and the guilt offering in chapters 4–5. There are also similarities to the burnt offering and the sacrifice of well-being. The reference to "the spot where the burnt offering is slaughtered" limits the comparison with the sin offering to the less serious offenses (4:22-35). The act of dashing the blood against the sides of the altar (7:2) recalls the burnt offering (1:5, 11) or the sacrifice of well-being (3:2, 8, 13), in contrast to placing the blood on the horns of the altar with the sin offering (4:7, 18, 25, 30, 34). The separation and burning of the fat portions (7:3-5) parallels the sacrifice of well-being (3:3-5) and the sin offering (4:8-10).

Verse 7 draws a direct parallel with the sin offering alone

regarding a portion that belongs to the priest who actually performs the ritual. There is an implicit connection between the functions of the sin and guilt offerings as rituals of atonement and their use by the officiating priest. This links 7:1-10 to 6:26 [6:19], which deepens the uncertainty about the authenticity of 6:29 [6:22]. The writer now extends the principle of reserving a portion for the officiating priest to the burnt offering and grain offering (vv. 8-10). For the first time the writer indicates that the officiating priest retains the animal hide from a burnt offering. Similarly, the writer makes a distinction between the grain offering of 2:1-3 and those of 2:4-10. The offerings mentioned in 7:9 (= 2:4-10) are reserved for the officiating priest, while "every other grain offering" (7:10 = 2:1-3) is available to all the males of the priestly families. This represents a clarification of 6:16-17 [6:9-10], bringing that passage more in line with 2:4-10.

Eating Sacrifices of Well-being (7:11-21)

The instructions for eating a sacrifice of well-being reveal its "less holy" status. There is no designation of it as "most holy," and there is a concern about it becoming an abomination (v. 18). The identity of the one presenting it is ambiguous, and most of the references to eating are voiced in the passive; commoner and priest alike may eat from this offering. The writer distinguishes the proper use of a "thank offering" (vv. 12-15), a "votive offering," and a "freewill offering" (vv. 16-18). There is no reference to these categories in the previous instructions regarding the sacrifice of well-being. There is only one other reference to the "thank offering" in Leviticus (22:29-30), and scarcely a dozen others in the rest of the Old Testament. Two in the Psalms identify it as a "sacrifice" (Pss 107:22; 116:17). Others simply associate it with occasions of joy (2 Chr 29:31; 33:16; Jer 17:26; 33:11). Amos refers to "a thank offering of leavened bread" (Amos 4:5), but the present law specifies the need for unleavened bread. The identification "thank offering" probably does not denote a distinct ritual, but rather a distinct purpose for an offering. Other passages point to a similar understanding of the votive and freewill offerings (22:18, 21). It is likely that worshipers could designate any of the three voluntary offerings as thanksgiving, votive, or freewill offerings.

In spite of this flexibility, the instructions attach considerable significance to these designations. A thank offering is more holy than a votive offering or a freewill offering. The law restricts consumption of the thank offering to the day one offers it. The stipulation, "you shall not leave any of it until morning," shows that the offering would take place during daylight, and consumption of the flesh could take place after sunset (v. 15; cf. Exod 12:8-10).

The writer gives attention in the first part of this law to the grain offering (vv. 12-14). It is similar to the grain offering of chapter 2, without specifying the flour to use. This suggests again that this offering is less holy than the others. The extension of rights of consumption to the second day also reflects the lesser significance of the votive and freewill offerings. There is a quadruple expression of rejection for those who try to extend this right (v. 18). Eating on the third day is not "acceptable" (cf. 1:4; 19:5, 7), it is not "credited" to the one offering it (Num 18:27, 30), it is an "abomination" (Lev 19:7), and it brings "guilt" on the consumer (5:1, 17).

The reference to "guilt" in verse 18 might have prompted the addition of verses 19-21. The latter contain the first mention of individuals who are to be "cut off." Four other passages link "guilt" to the threat of being "cut off" (19:8; 20:17; Num 9:13; 15:30-31). Other laws calling for expulsion omit any references to "guilt" (e.g., Exod 12:15, 19; Lev 17:4, 9). The pairing of these terms in verses 18-21 appears to be a result of redaction, but it is impossible to determine who is responsible for it.

The focus shifts here from the sacrifice one may consume to the topic of dietary uncleanness. Verse 19a concerns the cleanness of the food, while verse 19b concerns the cleanness of the consumer. The next two verses expand on a consumer's possible uncleanness. Both identify the food as the meat of the sacrifice, and both call for "cutting off" the offender. Their only difference is in the source of the worshiper's uncleanness. The first uncleanness originates in the worshiper (v. 20), the second is contracted from an external contaminant (v. 21).

The severity of the punishment is significant. Regulations regarding simple uncleanness call for a temporary quarantine. This law calls for permanent exclusion from the covenant people, probably because the offense involves deliberately ignoring known purity laws (cf. 19:5-8; 22:3; Num 19:13, 20). A lesser response would suggest a diminution in the holiness of the meal. The threat of cutting off an offender emphasizes the solemnity of the ritual act of eating in a worship context.

Prohibition against Eating Fat and Blood (7:22-27)

This unit continues the designation of certain dietary practices as warranting permanent expulsion. It is almost certainly a secondary addition (see "Literary Analysis"), probably inserted at the same time as 3:16-17 (cf. "settlements" in 3:17; 7:26; 23:3, 14, 17, 21, 31). This law is more fully developed, containing a narrative heading and dialogue heading. Its main body summarizes other regulations about the treatment of fat and blood. Prior regulations specify that fat portions are reserved for the Lord (4:8-9, 19; 7:3-5); this law explicitly prohibits human consumption of those portions. Later regulations expound on the prohibition against the consumption of blood (17:10-16).

The main discussion concerning this unit is the extent of the application of these prohibitions. Many contend that this law only prohibits the consumption of the fat of species that are eligible for sacrifice, thereby allowing the consumption of the fat of wild animals (vv. 23-25); on the other hand, the reference to "any of your settlements" forbids the consumption of blood from any animal (v. 26). Others interpret this law more broadly as a prohibition against the consumption of fat or blood from any animal in any situation. Some believe that the list of prohibited animals expanded over the years from sacrifices only to all animals. The general context might imply that the law only concerns the consumption of sacrificial animals, but it must be remembered that the law probably has been placed here secondarily.

Priestly Portions of Sacrifices of Well-being (7:28-36)

Leviticus 7:28-36 is in some respects an elaboration on Exod 29:26-28, which stipulates that the Israelites are to consecrate two parts of the "ram of ordination" (9:21; 10:14). There is a subtle hint in the wording of verse 29 that the portions of the animal designated for priestly consumption constitute an "offering," separate and apart from the rest of the sacrifice (vv. 31-34). The designation of this as an "offering" again recalls the offerings in chapters 1–5 and in 6:19-23 [6:12-16]. This supports the impression that 6:19-23 [6:12-16] and 7:28-36 once stood in a series of instructions regarding a priestly ordination ceremony, but they are included here as part of an expanded application to sacrifices in general. Most curious is the stipulation that the layperson bringing the animal is to bring forward one of the priestly portions as an "elevation offering" (v. 30; cf. 8:25-29; 9:18-21) and supply another as an "offering" (v. 32). In this instance, the layperson performs at least part of a ritual "before the LORD." The non-fat portions of these offerings are given to the priests for them to consume, as expected, but the text gives no explanation for allowing non-priestly persons to perform a ritual act at a place from which they are normally excluded.

The stipulation highlights the association between the priests and the Lord in the minds of those providing the sacrifice and, consequently, in the minds of the priests. The worshiper gives a sacrifice to the Lord, but the Lord then passes on portions of it to the priest to consume. This point is made clear in verse 34: God (and not the worshiper) has given these portions to Aaron and his sons.

It is clear that verses 35-36 constitute a summary, but it is unclear what they intend to summarize. Some see this as the first of a pair of summaries for all of Lev 1–7, because the designation "offerings made to the LORD" is common in the first three chapters. More conclude that verses 37-38 summarize all of chapters 1–7, while verses 35-36 summarize a latter section within this block. Some tie verses 35-36 to the "rituals" of 6:8 [6:1]–7:34, but others restrict this to the sacrifice of well-being (7:11-34). A similar suggestion is that verses 35-36 conclude an originally separate document connected with the priestly ordination ritual (perhaps including 6:19-23 [6:12-16]; 7:28-34). This suggestion rests primarily on the reference to anointing in 6:20 [6:13] and 7:36. Additionally, the reference to Aaron and his sons serving as priests in verse 35 is strongly reminiscent of Exod 28:1, which introduces the ordination instructions. The first ordination ceremony is described in Lev 8–9. If verses 35-36 once served as the summary to instructions for an ordination ritual that included portions of chapters 8–9, then the ordination ceremony described there probably intends to set the pattern for future ordination ceremonies.

Adding to the uncertainty about the origin of this summary is the Hebrew term for "portion" in verse 35, which stems from a homonym of "anoint," found in verse 36. This is the only occurrence of this term in the Old Testament. Other Semitic languages supply cognates that carry the meaning "share, allotment." It has become popular to translate it with the English word "perquisite" (think "perk"; Milgrom 1991, 433-34; Hartley 1992, 101). The rarity of the term suggests a different literary origin for verses 35-36 than the origin of most of chapters 1–7.

Summary of Laws on Offerings (7:37-38)

The summary in verses 37-38 serves as the conclusion to all of Lev 1–7. It lists six offerings, including the five common offerings detailed in these chapters plus an "offering of ordination." The order of the list essentially matches the order of 6:8 [6:1]–7:36, causing some to propose that verses 37-38 summarize the "ritual" laws only; however, other summaries in Leviticus mention only the latest groups of laws in the sections immediately preceding them (13:59; 14:32). The opening phrase ("this is the ritual") only coincidentally echoes the use of this phrase in chapters 6–7. It is part of a larger piece that has more in common on form-critical grounds with the summaries in the following chapters. Thus, it is reasonable to conclude that the redactor intended these verses to serve as a summary of all seven chapters that precede it.

The term for "ordination" comes from a root meaning "to fill." It probably stems from a pre-Israelite expression, "filling the hands," which denoted the conferring of a special status or office (Levine 1989, 53). The term also refers to the placement of a gem into its setting (Exod 28:17, 20; 39:13). The text does not identify the offering of ordination anywhere in these chapters. Some suggest that it refers to the offerings in 6:19-23 [6:12-16] and 7:28-34. Perhaps this item in the summary reflects an earlier state of the text, when there was a complete law for an ordination offering. Or perhaps the redactor recognized instructions for an ordination ceremony within this section, and so the designation "offering of ordination" was included.

Verse 38 first identifies Mount Sinai as the place where Moses received these laws, but the final clause modifies this to mean "the wilderness of Sinai" (cf. Num 1:1). The introduction to the book identifies the Tent of Meeting—not Mount Sinai—as the place where Moses receives these laws. Jacob Milgrom proposes that the reference to Mount Sinai originally had in mind chapters 6–7 only, but an editor awkwardly added the final clause to encompass chapters 1–5 as well (Milgrom 1991, 438; cf. Budd 1996, 128). On the other hand, the Hebrew expression "on Mount Sinai" can be translated "at Mount Sinai." This broadens the scope of this description to the mountain and its environs, where the Tent of Meeting stood at the time. The final clause of the verse thus parallels and specifies the earlier designation. The middle clause of verse 38 recalls 1:2, strengthening the sense of closure between the two passages.

Theological and Ethical Analysis

The general populace in Israel is expected to know the laws in chapters 6–7; therefore, they influence how the people view their priests. The laws restrict the priests' status as much as they elevate it in the eyes of the people. There is a close relationship between the Lord and the priests who officiate over God's offerings. This is seen most clearly in 7:34, where the Lord describes taking part of the divine share of an offering and giving it to the priests. Earlier references to the priests' share of the offerings to the Lord (6:18 [6:11]; 7:5-6, 9-10, 15) imply the same idea. These offerings are made to the Lord, but the Lord gives certain parts to the priests.

There are several implications derived from this that the general populace and the priests should not miss. One is how intimately intertwined are the welfare of the priests and popular acknowledgment of the blessings of the Lord. The people bring their offerings according to the measure with which the Lord has blessed them. The priests share in those blessings to the extent the people believe that the Lord is the one who provides them. If the people do not recognize the Lord as the source of their blessings, then they will not bring their offerings and the priests will not share in them. If the priests do not offer the sacrifices as these laws prescribe, then the people will interpret their actions as ingratitude or disrespect toward the Lord (cf. 1 Sam 2:12-17, 27-29). The proper recognition of God's blessings is just as vital today, as believers contribute to the needs of those who devote their lives to work in various religious communities.

The laws of chapters 6–7 primarily call for the consumption of offerings on the same day that they are offered, or the following day. This communicates to worshipers and priests alike that the Lord's provisions are a continuous blessing. Even though the agricultural cycle is seasonal, the Lord provides blessings in different ways during different seasons throughout the year. The Lord provides "daily bread." The worshipers should respond in kind, supplying the priests with provisions so that they can bring daily offerings and show the people's daily recognition of the Lord's daily blessings. The priests are to maintain the fire of the altar constantly, in the same way that the Lord constantly blesses the people. Even through the night—at times when (symbolically) people might not be able to see it—the Lord is blessing the people, and they maintain through the night the fire with which they present offerings to honor and praise the Lord. Similarly, these are "perpetual statutes" (6:18, 22 [6:11, 15]), suggesting the Lord's intentions to maintain this people for generations to come; so they should expect to acknowledge the Lord's blessings for generations to come.

The preceding remarks apply specifically to the burnt offerings, grain offerings, and sacrifices of well-being; but parallel ideas apply to the guilt and sin offerings. The latter remind the people that any offense is ultimately an offense against the Lord. The "ritual" laws communicate the Lord's constant willingness to forgive. When the priests eat a portion of the offerings, they show a parallel acceptance of the offerings by the Lord, an acceptance that can come only with forgiveness. The careful attention paid to the procedures for those offerings reflects the extreme care with which someone should petition God for forgiveness.

Permeating all these laws is the notion of holiness. Creating and maintaining a holy environment is the primary concern. Most of the burnt offering and portions of all other offerings are prohibited from human consumption because they are too holy. Parts that are not consumed are offered in a special way to the Lord, or they are disposed of in a clean place and in a special (holy) manner (6:11 [6:4]). Some portions are set aside for priests, because they are considered holier than other individuals in the community. The linen clothes that they wear are a reminder of the holiness of the items they handle (6:8-13 [6:1-6]). The offerings carry the designation "most holy" (6:17, 25, 29 [6:10, 18, 22]; 7:1, 6). Whoever touches them will become/must already be holy (6:18, 27 [6:11, 20]). The participants must eat the food in a holy place (6:16 [6:9]; 7:6). The food that is left unconsumed loses its holiness (7:18), and those handling or eating holy food must be holy (7:19-21).

Recognizing the holiness in offerings and the rituals for presenting them colors the way in which someone acknowledges the Lord's blessings. The blessings come from a being who is "totally other." The Lord's essential nature is so different that the recipients cannot expect to do anything that would compel the Lord to provide them with blessings; nevertheless, that is what the Lord does. The worshipers need to be aware of the inherent mercy in such blessings. Multiple reminders embedded in the rituals point to the holiness of these offerings and the need for holy priests to present them. In similar fashion, recognizing the holiness in these offerings dictates the care and solemnity with which worshipers address petitions for forgiveness or bring sacrifices of well-being.

This sense of holiness is often lacking in the worldview of Christians today. It is easy for Christians to emphasize the approachability of God that comes as a result of the work of Christ, and there is strong scriptural support for recognizing this approachability and celebrating it (Heb 10:19-22). At the same time, it is possible that the notion of God's approachability inadvertently minimizes the enormous significance of this blessing. The distinction between holy God and sinful humanity is just as marked as ever, and the right of individuals to approach God does not change that reality. Instead, Christians should appreciate more fully the magnitude of the privilege inherent in having such access to God, taking more seriously what is implied in Paul's admonition, "by the mercies of God, to present your bodies as a living sacrifice, holy and acceptable to God" (Rom 12:1).

LEVITICUS 8–10

Chapters 8–10 comprise the only extended narrative in Leviticus. Chapters 8–9 report the fulfillment of instructions given by Moses in Exod 25–30. Those instructions concern the establishment of the cult, which involves sanctuary, personnel, and ceremonies. Exodus 35–39 reports the construction of the pieces of the sanctuary, culminating with a call by Moses to erect the sanctuary (Exod 40:2-11) and ordain the priests (40:12-15). The former is carried out in Exod 40:16-33, intimating that the ordination of the priests will follow immediately. However, ordination involves offerings (ceremonies), so it was necessary first to prescribe the offerings in Lev 1–7. Now that those have been prescribed, the text can return to the topic of ordination.

Leviticus 8–9 relates the fulfillment of instructions that are not part of the book of Leviticus, and then there is an unbroken flow from chapter 9 to chapter 10. The latter reports a direct and serious trespass by Aaron's sons, producing consequences that are only partially resolved within chapter 10. The narrative introduction to chapter 16 suggests that its contents are a response to the trespass by Aaron's sons. Chapter 16 contains instructions for an atonement ceremony, which concerns atonement for priests. At some level, the atonement procedures resolve the problems raised in chapter 10. Chapters 11–15 constitute a coherent block. Chapters 8–10 and chapter 16 form a bracket around that block. Leviticus 8–10 is the only section of Leviticus for which there is no editorial summary. Chapter 8 begins with a narrative introduction that one finds throughout the Sinai laws (Exod 19–Num 10); and the clause, "as the LORD commanded Moses," is common in Lev 8–10 and in Exod 39–40.

Three important conclusions emerge from these observations.

First, the differences between chapters 8–10 and the rest of Leviticus could be the logical consequence of their contents and purpose, rather than a sign of variant sources. Second, the ordination of priests is a significant piece in the cultic legislation of the Sinai laws. Third, it is most likely that the same editor(s) who brought together the legal texts in Leviticus placed this narrative within them.,

LEVITICUS 8

Literary Analysis

Leviticus 8 is typical of the narrative style of the Hebrew Bible. The narrative heading leads into a short paragraph that relates a command by the Lord to Moses to install Aaron and his sons during an assembly at the Tent of Meeting (vv. 2-3; cf. 1:1). Verses 4-5 report the execution of the call to assemble. The summons of verse 2 mentions six items, listing them in their "order of appearance" on the first day of the ordination ceremony described in verses 6-30. The remainder of the chapter establishes the guidelines for the next seven days of the ordination process.

Statements about doing things "as the LORD commanded" are the primary structuring devices for this chapter. They are supplemented with statements about what Moses "brought forward" during each part of the ceremony. The people assemble "as the LORD commanded" (v. 4). Moses sets the tone in the next verse: "This is what the LORD has commanded to be done" (cf. Exod 16:16, 32; 35:4). Five clearly marked units describe the rituals conducted that day. In the first unit Moses "brought forward" Aaron and his sons, and he robed Aaron in priestly vestments, "as the LORD commanded Moses" (vv. 6-9). In the next unit he anointed the tent and Aaron, and he "brought forward" and put robes on Aaron's sons, "as the LORD commanded Moses" (vv. 10-13). The third unit relates how he "led forward" and sacrificed a bull as a sin offering to consecrate the altar, "as the LORD commanded Moses" (vv. 14-17). In the fourth unit he "brought forward" the first of two rams as a burnt offering, "as the LORD commanded Moses" (vv. 18-21). And in the fifth unit he "brought forward" a second ram and a basket of unleavened bread as an ordination offering, "as the LORD commanded Moses" (vv. 22-29). Moses consecrates Aaron and his sons with blood and oil (v. 30), and then gives them instructions regarding their activities over the following seven days. Three times he mentions that he is doing as the Lord "commanded" him to do (vv. 31-35). The narrator summarizes the whole procedure by saying "Aaron and his sons did all the things that the LORD commanded through Moses" (v. 36).

The "commands" to which the text alludes are primarily those of Exod 29. The arrangement of events in the two chapters is closely parallel. The introduction in Exod 29:1b-3 matches the second half of the introduction in Lev 8:2. The first half of 8:2 finds its antecedents in the prescriptions for the priestly vestments (Exod 28:2-40) and the anointing oil (Exod 30:23-25). Because the vestments and the anointing oil are prepared prior to the day of ordination, the narrator does not describe them here. The people assemble at "the entrance of the tent of meeting," as commanded (vv. 3-4; Exod 29:4). Moses places the vestments on Aaron, as commanded (vv. 6-9; Exod 29:4-6). The anointing of Aaron follows, but the text supplements that with information on the anointing of the tabernacle (vv. 10-12; Exod 29:7; 30:26-29). There is similar supplementation in regard to Aaron's sons (v. 13; Exod 29:8-9a; 30:30; cf. Exod 40:9-16). Then Moses presents three offerings, as commanded (vv. 14-29; Exod 29:10-26). The description of the first day of ordination concludes with instructions about eating from the offering, burning what is left over, and then remaining at the tent for seven days (vv. 31-35; Exod 29:31-35).

The places where this ordination ceremony varies from the one prescribed in Exod 29 expose possible redaction issues. The major differences involve 8:10-13 and 8:30. Verses 10-13 conflate two instructions regarding anointing, one drawn from Exod 29:7-9a and the other from Exod 30:26-30. The latter calls for the anointing of sanctuary items, and then follows that immediately with the anointing of Aaron and his sons. The prescriptions in Exod 29 call for the anointing of Aaron and then the dressing of Aaron's sons, without any reference to anointing them. They overlap in calling for Aaron's anointing. Leviticus 8:10-13 conflates Exod 29 and 30 by including the anointing of the sanctuary items and the anointing of Aaron, but it again mentions the clothing of his sons without any reference to anointing them. The information is not contradictory; however, the present arrangement of events creates some problems. In particular, it creates a time lag between the washing of Aaron's sons and their subsequent investiture by Moses (from v. 6 to v. 13; cf. Exod 40:9-15). The placement of verses 10-11 results from the redaction of the prescriptions in Exod 30:26-30 into those in Exod 29:7-9a (see "Exegetical Analysis").

Leviticus 8:30 mentions a second sprinkling. This verse has its antecedent in Exod 29:21, which stands in the midst of the instructions for the third offering of the ordination ceremony. (Blood from the third offering is mixed with oil for this sprinkling.) Based on Exod 29, this should occur immediately after Lev 8:24. It is likely that the current placement is the result of textual corruption, because this is the only instance in the chapter where there is no statement about following the Lord's command. Exodus 29 includes a short passage about passing the priestly vestments on to later generations (Exod 29:29-30). Leviticus 8 does not address that issue. The passage about vestments comes just before Moses' instructions about eating the ram of ordination (Exod 29:31-33). The parallel to the latter comes in Lev 8:31. Since instructions on vestments precede instructions on eating in Exod 29, instructions on sprinkling priestly vestments have been shifted to their present position in Lev 8:30, just prior to the instructions on eating the offering (Gorman 1990, 106; Milgrom 1991, 545-49; Hartley 1992, 109).

Other differences between Exod 29 and Lev 8 reflect differences in context. Exodus 29 prescribes future acts, while Lev 8 describes the execution of those prescriptions. For example, Exod 29:9b concludes one prescription with a reference to the priesthood as "a perpetual ordinance." That prescription is forward-looking, establishing the divine authority lying behind future practice. The corresponding section in Lev 8:13 includes the clause, "as the LORD commanded Moses." This looks back to the past, basing current practice on the divine authority of previous instructions. The repetition of this clause in Lev 8 reveals the importance of this divine authorization.

Exegetical Analysis

Summons to Anoint Aaron and His Sons (8:1-5)

The introduction summarizes the events that are to follow, in the order that they will occur. It offers no surprises, which contributes to the theme of doing what the Lord has commanded. The only additional element is that Moses conducts the ceremony in the presence of the whole congregation (vv. 3-4; cf. 1 Kgs 8:1-11). The location suggests that the "congregation" consists of tribal leaders, not the entire population (9:1-5). The presence of tribal leaders alone does not change the intended effect of the congregation's presence. The congregation bears witness to the ordination of the priests. The ceremony says to the people that the priests bear a special responsibility, for which they deserve respect. It also reminds the priests of their solemn obligations to "the whole congregation." The bridge statement in verse 5 reminds both priests and congregation that their actions are to be carried out in a way that is pleasing to the Lord.

Placing the Priestly Vestments on Aaron (8:6-9)

Moses now "brings forward" Aaron and his sons. The language is reminiscent of sacrificial offerings, suggesting that the priests are to be "unblemished" like sacrificial animals. This stage of the process begins with ritual washing, as Moses purifies their bodies before they don the holy vestments. It marks part of the passage from one state to another, from "common" to "consecrated" (cf. 16:4, 24). Details regarding the vestments are in Exod 28. The order follows the logical order in which the priests would put them on. Mention of the Urim and Thummim reflects the special nature of these enigmatic items (v. 8; Exod 28:30; Num 27:21).

Anointing the Sanctuary and Aaron (8:10-13)

Verses 10-13 conflate the instructions in Exod 29:7-9a with those in Exod 30:26-30, creating a curious situation in the flow of the ceremony. Moses washes Aaron and his sons (8:6), and then places vestments on Aaron alone (8:7-9a). The anointing of Aaron should follow immediately, so that Moses can turn his attention to Aaron's sons, who are washed but unclothed. Instead, Moses attends to the anointing of all the sanctuary items first. It is unlikely that the sons would actually be required to wait so long. The result is three separate acts—the anointing of the sanctuary, the anointing of Aaron, and the investiture of Aaron's sons—subsumed within one unit.

But why would someone conflate the two passages from Exodus? Perhaps the answer lies in the references to consecration in Exod 30. The ordination prescriptions mention consecration in the introduction and conclusion (Exod 29:1, 36), but the specific prescription on anointing does not mention consecration (Exod 29:7-9a); however, the instructions for making the oil mention consecration twice (Exod 30:29-30). The present unit links anointing and consecration three times, including a reference that is not in Exod 30. This suggests that the writer in Leviticus wished to emphasize the consecratory function of the anointing. The resulting text accomplishes this by grafting together anointing and consecration of the sanctuary with anointing and consecration of Aaron and his sons.

The reference to consecration of the altar and Aaron raises another problem in the ordering of these events. It seems inappropriate for Moses to anoint the altar before he purifies it with sacrifice (v. 15). Some argue that verses 10-11 are out of place sequentially, because purification should precede consecration (Exod 29:35-37). On this reasoning, the note that the anointing "consecrates" Aaron is also out of place, and the mention of consecration in connection with the third offering (v. 30) might suggest that this mention of consecration is secondary. One solution is to blame this on scribal carelessness. There is also the possibility that consecration and purification are essentially simultaneous events. In this vein, the first references to consecration (v. 10) might mark the beginning of the consecration process, while the reference in verse 30 marks the end of the process.

A Sin Offering for the Altar (8:14-17)

The description of the sin offering adheres closely to the instructions in chapter 4 and in Exod 29. The only real difference is the inclusion of purpose clauses here. Moses places the blood on the horns of the altar to "purify" the altar. Pouring out the blood at the base of the altar "consecrates" and "makes atonement" for it. The addition of the two clauses suggests the writer's concern to emphasize these aspects of the ceremony.

It is significant that the sin offering comes before the burnt offering. The burnt offering represents a gift to the Lord, but the priests must be purified before presenting a burnt offering, to avoid offending the Lord. When Aaron and his sons lay their hands on the head of the animal at the same time, they are seeking purification, even though no one charges them with specific sins. Similar assumptions are at work in Exod 29. Even though Moses has washed them, dressed them in new clothes, and anointed them with consecratory oil, the priests still need sacrificial purification and atonement. This might be a precautionary measure, but it suggests that even priests are assumed not to be holy in their natural state.

The Burnt Offering (8:18-21)

The description of the burnt offering parallels the instructions of Exod 29:15-18, even to the point of identifying it as "a pleasing odor, an offering by fire" (cf. 1:13). It is a gift from the priests to God. Neither text gives a reason for offering a ram, rather than a more valuable bull.

The Ram of Ordination (8:22-30)

The "ram of ordination" offering is more complicated. It involves laying hands on the animal's head, slaughtering it, daubing its blood on the extremities of the right side of the priests, dashing the rest of the blood against the altar, anointing Aaron and his sons with a mixture of oil and blood, offering portions of the animal's flesh and unleavened bread as an elevation offering, and then apportioning some of the offering to Moses (cf. Exod 29:19-26). Moses serves as priest to Aaron and his sons, performing for them the functions they perform for the rest of the people when presenting a sacrifice of well-being (7:30-34). Here, they lay their hands on the head of the animal, and Moses slaughters and dashes the blood against the altar (cf. 3:2, 8, 13; 7:14), turns the Lord's portion into smoke, and receives the elevation offering as his own portion.

There are no instructions for ordination offerings in Lev 1–7, although remnants of them might be preserved in 6:19-23 [6:12-16] and 7:28-36. The main distinction is the smearing of blood on the right-side extremities of Aaron and his sons (thumb, earlobe, and big toe). The prescriptions for purification from leprous diseases contain a similar action, although those instructions associate it with a guilt offering and include a parallel anointing with oil (14:14, 17, 25, 28). It is tempting to conclude that the smearing rite reveals an understanding of this initiation ceremony as an event that marks a priest's transition from ritually "leprous" to "clean," but this is purely speculative. Some interpreters believe the priests are simply being cautious, in case they are guilty of some unwitting sin. Others believe that the special circumstances of this event call for additional consecration.

Consecrating Aaron and His Sons (8:31-36)

The final paragraph brings to a climax the theme of obedience to divine commands and points ahead to their imminent completion. Aaron and his sons are to eat as Moses "was commanded" (v. 31; the NRSV reading reflects LXX, Syriac, and Targums [cf. 8:35; 10:13]; the MT adopts the active form of the verb, as in 10:18). As a counterpart to the statement in verse 5, the ordination ritual has been performed according to what the Lord "commanded" (v. 34), and Moses is communicating what he was "commanded" to say (v. 35). The anticipation raised by these three instances of "commanded" evokes a special sense of satisfaction at the summary report (v. 36). The significance becomes evident with the lamentable episode in Lev 10:1-2. The repetition of "commanded" is also a continuation of the renewal of creation theme (Exod 39:42-43; 40:33). The cultic apparatus that will facilitate a renewed relationship between the Lord and humankind is nearly in place.

One lingering question concerns what happens over the next

seven days. Some believe that Moses and the priests repeat the ordination offerings each day, while others conclude that one day of offerings was sufficient. The ambiguity arises in part from the curious way in which the text incorporates the events of the whole week within the instructions that Moses gives, rather than mentioning those events with the summary notice in verse 36. The crux stands in verse 34—"as has been done today, the LORD has commanded to be done to make atonement for you." It is unclear whether the first clause is the beginning of a new sentence, or the concluding clause of the preceding verse. The former means that the rituals of the first day fulfill the Lord's commands; the latter means that the Lord has given additional commands for Moses and the priests to perform the same acts for the remaining days. In support of the first opinion, Moses' instructions suggest that Moses will not be staying with the priests. He is simply instructing them to remain at the tent of meeting. If Moses is not staying with them, then he will not be there to present the installation offerings. On the other hand, the priests must eat for these seven days, and they are not yet consecrated for the purpose of offering other sacrifices (from which they could get food). It would make sense that they would eat from installation offerings like those just prescribed. The absence of any reference to Moses' whereabouts for this week provides nothing but an argument from silence. It is quite possible that he is commanding the priests to stay at the tent of meeting *with him*. This might be the meaning behind the final clause in verse 35, "for so I am commanded" (cf. Exod 29:35-37). Thus, it is likely that offerings are presented on each of the eight days.

A related question involves the performance of installation ceremonies in later generations. It is possible that this was the only installation ceremony ever performed. Some see in this episode a "rite of founding." Such a rite marks a permanent change in the world, as perceived by those performing it. All of creation was corrupted in one event (Gen 3:1-7), and the ordination of this priesthood constitutes the one-time establishment of the means to remedy that situation (Gorman 1990, 103-39). The text gives no instructions for subsequent ceremonies, and particularly problematic would be the designation of an individual to fulfill Moses' role. Instead, the offices of priests could have been inherited by subsequent generations, passing from fathers to sons. Such an informal process might lend itself to ambiguities, however, about who are the most worthy heirs. Such a system could foster an ever-lessening appreciation of the significance of priestly honor. Therefore, one cannot rule out the possibility that the description of this ceremony served as a model for future installation ceremonies (Num 20:22-29; 27:12-23).

Theological and Ethical Analysis

Concerns about an ever-lessening appreciation of the significance of priestly honor arise from a sense that honoring the crucial roles played by priests is the central concern of the ordination ceremony. At each step, Moses and the other players do "what the LORD has commanded." This suggests an awareness of the grave seriousness of what they do as priests. The well-being of the characters is at stake, because the priests' responsibilities affect the entire world. They work to fix a broken creation, all of which suffers because of the sin that humanity brought—and continues to bring—into the world. Correcting something that is utterly corrupted and utterly precious requires the utmost care and attention. Careful attention to detail sets the tone for how the priests are to fulfill their responsibilities.

The ordination ceremony changes the fundamental state of the priests. Ordination rituals "purify" and "consecrate" and "make atonement for" them. Prior to this ceremony, they possess the same (corrupted) human state as the rest of the nation. The closest parallels to these rituals are in the purification rituals for leprous diseases. Both involve a seven-day period of separation (13:6, 31-34, 50-51, 54), ritual washings (14:8-9), stationing the person at the entrance of the tent of meeting (14:11), and daubing blood on the right-hand extremities of the one being purified (14:14, 17, 25, 28). The priests' initial ritual state is somehow akin to that of a leper (cf. Isa 6:1-8).

Cognizance of the effects of priestly ordination should positively affect the attitudes of priests and worshipers alike when the latter come to seek the Lord's forgiveness. The priests have no justification for thinking of themselves as spiritually superior. More positively, the priests represent what all people can become. They are a living demonstration that lives can be changed, that those formerly offensive to the Lord can be made right. They represent hope for a fallen world.

For these reasons, it is important that the "whole congregation" be witnesses to the ordination. They confirm that the ceremony is carried out "as the LORD commanded," because the services that the priests render are of the utmost importance to the spiritual state of every person in attendance. The people witness an event that gives them hope that their corrupted human state can be made holy. If the priests, who are like lepers, can receive purification and sanctification and atonement, then anyone can be so blessed. One might expect, then, a growing anticipation as the conclusion declares, "Aaron and his sons did all the things that the LORD commanded." But the ceremony is not yet complete.

LEVITICUS 9

Aaron and his sons now assume their rightful place alongside Moses before the elders of the people. The priests demonstrate their worthiness to be there by pronouncing the first priestly blessings. The appearance of the glory of the Lord at the end of the chapter heralds the imminent restoration of an intimate relationship between the Lord and humanity, which the sins of previous generations had destroyed.

Literary Analysis

Leviticus 9 generally follows the structure of chapter 8. It begins with a summons and command from Moses for two sets of offerings (9:1-4; cf. 8:1-3). One difference is the promise that "the LORD will appear to you" (9:4b). Another is the inclusion of offerings from the people. The text is careful to distinguish between priests and people. Moses gives instructions directly to Aaron about what he is to bring, but Aaron is told to offer the sacrifices, and Aaron is to give instructions to the people about what they are to bring. These actions establish a hierarchy of authority that set the pattern for subsequent generations. The execution of these two commands (9:5) parallels the assembling of the people in 8:4; similarly, Moses' dual statements in 9:6-7 function as a bridge (cf. 8:5). The bridge shows how these events will go further than those of the preceding chapter. Moses sets the tone by framing these instructions with statements about the people doing what "the Lord commanded" (9:6a, 7b; cf. 8:5). He reiterates that the Lord's glory will appear to them as a result of their obedience (9:6b), but he also makes it clear that such an appearance will come only after the priests have offered sacrifices of atonement. This bridge leads into the account of the fulfillment of the command, which constitutes the main body of the chapter (9:8-21; cf. 8:6-30).

The main body proceeds from one offering to the next without the pattern of summary statements used in chapter 8. There is one instance of the clause, "as the LORD commanded Moses" (v. 10), but that is referencing earlier instructions regarding sin offerings (4:3-12); it is not a concluding statement. The only concluding statement comes at the end of the main body (9:21), and it cites Moses alone as the source of the commands. This maintains the sense of a hierarchy among participants. In the preceding chapter, the Lord commanded Moses, and Moses—and finally Aaron and his sons—did "as the LORD commanded." In this chapter, Moses commands Aaron, and Aaron and his sons do "as Moses had commanded." The chapter concludes by pointing the reader's attention toward the future (9:22-24; cf. 8:31-35). This conclusion consists of a blessing by Aaron and Moses (9:22-23a), the appearance of the Lord's glory (9:23b-24a), and the people's reactions in worship (9:24b).

The wording for the sin and burnt offerings here is slightly different from the instructions in earlier chapters. There is no mention of the priest placing his hand on the animal (cf. 4:15), and there is a different term for pouring out the blood. Nevertheless, in the majority of cases, the same terms are used here as in those earlier instructions.

The sequence of the offerings does not precisely match Moses' instructions. He calls first for a sin offering and a burnt offering for the priest. Aaron performs these in 9:8-11 and 9:12-14, respectively. He then calls for parallel offerings for the people, along with a sacrifice of well-being and a grain offering. Aaron performs the first two offerings for the people (vv. 15-16), but the grain offering is now linked to the burnt offering (v. 17) rather than to the subsequent sacrifice of well-being (vv. 18-20). As mentioned earlier, some believe that the placement of the instructions for the grain offering in chapter 2 reflects a time when burnt offerings and grain offerings had become more closely paired. It is possible that the command here represents the more original order, while the account of the performance of the rituals represents later convention. Then again, it could be that the grain offering is mentioned last because it is an ancillary offering rather than a primary offering, while the text reports the actual order in which the various parts of the ceremony are performed. There is no reference to the grain offering in the conclusion (v. 22). The mention of the wave offering is not unexpected (v. 21), since it is prescribed for every sacrifice of well-being (7:29-34). It forms another parallel with the ordination rituals in chapter 8 (8:29).

Exegetical Analysis

Instructions for the Eighth Day of Ordination (9:1-5)

The eighth day of the priestly ordination ceremony is one of several occasions when an eighth day marks a new beginning after a week of consecration (12:2-3; 14:8-10; 15:13-14; 22:27; 23:34-36, 39). Closely parallel to this ceremony are the dedication of Solomon's temple (1 Kgs 8:65-66) and the restoration of temple worship in Ezekiel's vision (Ezek 43:18-27), both of which conclude on the eighth day. The eighth day does not so much mark the conclusion or climax of the seven preceding days as it marks the beginning of a "new time" (Milgrom 1991, 571).

The instructions for the eighth-day rituals divide into two parts, one regarding the offerings from Aaron and his sons, and one regarding the offerings from the people. The identifiers for the people betray some inherent ambiguity. Moses summons "the elders of Israel" (v. 1), but then he gives Aaron instructions for "the people of Israel" (v. 3), and the execution of the summons involves "the whole congregation" (v. 5). The reference to "the elders of Israel" probably indicates more precisely who participates in this ceremony. The elders represent the entire nation (8:4).

The priests and the people are to bring separate sin offerings and burnt offerings, but Moses also requires the people to bring a sacrifice of well-being and a grain offering. There is no reason to assume that Aaron has committed some sin since Moses offered the sin offering for him at the beginning of the week (chap. 8), so some interpreters conclude that this text is redundant. Others propose that it shows a concern for the inherently sinful state of humans, or that it is a necessary preparation for the theophany at the end of the chapter. It could be that these initial offerings prove that Aaron now has the authority to present offerings at the sanctuary. The requirements of a bull calf for the priests' sin offering and a male goat for the people's offering might reflect the higher status of the priests in ritual matters (4:3-12, 22-26). On the other hand, the people must bring a more valuable burnt offering (an ox and a ram) than the priests bring (a ram). This simply means that the general populace has more to give than the priests alone have. The same applies to the call for additional offerings from the people. There is more specificity to the burnt offerings here than in chapter 1. These appear to be the most expensive types of burnt offering possible, which reflects the importance of this occasion.

The call for a bull calf for the sin offerings (vv. 2, 3, 8) is surprising; only two other texts in the Pentateuch mention a calf with legitimate sacrifices (Gen 15:9; Deut 21:3-6; cf. 1 Sam 16:2). The regulations in chapter 4 call for a "bull of the herd," and this is the term one finds throughout the Pentateuch, Chronicles, and Ezekiel. The term "calf" is used most often in references to the Golden Calf made by Aaron and the two calves commissioned by Jeroboam, and some rabbinic texts see an intentional irony in having Aaron offer a "calf" in this inaugural offering. Two prophetic texts mention a "calf" in connection with sacrifices (Jer 34:18-19; Mic 6:6). The use of this less-common term might indicate a different literary source for this chapter; others see in it another clue of the special value attributed to these offerings.

What lends special significance to the occasion is the impending appearance of the Lord. The Hebrew text of verse 4 literally reads, "For today the LORD has appeared to you," but this could be a simple mistake in the secondary pointing of the text. The LXX and other early translations reflect a participle here. A participle often denotes action that is imminent ("the LORD is about to appear to you").

Offerings for the Eighth Day (9:6-21)

The bridge into the main body of the chapter begins and ends by stating that Moses' commands originate with the Lord (vv. 6-7), which links these offerings with the offerings in the preceding chapter. They are the culmination of an entire week of offerings. The purpose of the offerings is to "make atonement" for the priests and the people (v. 7). (The Hebrew mentions "the people" twice here; LXX reads "for yourself and for your house," in the middle of the verse.) The priests have been offering sacrifices for themselves for a week (8:33-35), but they have not yet offered any for the people. The priests must make atonement for themselves before they can then turn their attention to the congregation (v. 7). The progression premieres what will happen in the cult from this day forward; the priests must keep themselves pure, so that they can make atonement for the people when they sin.

The descriptions of the priests' sin offering and burnt offering basically follow the regulations given in 4:3-12 and 1:3-9, respectively. Certain regulations are not mentioned, but it is likely that the writer felt it was not necessary to include them in this report. The succeeding references to the people's sin offering and burnt offering are even briefer, probably because sin and burnt offerings have just been noted. For the grain offering, the writer mentions only the part that is given to the Lord. There is a more detailed description of the dual sacrifice of well-being (vv. 18-21), mentioning every action that Moses prescribes in chapter 7.

The final clause of verse 17 mentions a "burnt offering of the morning." Moses does not include this offering in the introductory instructions, which is not completely surprising. The procedures here basically follow the prescriptions for ordination in Exod 29. Those include instructions for daily sin offerings "for atonement" (Exod 29:36), and then daily morning and evening offerings (Exod 29:38-41). The reference to the morning offering here confirms that all those instructions are carried out. The Lord promised then that God's "glory" would sanctify the sanctuary at the end of the ordination ceremony (Exod 29:43-44), just as the next paragraph describes.

The Glory of the Lord Appears (9:22-24)

The attention of the people moves from high to low in these verses. As Aaron completes the ordination rituals, he is at the altar platform, standing above the rest of the assembly (cf. 2 Chr 6:13). He has just "raised...an elevation offering," and the assembly maintains their elevated gaze as he blesses them. He then descends and, with Moses, enters the tent of meeting. The action now takes place at "eye level," as the divine glory appears to the people. Fire goes out from the tent, and they fall to the ground. The overall effect is that the reader recognizes how the Lord descends to be among the people and then goes out in their midst in a way that brings blessing to them.

This progression of movements marks the resumption of action that had been suspended at the end of Exodus. There, the activities of Aaron and his sons in the tent of meeting are anticipated, but not realized. The glory of the Lord had filled the tent, but there was still a barrier between the Lord and the people. The glory does not come out of the tent, and no one is able to go in. That changes with the ordination of Aaron and his sons. Once ordained, the priests are acceptable as mediators between the Lord and the people. Moses must accompany Aaron into the tent of meeting on this occasion. Moses alone had this right previously, but his ability to enter had been temporarily interrupted at the end of Exodus. Now Aaron and his sons are ordained, so they can enter with Moses into the inner chambers. The dual blessing that Moses and Aaron give when they emerge is a celebratory act (cf. Exod 39:43). The Lord shows initial approval by having God's glory emanate from the tent and consume the offering. The divine desire to "meet with" this people is now fully realized (Exod 29:42-43).

The emanation of the glory from the tent of meeting stands as a link in a chain of passages. It points back to the appearance of the glory at Mount Sinai (Exod 24:15-18). The glory was high up on the mountain, and there were clear indications that approaching the Lord then was a dangerous thing. Only Moses could draw near, and the people were afraid to approach him after Moses had a "close encounter" with the Lord's glory (Exod 34:29-35). The tabernacle was built to bring the Lord closer to the people, but the sense of separation was maintained, as even Moses was forced to leave upon the descent of the glory (Exod 40:35). This separation is all but eliminated with the ordination of the priests, who now are able to enter into the tent on behalf of the people. The Lord shows approval by sending forth the divine glory to consume their offering. Similar events transpire when Solomon moves the ark to the Temple (1 Kgs 8:1-11; cf. Judg 6:19-24; 13:15-23; 1 Kgs 18:30-39). Further parallels are suggested by dedication ceremonies for the Temple that take seven days to complete (1 Kgs 8:65-66; Ezek 43:18-27).

The reaction of the people to this series of events is celebration. The "shout" they raise is a shout of joy (cf. 2 Chr 7:3; Ps 105:43). They rejoice because they recognize the blessing the Lord bestows on them in appearing to them in this way. The Lord has previously maintained a distance, but now has graciously chosen to meet with the people. They show their recognition of this by falling to the ground in homage (cf. 1 Kgs 18:39).

Theological and Ethical Analysis

There is an important shift of cultic rights and responsibilities that comes with chapter 9. The sanctuary has been prepared (Exod 35–40), the rules for offerings have been given (Lev 1–7), and the priests have been ordained (Lev 8). Now they begin their vital role of facilitating reconciliation between the Lord and the people, with implications for all creation. It is tempting to suggest that the story of sin and its consequent curses in the garden constitute the "first eighth day," so that this eighth-day blessing marks a (symbolic) restoration of the state of creation prior to the events in the garden. The appearance of the Lord and the consumption of the offering by fire reveal the Lord's acceptance of their gift and affirmation of the blessing. The people's shout of joy comes at one level on behalf of all creation.

It is clear that this theophany and its accompanying blessing come as a response to obedience. The Lord gives a dual promise to appear in glory in response to the obedient presentation of these offerings. This sets a tone for occasions in the future when the people and priests will present similar offerings. If they act according to the Lord's commands, then God promises to respond with blessings and by living among them. The theophany confirms the Lord's faithfulness to those promises.

The events in chapter 9 demonstrate something of what is involved in "meeting with" the Lord. The Lord wants to meet with the people, but such a meeting is always a risky enterprise. The holiness of the Lord must be acknowledged through obedience. The progression of the offerings in this ceremony is from purification to gift for the Lord to sharing a meal with the Lord. Each step requires divine mercy. The Lord makes demands that the people must meet, but the Lord's acceptance of those obedient acts involves mercy. The people's response shows that they recognize this. They set a proper tone for worship by obeying him. Worship often involves looking up to the Lord and being grateful and humble when God responds positively to a meager gesture of apology and gift giving. The result is fellowship with the Lord and with one another. Gratefulness and humility arise from recognition that the Lord could reject their offerings and strike out in righteous punishment. The next event will demonstrate this, and there will be no further references to blessing until chapter 25.

LEVITICUS 10

The time of ordination began with obedience in chapter 8 and led to celebration by the end of chapter 9; but celebration turns to divine anger in chapter 10, with the resultant human responses of repentance and uncertainty. A rite performed by two of Aaron's sons runs contrary to what was commanded (v. 1). This provokes a reaction of retribution (vv. 2-3), which itself ceases when the survivors do "as Moses had ordered" (vv. 4-7). The attitudes of Moses and Aaron are strikingly different. Moses focuses on the big picture and what needs to be done to prevent similar incidents in the future, while Aaron is consumed with the immediate situation and his family. He is unable to eat, indicating a grief that he must justify to Moses. In the end, the writer leaves the episode unresolved, setting it aside until chapter 16.

Literary Analysis

There is no break literarily between chapters 9 and 10, implying that chapter 10 also relates events that occurred on the eighth day of the priestly ordination rituals (9:1). The chapter begins with the briefest of descriptions of Nadab and Abihu's offense (v. 1), the Lord's response (v. 2), and a poetic rendering by Moses of the rationale for that response (v. 3). The two units that follow suggest that Moses and Aaron and his sons act appropriately to remedy the situation. Each unit is framed by an introduction in the form of a new declaration from Moses and a conclusion consisting of an execution formula typical of chapters 8 and 9. Moses calls for Aaron's relatives to dispose of Nadab and Abihu's bodies, and they do "as Moses had ordered" (vv. 4-5). Moses tells Aaron and his sons to stay in the sanctuary, "and they did as Moses had ordered" (vv. 6-7). The next unit constitutes a departure from the natural flow of the story, as the Lord addresses Aaron directly with a prohibition against strong drink (vv. 8-11) that has no apparent connection to the immediate context. Verses 10-11 do not fit syntactically in their present context either. The two verbs in these verses are infinitives ("to distinguish between . . . and . . . to teach . . ."). The main clause to which they are subordinated is the clause prohibiting strong drink in verse 9. Many contend that verses 10-11 were originally subordinate to some other statement. The language of verse 10 foreshadows the purity laws of the following chapters. These factors combine to point to the possibility that an editor inserted this unit secondarily into this context.

The focus returns to the immediate situation in verse 12. As in verse 6, Moses speaks to Aaron, Eleazar, and Ithamar. This parallel might betray a clue that the redactor is resuming the main line of the story. Moses speaks to them about eating the grain offering and the sacrifice of well-being, "as the LORD has commanded" (vv. 12-15), but this time there is no report of the execution of this command. Instead, Moses rebukes Aaron and his sons regarding their failure to eat of the sin offering "as I commanded" (vv. 16-18). Aaron justifies his disobedience by suggesting that to eat would not have been "agreeable to the LORD" (good in the eyes of the LORD), and the chapter ends by reporting that Moses "agreed" (it was good in his eyes) (vv. 19-20).

Exegetical Analysis

Aaron's Sons Desecrate the Sanctuary (10:1-3)

The offering by Aaron's sons is something the Lord "had not commanded," indicating that it stands in direct contrast to the preceding ritual acts. Significant wordplays here highlight this contrast. The Lord shows rejection of the "unholy fire" with divine "fire." This contrasts to the Lord's acceptance and approval of Aaron's sacrifices when "fire came out from the LORD and consumed" the designated portions (9:24). But after the offering of Nadab and Abihu, "fire came out from the presence of the LORD and consumed them" (v. 2). The contrast in the Lord's reactions could not be clearer; the explanation for the contrast could not be more obscure.

Questions about the "unholy fire" have stymied interpreters for many years. The term for "unholy" ("illicit" in Num 3:4; 26:61 NOAB) refers generally to what is different or unfamiliar (Ps 69:8; Prov 27:2; Hos 8:12). It often refers to foreign persons ("aliens, strangers"—Isa 1:7; Jer 3:13; Ezek 7:21) or gods (Deut 32:16; Ps 81:9; Isa 43:12). Some translators give the term a negative connotation in denoting foreign women, rendering it "adulteress" or "loose woman" (Prov 5:3, 20; 7:5). The NRSV translation of "unholy" does not really resolve the problem, because it applies a religious connotation to a term that is not religious at its base. It suggests a dichotomy between this fire and "holy fire," an expression that does not occur in the Old Testament. The Lord's reaction shows that the fire is inappropriate, but the text never explains what makes it "unholy."

Interpreters look to what else is unusual in the description of this incident for an explanation. Early rabbinic sources reveal as many as a dozen possible rationales, involving the origin of the fire, the contents of the incense, the ritual state of the priests, the time of day, the motivation for their offering, and others (Milgrom 1991, 632-34). Several parallels with the account of Korah's rebellion in Num 16 might help to narrow the field of possibilities. There, the 250 members of Korah's group are told to approach the Lord, each man holding his own censer with incense (Num 16:15-18; cf. Ezek 8:11). The "glory of the LORD appeared to the whole congregation" at that time (Num 16:19), fire from the Lord "consumed" the group of 250 (Num 16:35), and Eleazar converts the censers into a shield as a reminder that "no outsider" (strange man) was to offer incense in worship (Num 16:40 [17:5]).

This points to the first of several proposed solutions to the issue of the "unholy fire" in Lev 10. There is no explicit mention of Nadab and Abihu in the preceding rituals, so perhaps the fire is unholy because they are unqualified to bring it. This does not seem to be the case, though. Their ordination process has just been completed, and the text identifies the fire—not the men—as "unholy." Many see a connection between this incident and warnings about "unholy incense" in Exod 30:7-9. That warning comes immediately after the lengthy prescriptions for priestly ordination, prescriptions that have just been fulfilled. Later in Exod 30, the writer gives strict instructions about the incense that is to be used, emphasizing that even the priests cannot use it for themselves (Exod 30:34-38). The story in Num 16 implies a strong correlation between a priest and his censer, so that an improperly prepared censer might be a strong indicator of corruption in the priest. It is possible that Nadab and Abihu present unauthorized incense. Leviticus 10 identifies the fire as the problem; but because the incense is placed on the fire, it is possible that unholy incense has polluted the fire. Another possibility is that the fire itself is the source of offense. This assumes that the fire comes from some source other than the sanctioned altar. Lev 16:12-13 would provide a contrasting example of the priests bringing authorized incense with coals from the fire of the altar. Finally, it is possible that the fault lies in the act itself, either that a fire ritual was not prescribed or that it imitates known foreign practices. The clause immediately following the mention of the "unholy fire" might be explicatory (10:1b), specifying that the fire is "unholy" because the Lord has not commanded anyone to bring it. Whatever the specific impropriety, it constitutes an offense serious enough to evoke an immediate and unequivocal response from the Lord.

The rationale Moses gives for the Lord's reaction affirms two complementary ideas (v. 3). First, there is a double entendre inherent to the main verbs in these parallel lines ("I will show myself holy" and "I will be glorified"). Both say that the Lord will be honored. Those who worship the Lord should show God honor ("glory"); but if they do not, then the Lord will punish them to assert divine honor (Ezek 28:22). Second, the reference to "those who are near me" has particular significance in the context of Leviticus. The offerings of Leviticus are "brought near." All worshipers "come near" with their sacrifices, but the priests are specifically ordained to "bring near" sacrificial animals on behalf of others. The poetic parallel to "all the people" betrays the belief that the priests are in some ways indistinguishable from the people when they approach God. Still, the sons of Aaron must take the greatest care in how they "come near" to the Lord, but now they have "brought near" an "unholy fire." Since they have not honored the Lord's holiness, the glory that had appeared as a blessing now takes on the necessary function of punishment.

Rounding out this picture is the use of "glory." The "glory of the LORD" appeared when Aaron offered the sacrifices properly (9:6, 23), because the Lord had been "glorified" in the sight of the people (10:3). Now, the text implies that the Lord has not been "glorified" by Nadab and Abihu (cf. 1 Sam 2:30), and so the fire—which represents divine "glory" (Exod 40:34-38)—becomes a destructive force to assert the Lord's holiness. The opposing nature of these two events is made manifest in Aaron's reactions. He had reflected the Lord's acceptance of the first offerings by pronouncing blessings (9:22-23), but now he reacts to the Lord's disapproval with silence (10:3).

Proper Disposal of Nadab and Abihu (10:4-7)

The silence of Aaron and the other priests constitutes half of a contrasting picture with Moses. Moses orders the removal of the bodies, and Mishael and Elzaphan silently comply. Moses orders the priests not to exhibit signs of grief, and they silently obey (vv. 4-7). The people can mourn (v. 6; cf. 21:10), but they mourn more than the deaths of two priests. They mourn the Lord's "burning." They mourn the dishonoring of the Lord, which prompted God to send fire in anger rather than in blessing. They mourn the rift between the Lord and the people that the burning represents. The priests are not to mourn, because this associates them with the dead. They must glorify the Lord again by showing their obedience to divine commands. Two commands follow.

Prohibition against Alcohol for Priests (10:8-11)

The relevance of the command in verses 8-11 to the immediate situation is difficult to perceive. Some interpreters conclude that alcohol might have contributed to the Lord's anger, but there is not much to commend this theory. The priests are rebuked for the fire they present, not their physical condition when they present it. The statute is not tied to one specific act, but applies to any occasion when the priests enter the sanctuary. The prohibition restricts the priests from drinking whenever they enter the tent, even though there is no mention that Nadab and Abihu entered the tent. So, this rule seems to be a general restriction, with no direct link to the immediate situation.

The same conclusion applies to the following verses. The instructions about discerning "between the holy and the common, and between the unclean and the clean" entail more general situations that will arise in the future, but they do not seem connected to what brought on the deaths of Nadab and Abihu. Instead, these instructions point to the dietary laws and other purity laws in the chapters ahead. There is a dual verbal link to the verses immediately following ("holy" and "clean"), which might explain the insertion of these instructions here. A redactor might have placed verses 8-11 here to strengthen a link between a story of priestly indiscretion and the purity laws of chapters 11–15.

Priestly Consumption of Offerings (10:12-15)

The commands in 10:12-15 signal a resumption of the (post-) ordination process. Moses calls on the remaining sons of Aaron to eat the portion of the sacrifice of well-being allotted to the priests. The stipulation to eat "in a holy place" recalls the law on the sin offering (6:26 [6:19]), but the parallel stipulation about eating "in any clean place" gives an additional piece of information (vv. 13-14). The parallel between "holy (place)" and "clean (place)" forms a link with verses 10-11, and the two together point back to the instructions on clean and unclean flesh in 7:19-21 and forward to the purity laws in the following chapters. The concluding formula ("as the LORD has commanded") hints at a deeper purpose in these instructions; they provide a corrective to the rebellious actions of Nadab and Abihu that incurred the Lord's wrath.

Aaron's Refusal to Eat (10:16-20)

It is logical to expect the priests to carry out Moses' instructions; but first, he wants to make sure they have already eaten—and thus completed—the people's sin offering. The priests must eat the sin offering before the sacrifice of well-being. Moses is angered to discover that this has not been done and, in fact, is no longer possible. The effects of Nadab and Abihu's disobedience persist; Aaron's sons are adding to their brothers' sin, rather than acting to atone for it. The concluding formula in Moses' remonstrance ("as I commanded," v. 18) implies that they are threatening to disobey. The nature of this disobedience might be twofold. First, eating the sin offering is part of the ritual by which atonement is achieved. Not eating the offering constitutes a disobedience that will deprive the people of forgiveness. Second, some see not eating as a sign of mourning (Deut 26:14), and Moses has specifically told Aaron and his sons not to mourn. In either case, Moses sees here the potential for a second offense.

Aaron's response answers Moses' concerns, but it does not answer the questions that interpreters have about it. The response suggests that it would have been "evil in the eyes of the LORD" if they had eaten. Some interpreters see in this a dispute between Aaron and

Moses (which Aaron wins) over the nature of the offering, whether it was the type that priests were to eat or not (6:24-30); but the text does not confirm that this is a type of offering they should not eat. Some say the sin of Nadab and Abihu interrupted the ritual process, rendering the offering unholy. In this case, one would expect the presentation of another offering, but that is not forthcoming. This makes it more likely that Aaron is convincing Moses that it is appropriate for him to mourn, in spite of Moses' command in verse 6. Moses appears concerned that the Lord will view Aaron's failure to eat the offering as another act of disobedience, a further dishonoring of the Lord. Aaron's response constitutes a claim of innocence. Even though they presented the prescribed offerings, the Lord still killed his sons. Aaron recognizes that the Lord wants something more than sacrifice; the Lord wants to be honored. Aaron's refusal to eat in this instance might defy Moses' order, but it is not an act of defiance against God (21:1-4). It is the natural reaction of a grieving man, but a man who seeks to honor the Lord. From this perspective, his grieving is not an act of disobedience.

This does not mean that Moses was wrong to give the commands that he gave. His reaction complements Aaron's reaction. Moses is looking at this situation from a broader perspective than Aaron is. Moses is considering how to move forward, while at the same time preventing something like this from happening again. He is concerned with how the actions and reactions of the priests affect the rest of the nation (cf. 2 Sam 14:1-24; 19:1-8). Moses' instructions imply that the disobedience of Nadab and Abihu does not mean the end of this ordination process or, more important, a break in the covenant relationship between the people and the Lord. His commands in verses 12-15 show that the Lord still intends to dwell in the midst of the people, still intends to have Aaron's family serve as priests, and still intends for them to bring offerings that will "remove guilt" and "make atonement" for acts of disobedience. It is still the responsibility of Aaron and his sons to set the example for the nation in regard to matters of ritual purity and dietary regulations. What they do ritually *in the future* still matters. This exchange shows the Lord displaying divine mercy as well as divine wrath by accepting a father's need to mourn his sons, even under these circumstances.

Theological and Ethical Analysis

The events of Lev 10 make important contributions to an understanding of Israel's cult. At the center—literally and figuratively—is the Lord. Drawing near to the Lord presents humans with opposing potentialities. The fact that these are represented as one and the same fire is quite appropriate. A fire in the fireplace is part of an idealized portrayal of home, even in this modern age. A fire represents protection from the elements and a necessary means for providing nourishment. A fire also represents danger. It can inflict immediate and permanent scars on those who do not respect its power. When not handled properly, it threatens to destroy the house in which it burns. The Lord's actions in the form of fire display a similar polarity in divine dealings with people (9:22–10:3). The fire at the end of chapter 9 represents God's acceptance of the people's worship and an intention to bless them in response. The same fire in chapter 10 demonstrates the Lord's disapproval and harsh punishment of those who dishonor God, particularly because the offenders had been entrusted with the responsibility of setting a proper example.

This new self-manifestation by the Lord is intended to send a strong message to the priests that they have been given great responsibilities, not just privileges. They alone have the privilege of serving "before the LORD." This privilege gives them status and honor in the Israelite community. They enjoy the blessing of approaching closer than anyone else to the Lord. But now they are reminded of the responsibilities such privilege involves, especially the responsibility of recognizing the honor due to the Lord. They must demonstrate to the people the importance of honoring the Lord through obedience. To take that lightly minimizes the mercy in the divine blessings; it is to lose sight of what is transpiring between the Lord and the people. If the priests do not appreciate the nature of this relationship, then it is more likely that the people will not appreciate it. This message must not be lost on the religious leaders of any time. Religious leaders can focus on their own rights and privileges as leaders, while neglecting the proper exercise of their responsibilities. The fire that blesses can also consume.

One function of Lev 10 is to remind religious leaders that there are limits to their authority. One cannot find a human authority in the Israelite cult higher than the priests. Even kings have reason to be careful when opposing a priest (1 Sam 22:17; 1 Kgs 2:26-27). But priests must remember that they serve the Lord; they carry out their responsibilities under the Lord's authority (v. 3; cf. 1 Sam 2:30, 35). To do otherwise incurs the Lord's wrath. Sadly, religious leaders often appeal to divine authority to exploit those whom they lead. Corrupt leaders can place demands on followers in the name of the Lord that really serve to satisfy their own selfish desires. This episode stands as a warning to such corruption, illustrating divine judgment on those who flaunt their power and privilege.

This episode also touches on some complicated issues regarding divine punishment, repentance, and grief. The deaths of Aaron's sons constitute punishment, and that inevitably provokes a human response. At one level, that can either be a response of anger and resentment toward the Lord, or a response of repentance and a desire to please the God in the future. The latter is the response represented by Moses, who advises Aaron and his sons on how to correct this mistake and work positively toward the future. It is in this light that the placement of verses 8-11 makes some sense. One implication is that the Lord will continue to provide for Aaron and his descendants (vv. 12-15). The verses point beyond the immediate situation to the future. They also foreshadow what is coming in chapters 11–15 and, in so doing, give a clue about how to read those chapters in the context of the whole book. The concern about purity aims to prevent the repetition of something like the calamity that has just happened to Aaron's family. Those laws will show what the people should do to bring divine blessing (the fire in 9:22-24) rather than divine wrath (the fire in 10:1-3).

At another level, the response to divine punishment can either be a response of grief over the pain that is suffered, or a response of acceptance that the Lord has justly humbled the disobedient. Divine punishment involves inflicting pain on wrongdoers. Ideally, the Lord's people would recognize the righteousness that is displayed against those who act contrary to the Lord's sovereignty. But this story reminds us that those receiving such punishment are not just sinners, deserving of our disapproval. They are often our own flesh and blood. Aaron demonstrates the appropriate grief that family members feel when their loved ones' sinful actions bring unhappiness on themselves. Grief is not a sign of approval for sinful actions, but rather a right reaction to the loss that has been suffered. In fact, there is plenty of evidence to suggest that God shares such feelings of grief. This episode shows that the God of the Bible understands the complicated world of emotions, in which righteous anger and grief for a sinner's suffering can coexist.

LEVITICUS 11–16

Leviticus 16:1 draws a direct line from the "unholy fire" episode of Lev 10 to the prescriptions for the Day of Atonement in chapter 16. Thus, chapters 11–15 initially appear to interrupt the narrative flow of the book. On closer examination, one recognizes that this interruption is really a pause. These are the only chapters in which the narrative headings refer to Moses and Aaron together as the direct recipients of the Lord's words. Chapter 10 describes an incident that threatens the cultic status of Aaron and his family, and chapter 16 provides the remedy. These intervening chapters constitute threats to the cultic status of any participants, and chapter 16 provides the remedy for them as well.

This block of instructions is often called "The Manual of Purity." There is a concentration in the use of "unclean" and "clean" here (approximately 160 occurrences in these five chapters). Three summary statements identify these as main categories of classification in cultic matters (11:47; 13:59; 14:57; cf. 15:31). From a cultic standpoint, impurities temporarily exclude individuals from the sanctuary, so the goal of the remedies is to include them again. These instructions involve food (11:1-47), women following childbirth (12:1-8), skin diseases and molds (13:1–14:57), and bodily discharges (15:1-33).

Chapters 11–15 deal with materials and substances that are "unclean" and "defile" ("make unclean") through contact. Other passages mention actions and words that "defile." There are competing schools of thought about the perceived relationship between these defilements. Some believe the Israelites recognized no difference between defilement by contact and defilement by sinful action, but others believe these were two separate but analogous classification systems sharing a common cult.

The ancient and medieval rabbis uphold a distinction between uncleanness and sin, arguing that uncleanness does not make one a sinner, but that sin makes one unclean. Impurities are lesser infractions that function primarily as metaphors for the more serious sins. Moderns assume that concerns about defilement by contact reflect "primitive" beliefs about magical powers inherent to certain substances, but recent anthropological studies expose weaknesses in such assumptions. More plausible is the idea that "unclean" and "clean" function as symbols that reveal a people's perceptions of the "real world" at the level of society or nature. An "unclean" body symbolizes a spiritual imperfection in the world around it. Impurities and sins are virtually indistinguishable. Some interpreters highlight the varying effects and remedies of impurities and sins. Impurities temporarily defile articles and people through contact, and the defilement is removed with time, washings, or offerings. Sin defiles not only the person but also the sanctuary and the land. Removal of the effects of sin requires rituals of atonement and divine forgiveness.

A recent treatment by Jonathan Klawans lays out the distinctions that are possible (Klawans 2000). Like others before him, he distinguishes between "ritual impurity" and "moral impurity." He sees these as "distinct but analogous conceptions of contagion." "Ritual impurity" entails people and things that possess an "impermanent contagion." Such a state is not sinful; in fact, it is often natural and unavoidable (e.g., childbirth). It does not immediately provoke divine punishment, and it can be rectified with time or prescribed sacrifices. "Moral impurity" is a direct result of sin. It does not contaminate others by contact, but it does impose "degradation" on the offender, on the sanctuary, and on the land. It is permanent, unless it is removed by punishment or ritual acts of atonement. While the biblical texts apply the term "unclean" to both categories, the terms "abomination" and "pollution" are applied only to sin. In the end, Klawans recognizes points that these categories have in common, but the differences warrant the recognition of two separate categories.

Others believe that the points these classifications have in common are significant enough to outweigh the differences. For example, acts of sin and the state of uncleanness both render one "guilty" (5:1-4). Persons who enter the sanctuary or who touch sacred objects while they are "ritually impure" are guilty of sin. Similarly, certain "ritual impurities" require atonement in their remedy, just like sins. This shows why it is difficult to establish whether these are "distinct but analogous" groups or "gradations" of a single group of "impurities."

The categories and labels suggested by the text are those in Lev 10:10, where the Lord tells the priests they are "to distinguish between the holy and the common, and between the unclean and the clean." The categories of "unclean and clean" (= "defile" and "cleanse") are primary in chapters 11–15, while "holy and common" (= "sanctify" and "profane") become more prominent in chapters 19–23. It could be that distinctions have been blurred as a result of redaction, but then one must explain why they did not maintain the distinctions. Both types identify grounds for separating people from the Lord. The Lord called for a sanctuary so that there might be a place to meet with the people, and each of these things precludes them from that communion.

This leads to a lingering question regarding these impurities: why do these things defile a person? The text often gives categorizations without accompanying rationales. Many of these are natural and unavoidable phenomena. Many distinctions appear arbitrary or, at best, they seem to represent attempts to give religious/divine authority to social customs. Interpreters often associate impurities with health concerns. They attribute these distinctions to practical motivations and known physical consequences that would confirm for the people the need for these restrictions. Others speculate that some distinctions reflect a simple desire to differentiate Israel's cultic rules from the cultic rules of Israel's neighbors. Unfortunately, there is not enough information available to confirm or deny such explanations. Others have abandoned the search for a practical explanation for these rules, turning instead to allegorical or metaphorical rationales. They assume that the Israelites viewed impurities as less significant than sins, and so they propose that the impurities served as allegories for vices and virtues or other more significant values. There is no textual support from Leviticus for this view, though. (For surveys of the main views, see Houston 1993, 68-122; Klawans 2000, 5-19.)

It is helpful to view these laws within the broader context of the Priestly texts of the Pentateuch. These laws function as cultic responses to the corruption of creation. Categories of "clean"/"unclean" and "holy"/"common" correspond to ideas about life and death. Things that are "clean" and "holy" promote life, while death and corruption accompany "unclean" and "common" things. There are enough linguistic links to the early stories of Genesis to imply that cleansing and sanctification remove persons and things from the realm of death and restore them to the realm of life that existed at creation (Milgrom 1991, 704-42). This does not explain *why* certain things belong to death and others belong to life, but it does provide a schema for understanding these categories that has a home in the overall message of the Torah.

LEVITICUS 11

Leviticus 11 introduces the dietary laws. The goal is to maintain the people's ritual purity before the Lord. Obedience will result in divine blessings, disobedience will incur divine wrath, as illustrated by events in the preceding chapters. Interpreters have developed a variety of explanations for these distinctions, but none that attempts to explain all the variations has won general acceptance.

Literary Analysis

The mode of address shifts here predominantly to the plural. The Lord is giving instructions to Moses and Aaron that they pass on to the people (cf. 13:1; 14:33; 15:1). The use of the plural verbs is more common in chapters 18–26. Similarly, the call to "be holy, for I am holy" in verses 44-45 has its closest parallels in those chapters (19:2-4; 20:7-8, 26; 21:8; 22:31-32).

Leviticus 11 begins with a typical narrative heading and discourse heading (11:1-2a). The mode of direct address to the people extends from verse 2 through verse 45; then the narrator provides a summary in 11:46-47. The summary groups living things according to land animals, birds, aquatic creatures, and animals that "swarm" (v. 46). This does not match the order of the laws in the chapter; instead, it reverses the order of creation (Gen 1:20-25). The author says the laws distinguish these according to "the unclean and the clean," and according to what may or may not be eaten. Though not in the summary, some of the laws apply the term "detestable" to unclean animals.

Stylistic features demarcate seven units, grouped into two movements. The first movement begins with land animals (vv. 2b-8), and then proceeds through aquatic creatures (vv. 9-12), birds (vv. 13-19), and "winged insects" (vv. 20-23 ["swarming creatures of the air"]). The second movement begins again with land animals (vv. 24-28), but then devotes two units to "creatures that swarm" (vv. 29-40, 41-45). The first movement differentiates between what one "may eat" and "detestable" creatures that one "may not eat." There are seventeen occurrences of these terms but only five of "unclean" (all in vv. 4-8). The second movement reverses these proportions; the primary dichotomy is between "unclean" and "clean" (thirty times), but only six references to what one "may eat" or what is "detestable" and one "shall not eat" (all in vv. 39-43). The first movement concerns defilement by eating (but see vv. 8, 11); the second identifies things that make people and objects "unclean until the evening" by contact (vv. 29-38), and then those that defile by either touching or eating, or both (vv. 39-45).

These differences between verses 2-23 and verses 24-45 lead source and redaction critics to posit different sources for these two parts. Deuteronomy 14:3-21 parallels this chapter, excluding verses 24-38. The similarities between verses 44-45 and key passages in chapters 18–26 add to the impression that two sources have been combined (19:2-4; 20:7-8, 26; 21:8; 22:31-32). On the other hand, the delineations of this chapter match the summary of verse 47, but in reverse order. The summary has both parts of the chapter in mind; therefore, it is part of the final redaction.

Various literary features demarcate smaller units within the main body. In the first unit, the Hebrew distinguishes between land animals that the people can and cannot eat (11:2b-8), beginning the first part with "These are the creatures that you may eat" (v. 2b, emphasis added), and then the second part with "But [*these*] you shall not eat" (the NRSV moves this phrase down to the middle of v. 4). Verses 4-8 include a fivefold repetition of the phrase "it is unclean for you"; a general prohibition and summary close out the unit (cf. vv. 11, 24-28). The second unit distinguishes between aquatic creatures that can or cannot be eaten (11:9-12). Its structure is similar to the first unit. Clauses using a common verb bracket verse 9 ("*These/such* you may eat"). In verses 10-12, the same formula stands in the first and last sentences ("Anything/Everything . . . that does not have fins and scales"; cf. v. 9). The creatures so classified are characterized as "detestable to you" four times.

The third unit envelops the prohibitions against eating certain flying creatures with the designations "detestable" and "abomination" (v. 13a; these derive from the same Hebrew root). This succinct dictum leads into a list of the flying creatures the people are not to eat (vv. 13b-19; cf. vv. 29b-30). The final unit of this movement distinguishes between "winged insects" that are "detestable" and those that the people may eat (11:20-23). Like the second unit, the first and last sentences begin with the same phrase ("All winged insects"). In between, two sentences begin with a demonstrative pronoun ("you may eat *those . . . them* you may eat"). These internal clauses identify exceptions to the surrounding general rule.

The shift in terminology that begins in verse 24 is quite marked, showing the transition to a new movement of units. Verses 24-28 form the first unit here, consisting of the following chiasmus:

- general statement of uncleanness (v. 24a)
- "whoever touches . . . unclean until the evening" (vv. 24b-25)
- what is "unclean for you" (v. 26a)
- "everyone who touches . . . shall be unclean" (v. 26b)
- what is "unclean for you" (v. 27a)

- "whoever touches...unclean until the evening" (vv. 27b-28a)
- general statement of uncleanness (v. 28b)

This chiasm alternates between references to what is "unclean" and statements that link "unclean" and "touch."

An initial demonstrative pronoun marks the introduction to the next unit, dealing with "creatures that swarm upon the earth" (v. 29). The extent of this unit is not easily discerned. The initial clause in verse 29 serves as a brief heading that leads into a list of unclean, "swarming" land creatures. A second (or secondary) heading in verse 31 turns to ways in which these creatures defile by contact. At one level, there is a twofold progression, involving verses 31-34 and then verses 35-38. Each part moves from external contact (carcasses that fall upon) to internal contact (carcasses that fall into). The heading in verse 31 governs a series of statements that are linked syntactically (vv. 32-34 + v. 35). Each statement begins with "anything/any/ everything" (each translates the same Hebrew word). A turn comes with verse 36, which begins with a strong adversative, "But" (cf. v. 4). This ushers in a short series of exceptions. This series is carried forward with three statements that begin with "(but) if" (vv. 37-39). Many argue that verses 39-40 are a late interpolation (Milgrom 1991, 63, 681-82, 693-94). The syntactical progression argues against a complete separation, even though verses 39-40 concern land animals like those in verses 24-28, rather than "creatures that swarm."

The reference to "an animal" in verse 39 signals a return to land animals. The difference is that verses 39-40 consider otherwise "clean" animals that have died, while verses 24-28 refer only to "unclean" animals. The phraseology of verses 39-40 imitates that of verses 24-28. For example, only these two passages call for washing contaminated clothes. Some source critics argue that verses 39-40 once stood directly after verses 24-28, but it is possible that the redactor wanted to lump all the unclean animals together (vv. 24-38). There is an AB/AB structure to 11:24-45 (24-28 and 39-40 concern land animals, 29-38 and 41-45 concern "creatures that swarm"). On the other hand, the repetition of the phrase "shall be unclean (until the evening)" ties together verses 24-40, but this separates them from verses 41-45.

The repetition in verse 41 of a phrase from verse 29 ("creatures that swarm upon the earth") probably marks a new beginning. The explication of what constitutes "creatures that swarm" (v. 42) indicates a different origin for this unit. The repeated use of "detestable" in verses 41-43 shows a link to verses 2-23. These features betray attempts to tie this unit to all that precede it in the chapter. Verses 44-45 put an important twist on this. These lines have close parallels in chapters 18–26. The two clauses "I am the LORD" and "you shall be holy for I am holy" occur twice each and at key points in those later chapters. This points to the probability that verses 41-45 were added secondarily to the chapter.

The narrative summary brings together several important terms in the chapter (vv. 46-47; e.g., "swarm," "unclean," "eat"). The variety of literary styles and the overlap in contents supports the conclusion that this is a redacted collection of previously independent instructions. No proposal about when each portion enters has won general acceptance; therefore, it seems unwise to try to distinguish between a more original intent and later modifications.

Exegetical Analysis

Guidelines on Eating Land Animals (11:2-8)

The range of animals from which the Israelites may eat is relatively narrow. The term translated "land animals" refers more specifically to quadruped mammals. Verse three identifies three physical characteristics that such animals must exhibit: they must have hooves, the hooves must be cleft, and they must chew their cud. The prohibitions that follow verify the need for all three characteristics. The absence of any one of them makes an animal "unclean." This list considers domestiMcated species; the corresponding list in Deut 14:4-8 mentions wild species that would be "clean" as well.

Verse 8 expands the prohibition from eating unclean animals that have been slaughtered to touching unclean animals that die naturally, a distinction suggested by "flesh" and "carcasses." The latter represents the only mention in the first half of this chapter to prohibitions against touching animal carcasses (but see v. 11). The text addresses that concern more fully in verses 24-28 and 39-40. This might reflect the disparate nature of sources, or it could be that a redactor has added the verse to tie this opening unit to those later ones.

Guidelines on Eating Aquatic Life (11:9-12)

The principle of evaluation established in the first unit applies here too; only creatures that meet all the criteria may be eaten, that is, they must have fins and scales. This section excludes fishes that have only one of these characteristics, in addition to all non-piscine water creatures. This unit identifies prohibited creatures as "detestable" rather than "unclean," which raises questions about possible differences between the reasons for the prohibitions. A few scholars raise questions about the applicability of these restrictions to the average Israelite. Marine creatures were available to a small segment of the population. Perhaps this shows the writer's desire to be comprehensive, or it reflects a concern to consider all the categories of animal life mentioned in Genesis.

Guidelines on Eating Birds (11:13-19)

Although the law refers to these birds as "detestable" and "abominations," it provides no explanation for this designation. Lists of other animals indicate that these birds are merely examples. Many interpreters assert that they are examples of carnivores and carrion eaters, who would be unclean because they have eaten blood. This cannot be confirmed, because half of the birds listed are unknown outside these lists.

Guidelines on Eating Winged Insects (11:20-23)

The guidelines for "winged insects" speak of what may be eaten, rather than what must be avoided. The text mentions four kinds, and a precise identification of each eludes the modern reader. The description of these as creatures that "walk on all fours" is curious, since insects have six legs. Apparently they considered the larger ("jointed") hind legs to be different from their four normal "feet." The text provides no explanation for why these characteristics permit the people to eat these creatures and not others.

Unclean Land Animals (11:24-28)

These creatures are the same as those in verses 2-8. The instructions elaborate on the middle clause of verse 8. The focus shifts to contamination caused by contact. The carcasses of "unclean" land animals render persons and their clothing unclean "until the evening." This defilement dissipates from human skin over time, but it clings to fabric. The same criteria apply to "clean" land animals in verses 39-40. The writer mentions a different physical characteristic in verse 27—"all that walk on their paws." These animals are unclean because they have none of the three criteria for clean animals given at the beginning of the chapter. Mary Douglas attributes the uncleanness to the fact these animals use their "hands" (paws) for walking, but this cannot be sustained. The Hebrew term (*kap*) can refer to "palms" or "soles," but it is not exclusively a reference to "hands."

The mention of "carcasses" indicates that these animals have died of natural causes. Contact with them does not defile because of the physical characteristics of their bodies, but because they are dead. Not only can they not be eaten, now they cannot even be touched without defiling. Touching them while alive does not defile, but touching them after they have died does defile. There is an additional notion at work now. That notion sees a direct connection between uncleanness and death.

Unclean Swarming Creatures (11:29-40)

Attention now turns to "creatures that swarm upon the earth." These land animals are not mentioned previously in the chapter. They too are obviously "unclean," based on the earlier criteria; a brief list provides typical examples of such creatures (vv. 29-30). It is curious, though, that any list at all is given since, as verses 41-45 make clear, all are unclean. This list seems superfluous. Some contend that only those listed are unclean, and that all other swarming land animals are clean. The discrepancy with verses 41-45 is attributed to a difference in sources. On the other hand, there is no text that speaks of swarming land animals that are clean. Therefore, although these two paragraphs might derive from different sources, they do not contradict each other.

The main instructions begin with a return to the concern not to touch animals that die naturally (v. 31). These verses go beyond verses 24-28 by identifying other ways defilement can pass to humans. Such carcasses defile household articles of wood or cloth, just as they defile clothing (v. 32; cf. vv. 25, 28), and one purifies the article by the same means (washing). Defilement cannot be removed from earth-based materials, so they are smashed (vv. 33-35). The primary focus then turns to distinguishing the effects of water on the potential to defile. Water from a spring or cistern restricts the defilement to what a carcass touches directly (v. 36). On the other hand, a carcass does not defile seed outside a container, unless that seed is wet (vv. 37-38). In all this, the defilement is "until the evening" (cf. vv. 24-28). The final unit reveals that defilement brought on by natural death is supplementary to ritual defilement. Touching or eating clean animals that die naturally defiles the handler/consumer, but only "until the evening" (vv. 39-40). Eating clean animals that die naturally does not defile like eating unclean animals defiles.

These guidelines reflect interconnections between the binary concepts of unclean/clean, death/life, and earth/water (Milgrom 1991, 656-59). Life, water, and cleanness are intertwined, while death, earth (dirt), and uncleanness are intertwined. Natural death—which involves turning to dust—makes animals unclean, and their uncleanness is transferred to animate and inanimate objects by physical contact. The nature of those objects is a factor in whether they can be purified. Water from a spring inhibits defilement. Running water is sometimes called living water ("fresh water" in 14:5-6, 49-53; 15:13); it possesses life, and it sustains life. The "life" in the water negates the "death" that has claimed the animal. The amount of water seems to be a significant factor. Clothes "dipped" in water are purified (v. 32), but seeds merely wetted by water are more susceptible to contamination (v. 38). Water in a small vessel is contaminated by contact with a dead animal (v. 34), but water in a cistern remains clean (v. 36). Water can cleanse impurities from wood and cloth (v. 32), but items made of earth materials cannot be purified (vv. 33, 35). Thus, it is possible that uncleanness comes upon and clings to certain things because of an assumed association between death and earth, while cleansing is based on an association between life and water.

Ideas about blood seem to parallel their understanding of these rules. They apparently associate the flowing of blood in the human body and the flowing of water. Water that flows "lives" and therefore purifies, so blood that flows inside the body purifies. This might explain why unclean animals do not defile while they are still alive, and why external contact with their carcasses defiles only temporarily. The blood that flows inside humans purifies them, but inanimate objects have nothing flowing in them to purify, so an external purifier is needed. The blood inside animals that die naturally is no longer flowing. Like water that does not flow, blood that does not flow becomes unclean. The blood that drains from an animal in sacrifice or during food preparation is still flowing; thus, it does not turn to its unclean state while still in the body, and the flesh is not defiled. Assuming that blood becomes "unclean" once it dries explains why all animals that die—even clean animals—become unclean.

Prohibition against Eating Swarming Creatures (11:41-45)

This paragraph elaborates on verses 29-30. Verse 42 expands on what constitutes "creatures that swarm"; verses 43-44 use the terms for "detestable" and "unclean" in a different manner than previous constructions in the chapter; verse 44 identifies swarming creatures as those that "move" ("creep") on the ground; and verses 44-45 link purity to holiness for the first time in the chapter. This is the only passage in Exod 35–Lev 17 that mentions Egypt, connecting the exodus and calls for obedience.

The infusion of language regarding holiness puts the concerns of this chapter in a different light. Without it, it would be easier to accept Klawans's contention that "ritual impurity" (in this chapter) and "moral impurity" (in chapters 18–26) are "distinct but analogous" categories. This paragraph suggests that the two overlap in the minds of the biblical writers. A person acquires and maintains holiness in part by avoiding physical contact with things that are ritually impure, not just through adherence to moral standards. Physical impurities compromise the Lord's holiness just as immoral behavior compromises holiness. Many interpreters try to negate this impression by attributing these verses to a later redactor, but their efforts betray a level of hubris, as if modern interpreters are better able than the ancient writers to judge what beliefs are more "biblical" or more "inspired" than others.

Summary (11:46-47)

The phraseology in this summary is closer to the language of Gen 1–2 than any other part of this chapter. The expression for "living creature" has its antecedents in Gen 1:20-21 and 2:8. The connection between things that "move" and "water" is not made previously in Leviticus as it is in Gen 1:21, and the call to "make a distinction" (*hibdîl*) between animals echoes the times when God "separated" (*hibdîl*) light from darkness and "the waters from the waters" (Gen 1:4, 6-7). The Israelites would see these dietary rules as ways in which humans participate with God in blessing through creation.

The summary brings together the two operative dichotomies that are held separate for most of the chapter. The regulations in verses 24-40 distinguish "the unclean and the clean," while those in verses 9-23 separate what may and may not be eaten. These pairs of descriptors are mixed elsewhere only in verses 2-8, while "defile yourselves" ["make yourselves detestable"] is used in reference to dietary restrictions in verses 41-45. There is much to suggest that these features betray the hand of a redactor, but one must be careful about how to interpret that editorial activity.

Theological and Ethical Analysis

The most exasperating aspects of verses 2-23 arise from what is not said. There are no theological explanations for what is permitted and what is prohibited. It would be easy to assume that these rules represent theological affirmation of practices previously based on physical observations and health conditions. Modern understanding of diseases can contribute to this assumption, but it is suspect because it is not applied consistently. Some attribute food taboos to associations between certain animals and the religious beliefs of Israel's neighbors (18:24-30; Deut 12:30-31). This principle is not applied evenly either, because many of those neighbors used cattle, sheep, goats, and doves in their sacrifices, just as the Israelites did. Still others hold that these dietary rules identify foods that the Lord enjoyed, and so the Israelite diet mirrors the Lord's food preferences. This creates its own problems, particularly in the light of passages such as Ps 50:13-15 and Mic 6:6-8.

Jacob Milgrom sees here a narrow restriction in the number of consumable animals. The goal is to balance between a reverence for life and the nutritional needs of humans. The people must remove the blood to show that they do not benefit from the animal's "life" but merely from its flesh (17:10-14; Milgrom 1991, 718-36). Douglas suggests that clean animals represent "unblemished" species, while unclean animals possess physical abnormalities that blur the boundaries between species (e.g., aquatic creatures that crawl are acting like land animals). Douglas then argues that unclean animals are excluded as a sign of divine mercy to things that are imperfect. They are not "detestable" so much as they are "off limits." This dovetails into her belief that the dietary laws are part of a broader socioecological system. The parts of this system fulfill dual roles, conveying their own realities but also serving as symbols of other parts of the system (Douglas 1999, 134-75).

The most attractive aspects of these interpretations are those that find support in other Priestly texts. The closest linguistic connections are in Gen 1–2 and 8:20–9:17. Perhaps Lev 11 is drawing on Gen 1–2 to suggest an explication of humanity's governance of creation through dietary practices. On the other hand, if distinctions between "unclean and clean" are based on the perception of abnormalities, one must ask when these abnormalities emerged. If God created some creatures "abnormal," then why does God declare everything "very good" (Gen 1:31)? If the abnormalities arose later, then why did the writers of Genesis not note this change? As for Gen 8–9, it is curious that an early narrative mentions distinctions between clean and unclean before the laws identify such distinctions. Perhaps the reasons behind "clean" and "unclean" were felt to be obvious.

Genesis 8–9 suggests possible connections between the promises of the Noachic Covenant and Israel's dietary laws. The Lord's words to Noah give divine permission for eating meat, while giving strict warnings against the consumption of blood (Gen 9:3-5). The Levitical laws narrow the field of foods, supporting Milgrom's suggestion that these laws exist in part to promote reverence for life. The mandates in Genesis also show that some of these laws apply to all humans, inferring that all humans will be judged by Israel's dietary laws. The usual contention is that this was not the case (Deut 14:21), but that these laws distinguish the Israelites from their neighbors. Finally, connections to Gen 1–2 and 8–9 point to deeper connections between what the Israelites do to be "clean" and the reception of divine blessings. God announces blessings in Gen 1–2, but the tone of their reiteration in Gen 8–9 betrays how tenuous they are. These laws show how humans can secure blessings in the present.

These dietary laws present difficulties on several levels. First, there are pragmatic questions about what is to be done. Like the other purity laws, some of these laws involve nondeliberative acts that defile a person (11:24-40). This defilement is often unavoidable; it has temporary consequences, and remedies are relatively simple. The only concern is whether a defiled person might enter the sanctuary (7:19-21). For this reason, some wonder how these laws affected the lives of Israelites beyond the priests. Laws concerning what may not be eaten suggest more serious consequences (vv. 2-23), but the text does not indicate what those might be. To eat unclean foods assumes an awareness of the gravity of the act. Leviticus 5 prescribes how to deal with unintentional defilement, but there are no instructions there for dealing with deliberate sins. Perhaps this is part of the reason for the establishment of the Day of Atonement (chapter 16).

Readers have long puzzled over the rationale for these rules. Christians tend to dismiss any significant motivation for observing these laws, because of New Testament teachings (Matt 15:10-20;

Mark 7:14-23; 1 Tim 4:3-5). The restrictions hindered the uniting of Jews and Gentiles into a single community (Acts 10:1–11:18). Dietary laws were a major component in identifying what distinguished Israelites/Jews. Over the centuries, developments in scientific reasoning have steered people to prefer scientific explanations for these regulations, so that many Christians typically regard them as remnants of a more primitive worldview.

This focus on scientific explanations diverts attention away from the theological foundations of the laws. The laws assume the need to distinguish between God's people and nonbelievers. Jesus and his disciples eliminate distinctions based on physical criteria, but they still expect Christians to be a distinctive people (morally and spiritually). Walter Houston is probably right to propose that the purity laws promote monotheism (Houston 1993, 181-282). The critique of Jesus and his followers is a call to recapture the original intent of these laws, a call to associate with life rather than death (Matt 5:13-20; 23:27-28; 1 Tim 4:1-5). The physical should reflect the spiritual, and the essence of the spiritual is life and blessing and holiness. The Lord is a God of life, so it is inappropriate for the Lord's people to associate themselves with the things of death.

The food laws exemplify the differences between life and death, not just between one people and others. Blood functions as an important boundary marker between life and death, but it is not the only marker in these laws. If Douglas is correct, the Israelites and their neighbors associated physical abnormalities (suffering) with death. This involves orderliness, as illustrated in the creation account of Gen 1. The stories of Gen 1–11 lay the foundation for ideas of life and death, divine blessing and curse, order and chaos. These laws show how the Israelites affirm and participate in the things of life and blessing and denounce and avoid the things of death and disorder.

Maintaining a proper perspective on the relationship between physical matters and spiritual matters is a never-ending task. No generation—and no group of believers—can avoid this struggle. The principles of affirming life over death, blessing over curse, and holiness over impurity can be applied today, for example, to issues of worship styles. These are matters more closely akin to ritual concerns than moral concerns. This does not make them unimportant, but physical practices should affirm and promote the spiritual qualities of life over death, blessing over curse, and holiness over impurity. One would expect this to involve distinctions between believers and nonbelievers, but such distinctions must go beyond physical distinctions to more fundamental spiritual qualities.

LEVITICUS 12

Leviticus 12 prescribes the purification process for a woman who has just given birth. The woman is impure because of the bleeding she naturally endures. The concern is defilement caused by bodily discharge, and references to menstruation (vv. 2, 5) assume the reader is familiar with the laws of chapter 15. Additional regulations given there apply here as well. One curious aspect of this passage is its current placement. It creates a bracket with chapter 15, but the purpose for this bracketing is not apparent.

Literary Analysis

This chapter's literary features are typical, except for the placement of the final verse (12:8). The two-part heading (vv. 1-2a) is similar to others in the book. The structure for the instructions follows a typical pattern. The primary law begins with "if" (*kî*, v. 2b), and "if" (*'im*) introduces a subordinate provision (v. 5). Verse 6 begins with "when," which introduces the situation that follows either of the two preceding circumstances (vv. 4-5; the Hebrew construction underlying "when" in v. 6 is different from "when" in introductions to primary laws earlier in the book). The language of verses 6-7a is typical for sacrifices: the woman "brings" the animals, and the priest "offers" them and "makes atonement." Verse 7b provides a short narrative conclusion, reminiscent of earlier conclusions in the book (6:2, 7, 18; 7:1, 11, 37).

Verse 8 stands out from such typical formulations. It follows the pattern of an alternative or subordinate law. One would expect to find this before the concluding formula of verse 7b;

therefore, verse 8 represents a secondary addition. The formulation of verse 8 is indistinguishable from similar clauses in other laws, yielding four possible explanations: (1) a redactor perfectly matched the form of existing regulations, (2) a redactor rearranged existing material without altering its wording, (3) a copyist misplaced the verse, or (4) such a variation is not an indication of a different author.

Exegetical Analysis

Female Uncleanness Resulting from Childbirth (12:1-5)

Leviticus 15:19-30 attributes a menstruant's impurity to her discharge of blood. There has been speculation about why the natural discharge of blood defiles, whether the defilement derives from the blood or from discharges in general (chap. 15). Other questions involve matters of time in this law. It first mentions a seven-day period when the mother is considered "unclean," followed by a period of thirty-three days ("her time of blood purification"). Most interpreters agree that the woman is unclean for the first seven days only (15:19), but that she is between unclean and clean for the remaining days. The text provides no explanation for this in-between status, except to say that she is not allowed contact with things that are "holy." Many assume that contact with her defiles others, and they deduce that this precludes sexual contact between the woman and her husband (cf. 15:20-24). Such a provision might intend to protect the woman at a time when her overall health was more precarious.

The reason for mandating thirty-three days of "purification" seems at first to be simply to achieve forty days, a period known as a time of separation and renewal. The primary concern expressed has to do with blood, though (vv. 4, 5, 7). Perhaps the forty days provides time to ensure that no complications involving the woman's flow of blood persist after childbirth. There is no generally accepted explanation for doubling the periods of uncleanness and purification when the baby is female (v. 5). Theories claiming that this reflects ideas about the cultic inferiority of females are purely speculative. Early Jewish legends connect the different lengths to the time Adam and Eve spent in the garden before being tempted. More recent interpreters attribute it to slight physical differences occasionally accompanying the births of girls, but these involve such small percentages that it is hard to accept this as a viable explanation. A few wonder if the eighty-day period is more natural, and that circumcision of males accelerated the process with boys. One must be careful not to assume that the child defiles the mother; there is no purification ritual prescribed for the child, only for the mother. Some Christian groups have cited this passage as a precedent for excluding mothers from the sanctuary for several weeks following childbirth (Schearing 2003, 429-50).

Ritual for Purification from Such Uncleanness (12:6-8)

The law concludes by calling for a burnt offering and a sin offering at the end of the mother's purification period. This procedure is intriguing because it calls for the burnt offering first; normally, one finds the reverse. This reversal supports the notion that purification is accomplished with the passage of time; so, the sin offering does not actually serve as the cleansing mechanism. Like the priests' offerings in chapter 9, these offerings mark the completion of the purification process and the renewal of the woman's right to enter the sacred space of the community. The term for "flow" of blood differs from the term in chapter 15, but both are used in reference to water; therefore, it is likely that they are synonyms. The exception in verse 8 prevents these required offerings from being overly burdensome to poorer families. They are comparable to offerings for other bodily discharges (15:14-15, 29-30).

Theological and Ethical Analysis

The ultimate motivation for this law is elusive. Its basic premise is that a woman becomes unclean by virtue of a natural—and "blessed"—process. There is no reference to defilement carried by the child or by anyone assisting in the birth. Additional guidelines in chapter 15 imply the latter, but the defilement considered there is minimal. This makes it all the more difficult to find a rationale for excluding the mother from the sanctuary for several weeks. It is tempting to accept the proposal that this law protects the woman from having to perform many tasks, except that the text only mentions concerns about blood and the sanctuary. It forbids no other activities.

This law is most suggestive about the thin line between life and death in association with blood. Leviticus 17:11 proclaims, "the life of the flesh is in the blood," explaining its atoning quality; but the present passage portrays blood as a contaminant, even when it flows involuntarily and by necessity. Blood carries life as long as it flows within flesh; the expulsion of the blood indicates that it no longer carries life within the body (cf. 15:19). The mother's body expels the blood that has been nourishing the unborn child but is now spent; it has lost its life-giving function and thus becomes a contaminant. The mother's blood represents life and death at the same time, life in the blood now flowing in the child and death in the blood that is expelled. Perhaps it is the close proximity of life to death that gives the blood of childbirth a greater significance, resulting in the need for an extended separation between the woman and the sanctuary.

If this understanding is correct, the event of childbirth illustrates the struggle between life and death that has existed since the eating of the forbidden fruit. The Lord warned that eating of the fruit would result in death, but then the Lord provided a way of perpetually counteracting that sentence—through childbirth. In a single act, a woman produces life and death, perhaps as a profound reminder of how precarious is the human condition and how precious is the merciful gift of life.

LEVITICUS 13

Chapters 13–14 address related conditions rendered collectively as "leprous disease." This could be misleading, because the Hebrew term does not refer to Hansen's disease, the scientific designation for leprosy. Instead, it denotes several conditions (such as psoriasis, vitiligo, eczema) that might afflict human skin, as well as various forms of mildew in cloth (13:47-59), and in wood, plaster, and other building materials (14:33-53; Wright 1987, 75; Milgrom 1991, 773-75; Hartley 1992, 186-89).

At the stylistic level, Lev 13 and 14 are linked together in the same way that Lev 1–5 and 6–7 are linked together. Chapter 13 consists of primary laws and their subunits concerning skin diseases on persons (vv. 2-46) or mildew on clothing (vv. 47-59). Chapter 14 contains two related sets of "rituals," one set for offerings and other acts for cleansing skin (vv. 2-32), and one set for the cleansing of a mildewed house (vv. 33-53). It is likely that these sets of regulations were originally separate, but they have been brought together here because of their common subject matter.

Literary Analysis

The style in chapter 13 is most similar to that in chapters 1–5. Between a typical narrative heading (13:1) and a typical narrative summary (13:59) there are eight (or nine) distinguishable units: 13:2-8, 9-17, 18-23, 24-28, 29-37, 38-39, 40-44, 47-58. A great deal of repetition or near repetition characterizes these laws. A typical introductory formula for primary cases marks the beginning of each unit. In seven units, the primary case is followed by two or three subordinate cases (vv. 38-39 provide the lone exception). The typical formula for subordinate cases, "(but) if," is used in most instances.

The first seven units deal with cases of a "leprous disease" on a person, while the final unit (vv. 47-58) considers infected clothing. Verses 45-46 reflect a somewhat different style, pointing to their function as a transition unit that brings together the "leprous disease" and the clothing of those afflicted. Most of these units progress in pairs, according to their initial subject. The subject of the first two units is "a person" (vv. 2-8, 9-17); the subject of the next two units is "a body" (vv. 18-23, 24-28); the next two units concern "a man or a woman" (vv. 29-37, 38-39); the seventh unit concerns "anyone" who is balding (vv. 40-44); and the final unit concerns clothing (vv. 47-58). The "person who has the leprous disease" in verses 45-46 refers to any individual from any of the preceding units; verses 47-58 concern mildewed clothing.

In all the cases prescribed there is a consistent sequence to the procedures. The person comes to the priest, who is to "examine" (see) the suspicious feature on persons or cloth and make a diagnosis. Every unit mentions from one to five times when the priest conducts such an examination. These statements of examination and diagnosis are followed by common formulas reporting the medical/ritual state of the person or clothing. The priest "pronounces" the person "unclean" or "clean." Most of the units and subunits include one or two clauses that identify the nature of the condition (e.g., "it is a leprous disease," or "it is [just] the scar"). This typically is a verbless clause that includes a demonstrative pronoun ("he/it is . . .") and states the priest's findings. This construction lends a sense of finality or certitude to the diagnosis.

There are a couple of variations to this pattern. In five of the eight cases, the priest's initial examination is inconclusive, leading to one or two seven-day waiting periods. A subsequent examination yields the ultimate diagnosis and pronouncement. There are two instances in which the instructions call for the person to wash his or her clothes after being declared "clean" (vv. 6, 34).

The construction of verses 45-46 constitutes a significant deviation. Typical introductory and concluding formulas are lacking. No main clause begins with a verb (verb-initial clauses predominate in Hebrew), and in many cases the verb closes the clause. In their present location, these instructions apply to all the preceding units. They also serve as a transition from those units to the following unit. Only a couple of previous units refer to the clothing of persons examined. Verses 45-46 give remarks regarding the clothing of anyone with a "leprous disease." This opens the way for further instructions about the handling of clothing that carries a leprous disease.

Lesser deviations exist in the concluding formulas of the final unit (vv. 47-58). While the verbless clauses typical of the earlier units appear once again, in this unit additional instructions follow in all three cases (vv. 52, 55, 57). These additional clauses call for the burning of contaminated clothing. In the latter two instances, the text unexpectedly shifts to the use of plural verb forms. This might indicate a different source, or it might reflect specific circumstances of the case (multiple members of a domicile typically store their clothing together). Verse 58 ends with a call to wash clothing that is declared "clean" (vv. 6, 34).

The summary raises questions about the chapter's unity (v. 59). It mentions only "leprous disease in a cloth... or in anything of skin"; thus it summarizes verses 47-58 while apparently ignoring verses 2-46. Perhaps verses 47-58 originally existed alone, and perhaps verses 45-46 originally served as the conclusion to the first seven units. It is also possible that the "ritual" in 14:1-32 once followed immediately after 13:1-46. But that does not provide much help, because 14:32 summarizes the items in 14:21-31 alone. This brings us full circle, as these two summaries provide parallel examples of summaries that mention only the final cases from the series of laws that precede them.

Exegetical Analysis

Priestly Evaluations of Various Skin Diseases (13:2-44)

The text presents seven cases concerning skin diseases. The first unit (vv. 2-8) sets two primary criteria: (1) the color of any hairs in the affected area, and (2) the depth of the affliction. These symptoms are regularly paired in the chapter. The color of the hair was thought to reflect the health of the flesh beneath the skin. The depth of the affliction is the main concern. Discoloration on the skin's surface indicates only the potential for uncleanness (v. 4). This results in a one-week waiting period. Subsequent observations determine whether the problem is arrested or advancing. This determination lies at the heart of these regulations. A skin disease that is temporary is a disease that the body is expelling. A disease that goes deeper penetrates to the "flesh," where its effects are more serious. This suggests that the Israelites recognized a distinction between a living being's "skin" and its "flesh" ("flesh" can denote the whole body or just what lies beneath the skin; Lam 3:4; Ezek 37:6, 8). Sores that are deep and chronic indicate a more serious problem in the health of the body. This deeper physical problem is considered an indicator of spiritual imperfection, and this yields a diagnosis of "unclean."

The second unit (vv. 9-17) emphasizes the depth of the condition as a primary criterion for determining its nature. It opens by mentioning two criteria that are similar to those given in the preceding law. The hair has turned white, as before, but now there is the appearance of "raw flesh" (living flesh) (vv. 10, 14, 15, 16); flesh beneath the skin is exposed. This unit emphasizes the latter symptom, as there are no references in this unit to the hair, after verse 10. The appearance of whitened skin is a cause for concern, but by itself it might indicate a temporary condition. The diagnoses based on the presence of white skin stand in contrast to diagnoses in the first unit. The previous unit implies that the spread of the whitening signals a worsening condition, because the spread of the disease below the skin is expected to follow. But in this case, the deeper problem of visible "raw flesh" exists already, so the spread of whitened skin suggests an improving condition. The skin is covering the "raw flesh." This confirms that the condition of the flesh beneath the skin is the primary concern. The second subordinate case (vv. 16-17) does not mention that the whitening spreads over the entire body, only over previously diseased areas. It could be that the point of verses 12-13 is that the spread of whitened skin on diseased flesh is a good sign, *even if* the whitening covers the entire body ("from head to foot").

This allows for an educated guess about why these persons are considered to be "unclean," while those with other symptoms are "clean." The "raw" flesh is where the blood is, and the blood carries the life of the body (17:11). In a healthy body, the skin encases the flesh. "Leprous diseases" involve conditions where the life-giving quality of the blood is corrupted; "death" is taking over. The flesh is acting as if it were dead. One external sign of this is the condition of the skin. "Death" within the body first causes the skin to turn white, and then decay allows the exposure of the flesh beneath (cf. the description of Miriam, Num 12:9-12). When the skin regains its healthy function, then the "life" of the body is reasserting itself. The blood is giving life once again, and there is a reversal of the mortifying process in the skin. These laws include an additional layer in the Israelite conception of these diseases. They make a connection between the body's physiological condition and the cultic/ritual state of the affected person. Bodies that manifest conditions of life are "clean," while those that manifest death are "unclean."

The next two units consider parallel circumstances (vv. 18-23, 24-28). They stipulate how a priest evaluates the aftereffects of skin damaged by a boil or a burn. The criteria are the same as before: if the affected area spreads beneath the skin, then it is a "leprous disease"; otherwise, following a seven-day waiting period, the priest pronounces the person "clean" because the affected area is merely a "scar." A scar indicates that, though imperiled to some degree, the "life" of the body has asserted itself.

The remaining units consider variations on these symptoms. The fifth (vv. 29-37) concerns cases where the discoloration of the skin is yellow rather than white (indicating eczema?). If the symptoms spread on the skin or penetrate beneath the skin, then the disease is "leprous." Otherwise, the condition is temporary and the person is "clean." There is a longer waiting period here (two weeks) before the priest renders a diagnosis, and the victim must shave the hair near the affected area in the middle of the waiting period. The end result is the same as before. The sixth unit deals with what should be obvious; if the only symptom is white spots on the skin, then the person is clean (vv. 38-39). The seventh and final scenario also begins with a single symptom: hair loss (vv. 40-44). This also might point to a deeper problem, but only if there are additional symptoms. Without them, the person is merely bald (vv. 40-41). If sores and lesions accompany the loss of hair, indicating that the problem extends beneath the skin (vv. 18-20, 24-25), then the priest declares the person "unclean."

Restrictions on Those Pronounced Unclean (13:45-46)

This brief unit might have been composed to bring together the preceding units, which had been separate from one another; or it could be that this unit originally stood as a final, overarching rule for all that precedes it. In either case, the directive applies to everyone pronounced "unclean" in the preceding units. These measures effectively declare someone to be "dead." The prescribed actions are more typically associated with grieving for the dead (Gen 37:34; Lev 21:10; Ezek 24:17, 22). Like other "unclean" things, those with leprous diseases are placed "outside the camp." It is logical to draw a connection from the physical ailments to a deeper, spiritual ailment, which is part and parcel of the Israelite concept of "death."

Evaluation of Diseased Clothing (13:47-59)

It is generally agreed that the writer uses the term for "leprous disease" in these verses to refer to form(s) of mildew or mold that can develop on clothing. The seriousness of the problem is described in three descending levels. These are determined by two examinations, the second coming seven days after the first. If the condition spreads over that time, the clothing is "unclean" and they burn it (vv. 47-52; also v. 57). If it is not spreading but cannot be removed by washing, the clothing is also burned (vv. 53-55). If washing eliminates it, then a second purification washing follows and the clothing can be used again (vv. 56-58).

The text indicates no direct cause-effect relationship between the diseases in the cloth and the preceding leprous diseases. The people apparently believe that these conditions portray a common problem—an abnormality associated with "death" that either displays or elicits divine disapproval. In both cases, the disease threatens the sanctity of the community, and so their carriers are removed from the community. Clothing cannot reassert "life" through healing, so the clothing is destroyed rather than being temporarily separated from the community.

Theological and Ethical Analysis

For modern interpreters, these instructions probably produce more questions than insights. The most tantalizing questions consider connections between physical ailments, ritual imperfection, and spiritual imperfection. While none of these instructions indicate that wrongdoing precipitates these diseases, there are examples of the Lord striking individuals with leprous diseases as punishment (Num 12:1-10; 2 Chr 26:16-21). Moreover, the cultic diagnosis and treatment of these diseases assume a spiritual component to the diseases. It is possible that the people regarded these diseases as a means of exposing an unwitting or hidden sin. It is significant, though, that these instructions do not expect a confession of sin or the identification of wrongdoing. Instead, the primary concern is to circumscribe the physical effects of the impurity by isolating the diseased individual.

It is not disease in general that yields uncleanness; only these specific leprous diseases have that effect. It is tempting to assume a parallel between the symptoms of disease and the designation of uncleanness. The temporary skin diseases require time to heal, just as previous forms of uncleanness persist only "until the evening." Leprous diseases are deeper and chronic. This suggests that the (unmentioned) offense is more serious than usual and forgiveness is more difficult. The two cases mentioned above involve individuals who demonstrate a lack of respect for God's duly appointed representatives, a grievous offense to priestly groups.

This line of reasoning is based on associations between holiness and life, and between defilement and death. The Lord is the God of life and therefore holy, and that is reflected in the community of believers among whom the Lord has chosen to reside. These particular diseases connote death to the Israelites, and death stands in opposition to the Lord; so, the community must exclude persons and objects bearing these diseases. These diseases indicate chronic and deep-seated problems, conditions that communicate the dominance of death over life. It is possible that the life in a body will one day regain the upper hand, showing that the body is clean again; but for the foreseeable future that is not the case, and so the person is unclean and unwelcome in the community.

Most modern readers do not automatically attribute physical diseases to spiritual failings. While many think that a physical condition can influence one's spiritual well-being, and feelings of guilt or participation in immoral activity can have physical consequences, moderns do not usually see physical well-being as a direct reflection of spiritual well-being. Some might conclude that these laws imply such a correlation, but the present considerations caution against generalizations. Nevertheless, the separation between the physical realm and the spiritual realm assumed today was not assumed then. Does this suggest that they were "primitive" in their worldview? Or should it challenge modern people to reconsider their own worldview? This passage might spur some healthy discussion in that regard.

LEVITICUS 14

Leviticus 14 functions as a partner to chapter 13. Chapter 13 speaks to the issue of diagnosis, while this chapter provides the guidelines for ritual purification once physical healing has occurred. In particular, it concerns the functions of the priest in this process.

Literary Analysis

There are two narrative headings in chapter 14 (vv. 1, 33) and two narrative summaries (vv. 32, 54-57). This breaks the chapter into two sections (vv. 1-32, 33-57).

The introduction to the first section (v. 2) parallels the introductory formulas of the five "rituals" in chapters 6–7. The summary in verse 32 is similar in construction to 7:37-38; 11:46-47; 12:7; and 13:59. There is only one subordinate law in the first section. It is marked by "but if" at the beginning of verse 21. Immediately preceding this is the concluding clause, "and he shall be clean" (13:6, 13, 17, 23, 34, 36). This clause also stands at the end of 14:9. The latter suggests two parts to the primary law (vv. 2-9, 10-20). This demarcation matches the shift from the seventh day to the eighth day. The subordinate law is similar to the subordinate laws in chapters 1 and 3. The general style of this instruction is similar to that of much of chapters 1–7. The structure involves an initial cleansing ritual and seven-day waiting period (vv. 2-9), then a second cleansing on the eighth day (vv. 10-20). The subordinate law explains what animals a poorer person might use in the cleansing ritual (vv. 21-31). In both cases, the writer gives more details about the second ritual than the first.

The narrative heading and summary of the second section (vv. 33, 54-57) are typical, although there is a "ritual" clause at the beginning and end of the latter. This summary, like the one in 13:59, describes what precedes as distinguishing between "unclean" and "clean." This summary refers to diseases on clothing, houses, and persons, but the subject of 14:33-53 is disease in houses; so, the inclusion of clothing and persons suggests that this summary might have encompassed both chapters at some stage in the book's development.

Some features hint at a redactor's hand in verse 34. There is a step missing in the presentation of the process of oral transmission. The narrative introduction says the Lord is addressing Moses and Aaron, yet the Lord addresses the nation in verse 34. What is more, verse 34 is one of the few occasions in this half of Leviticus that uses the second-person plural. The writer reverts to the third-person singular form from verse 35 through the rest of the chapter.

There are indicators of two subordinate laws in this section, with the particle "if" at the beginning of verses 43 and 48. The primary law considers the possibility of disease appearing in the walls of a house (vv. 34-42). The law prescribes a seven-day waiting period before the priest takes action. The first subordinate law explains what to do if the first cleansing is ineffective (vv. 43-47), while the second subordinate law prescribes a final sacrifice in cases where the cleansing is effective (vv. 48-53). The law ends with the statement "and it shall be clean" (cf. v. 20).

Exegetical Analysis

Purification of Skin Diseases (14:1-20)

The first part of the purification ritual shares general similarities with the ritual for bodily discharges. Both call for two birds, and both involve the washing of clothes and body (chap. 15; cf. 12:6-8). There are significant differences, though. This ritual involves an unusual manipulation of the birds, as one is slaughtered and the other released. This is similar to the two goats of Yom Kippur; the text, however, does not mention whether the released bird carries away the leper's sins. The association of the living bird with fresh ("living") water and red materials (cedar and scarlet yarn) points to the association between blood and life and death. The blood of the dead bird and the "death" of leprosy are linked, and the living bird and the water symbolize how "life" carries away "death."

The seven days of waiting reveal a deeper significance to this ritual. This parallels the priestly ordination process (chap. 8), signifying the reintegration or "aggregation" of the leper back into the community of the living. The leper is moving from the state of unclean to clean, just as the priest was transitioning from a common priest to one consecrated for the task of offering sacrifices.

The completion of the process on the eighth day also marks a person's migration across symbolic boundaries, in this case from the realm of death to the realm of life. The ceremony takes place at the entrance of the tent of meeting, just like the ordination ceremony. There is a sin offering, a grain offering, a burnt offering, and an elevation offering in both ceremonies. Both involve the triple daubing of blood on the one undergoing the purification/consecration process, and both involve placing oil on the person's head and in the sanctuary. The primary difference is the inclusion of a guilt offering in this process. It is often thought that this offering implies a serious offense against the Lord, but some argue that it is reparation for offerings to the sanctuary or services to the community that were lost while the leper lived outside the camp.

Alternate Offerings (14:21-32)

The guidelines for offerings brought by a poor person are consistent with earlier regulations; the differences appear in the offerings of the eighth day. The poor person is to bring only one lamb rather than three for the elevation offering, and the grain offering is one-third the size of the usual grain offering. The law also calls for the use of doves or pigeons in the concluding sin offering and burnt offering, in line with other special considerations for the poor (1:14-17; 5:7-13).

Purification of Houses (14:33-55)

Mold in the walls of a house is regarded as a "leprous disease," and it is treated according to similar guidelines. The diagnosis requires two inspections, seven days apart (vv. 34-42). The priest is concerned with the depth of the disease and whether it is spreading. If it is on the surface and not spreading, no further action is required; if it spreads, the diseased portions are removed and it is hoped that no further measures are required (cf. 13:4-6, 50-51).

The subordinate law of 14:43-47 concerns further spread of the disease (cf. 13:7-8, 51-52). As with the leprous person or clothing (13:45-46, 52, 55, 57), the house is considered permanently "unclean" and it is removed from the community. This law considers the possibility of contamination from house to persons (vv. 46-47), although this is not regarded as a serious threat. Even though it is a "leprous disease," the persons in the house must simply wash their clothes for cleansing. The cleansing ritual for the house (vv. 48-53) is virtually identical to the cleansing ritual prescribed for leprous persons (vv. 2-9), omitting the second phase of that ritual (vv. 8-9). That phase accomplishes reintegration of the person into the community. In the case of the house, a reintegration is not necessary because the house was never removed from the community.

Theological and Ethical Analysis

These matters of impurity and cleansing raise questions about the Israelite understanding of the interaction of the physical and spiritual realms. The assumption is that the physical diseases considered here betray the presence of spiritual disease. Western thinkers wrestle with this on two levels. From a scientific point of view, they do not normally attribute physical diseases to spiritual imperfection. A physical disease has a physical origin. Westerners also object to this association on theological grounds. Jesus' comments concerning the man who was born blind provide but one example of New Testament teachings on this subject (John 9:1-3). Most Christians believe that it is wrong—even hurtful—to attribute physical infirmities to spiritual failings. These chapters seem to assume a direct link between a person's physical and spiritual conditions, but the nature and extent of this link demand clarification.

These laws do not explicitly link disease to any sinful act. The disease simply appears. There are occasions when the Lord places diseases on individuals because of their sin, but this does not justify generalizations. A central concern here is that the disease might spread through physical contact or close proximity to the disease. This is not a concern about the spread of sin but about the spread of uncleanness. Similarly, one should consider the purpose

of the purification rituals. The rituals do not bring physical healing, they come after the healing has occurred. They certify that the
healing has taken place, or they bring spiritual healing to the one
enjoying restored health. The function of sin offerings elsewhere
argues for the latter.

These observations point to greater integration between the
physical realm and the spiritual realm in the minds of the Israelites.
They did not simply believe that sins produced physical ailments.
Instead, they believed that physical ailments were signs of imperfections or blemishes in the created order. These particular ailments
are of special concern because they are suggestive of life and death.
Such imperfections naturally include a spiritual component,
because life is an inherently spiritual matter; but it is the imperfection, regardless of its cause, that necessitates spiritual purification.

It is important to recognize the difference between the fate of an
infected person and the fate of an infected object. Both require
removal from the camp, but there is hope for future reintegration
for the person. Objects are declared clean, or they are removed
from the camp and destroyed. The chapter begins from the premise that persons with "leprous disease" can be restored to the community. This is a passage of hope. The ritual involving the two
birds furthers this tone. Just as the living bird carries away blood
from the dead bird, so life carries away death. Daubing the
cleansed person with blood intimates parallels between the changing status of the one who is healed and the priest. Just as the priest
approaches the Lord after receiving the blood, so the one who is
healed can come closer to the Lord after receiving blood on his or
her body.

LEVITICUS 15

This chapter closes the block of laws on physical impurities. It
shares concerns with the discharge of blood during childbirth in
chapter 12, and with things that make one "unclean until the
evening" in chapter 11. This suggests a general structure to chapters 11–15. Chapter 11 concerns defilement that is common and
temporary. Chapter 12 considers defilement that is limited (and

predictable) in occurrence, but it is of longer duration. Chapters 13–14 involve impurities of varying occurrence and duration, and chapter 15 returns to defilement that is common and temporary.

Literary Analysis

Typical narrative formulas frame chapter 15 (vv. 1, 32-33). Following the narrative heading is a typical discourse heading (v. 2a), and corresponding to that is a summarizing instruction to Moses and Aaron (v. 31). The latter stands out because the Lord again addresses the two with plural verbs, and the Lord refers to the Israelites with plural pronouns. The main body refers to the ultimate recipients in the more common mode of the hypothetical individual.

The main body consists of five units (vv. 2b-15, 16-17, 18, 19-24, 25-30). A common casuistic construction introduces the first, second, fourth, and fifth units; a less common construction marks the central unit (v. 18). The narrative summary identifies the topic of concern as "anyone, male or female, who has a discharge" (vv. 32-33). The subject of the first two units is "any/a man," and the subject of the latter two is "a woman." The middle unit facilitates the swing from male to female by beginning (more literally) with "a woman with whom a man lies" (v. 18).

The "swing" of verse 18 is part of the chiastic organization of these five units (arranged ABCB'A'). The first unit concerns abnormal male discharges (vv. 2b-15), and the second addresses any normal case of semen discharge (vv. 16-17). The hinge in verse 18 concerns male and female united as one. The fourth unit concerns the normal female discharge of menstrual blood (vv. 19-24), and the fifth unit concerns any abnormal female discharges (vv. 25-30).

The first and fifth units conclude with parallel prescriptions for atonement offerings following cleansing (vv. 13-15, 28-30; cf. 12:6-8). These passages are virtually identical in content and style. The one significant difference is the command that the man wash himself and his clothes (v. 13). Although washing might be implied for the woman, that law specifies that "anyone" (male/generic) who touches anything upon which she sits or lies must wash himself and his clothes. As if to balance things out, the text identifies only the female discharge as "unclean" (v. 30), but again this is probably implied with male discharges (v. 15).

The dominant term in this chapter is "unclean," but this again is temporary uncleanness. The most common concluding formula states, "he/she/it is unclean until the evening." This clause is also prevalent in 11:24-40, strengthening the sense of unity between these two chapters. (This clause occurs only twice else in Leviticus—17:14 and 22:6.) The animals in chapter 11 are thought to be "unclean" because of their association with death, and the particular concern in 11:24-40 is regarding contact with carcasses. This suggests that the concern with emissions in chapter 15 derives from an assumed connection between emissions and death.

Exegetical Analysis

Impurity Resulting from Abnormal Male Discharges (15:1-15)

The first unit gives the most details about what things and persons are defiled by abnormal genital discharge. Discharges defile anything on which the man sits or lies and anyone who touches him or the defiled items. Even someone touched by the spittle of a man with an emission is rendered unclean (v. 8). This shows that it is the man—and not the emission—that defiles; the emission reveals an impurity inherent in the man. A single remedy applies to all persons who come into contact with such a man. The differences in cleansing an earthen dish and cleansing a wooden dish parallel the guidelines in 11:32-33 (v. 12).

The primary reason for assuming that this is a genital discharge is the parallel to female discharges. The Hebrew word rendered "member" is the word for "flesh" (v. 3), which most scholars regard as a euphemism for sexual organs in this case. Most now agree that the disease is not the more virulent strain of gonorrhea, which came from the Americas, but a weaker malady with similar symptoms (Milgrom 1991, 907).

The ritual for cleansing a man from an abnormal discharge involves a seven-day waiting period (chaps. 8–9, 13–14). This indicates a transition from one state to another, in this case from exclusion outside the sanctuary precinct to inclusion inside it.

There is no indication that the afflicted person must live outside the camp. This indicates that a discharge is considered less offensive than a leprous disease.

Impurity Resulting from Normal Male Discharges (15:16-17)

This brief secondary law reveals some basic beliefs about sexuality. Most important, it suggests that the primary purpose in the emission of semen is procreation. Emission for any other reason—even involuntary—constitutes the loss of potential life, which is acknowledged (lamented?) by declaring the man momentarily unclean. What the text envisions is considered "normal," in contrast to the emissions considered in verses 2-12. Normal physical phenomena can render one unacceptable for admission into the sanctuary but still acceptable for life in the broader community.

Impurity Resulting from Intercourse (15:18)

The main point of this stipulation is that a woman who lies with a man with a semen emission is defiled by his emission. Most interpreters infer from this that intercourse renders a couple temporarily unclean. There are ample parallels to support the idea that sexual activity can exclude persons from a sacred place, so this would make sense. There are a couple of aspects of this statute that raise questions of interpretation, though. Some interpreters assume that, because marital intercourse is divinely ordained, this statute must refer to extramarital intercourse; however, to confer such a minor effect on such a serious transgression seems inconsistent. If the defiling act is intercourse, then it seems unnecessary to mention that the man emits semen. Perhaps "has an emission of semen" refers to something other than what normally occurs during intercourse.

Impurity Resulting from Normal Female Discharges (15:19-24)

The text in verses 19-23 lists the same possibilities for contamination that one finds for a man in verses 3-7. Like the emission of semen, the emission of menstrual blood renders one unclean (chap. 12). The most obvious difference is the duration of the uncleanness (seven days). This is probably a reflection of the duration of a woman's menstrual period. The defilement resulting from intercourse during a woman's menstrual period might appear to mirror the situation envisioned in verse 18, but it actually goes further (v. 24). This verse speaks of contact with the emission itself, not just contact with the woman. This contrasts with the concerns about contact with a man who has an abnormal emission. In this case the man essentially joins with the woman in her defilement, sharing its effects with her. While a man's abnormal emission necessitates the offering of sacrifices after seven days (vv. 13-15), the woman's normal discharge merely requires the same passage of time before its effects are spent. There is no need for sacrifices.

Impurity Resulting from Abnormal Female Discharges (15:25-30)

Abnormal discharge of blood renders a woman unclean to the same degree that a male's abnormal discharge defiles him. The consequences are the same as detailed in verses 3-7 and 19-23, so here they are given in more summary fashion. The cleansing ritual for the woman is no different than that for the man.

Summary (15:31-33)

The motive statement in verse 31 points to a deeper concern underlying these instructions. That concern is the contamination of the sanctuary. The people are to keep themselves "separate" (from *nazar*, the root for Nazirite) from their uncleanness so that they do not defile the Lord's dwelling place. This raises the broader issue of how human impurity defiles the sanctuary. Jacob Milgrom asserts that contamination is airborne, and that it comes to the sanctuary from anywhere in the land. The concern in this chapter associates contamination with direct contact with the contaminating persons or, at the least, with those in close proximity to them. They are not required to separate themselves from the camp. It is unreasonable to conclude that the contamination of one type of uncleanness is physically lighter than and travels farther than another. This shows the need to be careful not to conceive of the "contamination" in more physical terms than they did.

The summary statement in verses 32-33 applies the priestly ritual for abnormal discharges to all discharges. This is the last in a series of such summary statements in Leviticus (6:2, 7, 18; 7:1, 11, 37; 11:46; 12:7; 13:59; 14:32, 54, 57). Those in chapters 6–7 concern the five main offerings, while those in chapters 11–15 mark cleansing rituals. What these have in common is that they are offerings made by the priests before the sanctuary on behalf of other members of the community. These are not the only examples of such offerings, however, so this probably points only to a common redactor's hand.

Theological and Ethical Analysis

At first blush these regulations appear to be fairly straightforward. Various forms of genital emissions all lead to the same result—the temporary defilement of people and objects touched by the person with an emission. The duration of the defilement varies according to the type and duration of the emission. There are a few deeper matters to recognize, though.

First, it is the person who is unclean; the emission exposes the person's uncleanness. As with other situations of uncleanness, this might imply that the person is guilty of some wrongdoing, which the defiling emission is exposing. This might be so, but only in some cases. The text makes no explicit mention of any wrongdoing that might explain the occurrence of an abnormal emission; it is simply there. In cases of natural emissions, there is defilement, but the text attaches no fault or guilt to this defilement. If the defilement derives from the loss of potential life, then the temporary period of separation serves as a reminder of the importance and sacredness of life, not as a punishment. These regulations presume no significant difference between female defilement and male defilement. The only noticeable distinction is the duration of the defilement, but this reflects the duration of their respective discharges. Men and women attain purification through the same means, depending on the nature of their defilement.

What ultimately lies behind these guidelines is the belief in the sacredness of sex between a man and woman. These guidelines do not derive from a view of sex as an inherently defiling act. The crux of the matter is that the primary goal of sex should be the furthering of life. This is a sacred trust, shared by male and female equally. An emission constitutes a loss of potential life, and these regulations call for all those who come into contact with this loss to acknowledge that fact. These rules reflect the idea that men and women should regard sex first and foremost as a life-giving act. This is not to deny or reject other aspects of sex, but it does give priority to this aspect over all others. Such a perspective could have far-reaching implications, particularly in modern societies, where a different set of priorities concerning sex tends to prevail.

One other aspect of these regulations is disquieting to some in the modern Western world. This is the apparently public nature of things that Westerners tend to regard as private. These rules assume that a man's emissions and the time of a woman's menstrual flow are known to those around them; otherwise, their associates would not know to take the "necessary precautions." On the other hand, only priestly families needed to be concerned with such things most of the time, because most families would not go to the main sanctuary on a regular basis. Defilement from natural emissions would take care of itself with the passage of time, so that only abnormal emissions would require much, if any, further attention.

Beyond that, these observations reflect some ironic cultural differences between modern sensibilities and attitudes in biblical Israel. Westerners tend to be more protective of these aspects of their lives than the Israelites were. The irony is that both attitudes derive from a fundamental desire to honor the sacredness of sex. Westerners are highly influenced by Christian ideas of morality, which include the belief that the sanctity of sexual activity is upheld to the degree to which sex is kept private. The relationship between sex and life predominates in Israel, so that the sanctity of sex is directly tied to its ability to perpetuate life. Sexual activity carries implications for life and the perpetuation of life, in their minds, and so anything concerning sex that threatens life makes it a public concern. Sex is of concern to the biblical writers because of the sacredness they associate with sex, not because they see an inherently defiling component to sex.

More generally, these regulations assume a sense of corporate responsibility and accountability. The uncleanness of an individual can affect the relationship between the entire community and the Lord. It is for this reason the biblical writers assume that there needs to be public awareness of private impurity. The next chapter addresses this sense of corporate responsibility more directly in the Yom Kippur ceremony.

LEVITICUS 16

The narrator links the rituals of Lev 16 to the sinful offering of "unholy fire" by Aaron's sons (10:1-2), implying that these rituals were designed as a cultic response to that sin. Direct movement from chapter 10 to chapter 16 conforms to the pattern of diagnosing a sin or impurity and then prescribing remedial rituals. This raises questions about the placement of chapters 11–15. A part of the answer comes in the closing paragraph (vv. 29-34), which presents these rituals as an annual, national purification ceremony. Other passages identify this as "the day of atonement" (23:26-32; 25:9). The overall inference is that the offense of Aaron's sons in chapter 10 and the impurities dealt with in chapters 11–15 all have a similar effect, an effect that requires the rituals of chapter 16. There are also links to the laws of Lev 1–7, giving the impression that chapter 16 serves as a culmination to all of chapters 1–15. It is no surprise that the rabbis devoted an entire tractate of the Mishnah to this day (*Yoma*).

The significance of this chapter broadens in view of the relationship between Lev 1–16 and the closing chapters of Exodus. Exod 35–40 describes the construction of the Tabernacle. The laws of Lev 1–15 prescribe how the Israelites should conduct themselves in the Lord's dwelling. The primary concern is to keep the house clean, so that the Lord will "feel at home" there. Chapter 16 concludes this section with rules about how the people are to "clean up" the house after they have been there. It also begins to shift attention beyond the Lord's home to the rest of the community.

Literary Analysis

The stylistic features of these prescriptions are typical of the first half of the book. The mode of address in the main section is third-person masculine singular, because Aaron is the primary actor. The narrative heading (1:1-2a) is extended and doubled. A temporal setting accounts for the extension (v. 1), presenting these instructions as a divine response to the offering of "unholy fire" by Aaron's sons. A variation on the direct address introduction ("The Lord said," rather than "The Lord spoke") and a specific prohibition set the stage for the main body (v. 2; cf. 21:1). The prohibition, "Tell your brother Aaron not to come just at any time," has its opposite in verse 3, "Thus shall Aaron come." The next twenty-five verses prescribe how Aaron might enter the holiest part of the sanctuary.

Verses 3-5 serve as introduction to the offerings proper, identifying the animals that Aaron and the people are to bring for this special occasion. The syntax further isolates these verses as providing preliminary information. All of the clauses place the verb at the end, rather than at the beginning (cf. 13:45-46). This sets them off from verses 6-28, where the more typical word order is the rule (verb-subject-object).

The only surprise in the main body (vv. 6-28) is the duplication between verse 6 and verse 11a. Verse 6 introduces the instructions for sacrificing the priest's bull. This signals that the instructions follow the order set out in verses 3-5. However, the subsequent verses explain how Aaron determines the respective functions of the two goats that the congregation provides (vv. 7-10). Verse 11a repeats verse 6, introducing again the instructions for the priest's bull. There are various explanations possible for this duplication. (1) The least likely explanation is that the duplication arose because of carelessness on the part of a copyist. (2) Gordon Wenham suggests that verses 6-10 function as an outline for verses 11-22 (Wenham 1979, 228); however, these verses do not outline all the steps that follow. (3) It is more likely that the text seeks to describe simultaneous events. Aaron would perform the sin offering first, but he would have to designate the respective functions of the two goats at roughly the same time. The designation of the goats is a preliminary action, but it does not occur until the ceremony has begun; so it does not fit in the introduction (vv. 3-5). To indicate this, the author introduces the bull of the sin offering—the first ritual in this ceremony—and then follows that with a parenthetical note about the designation of the goats. Mentioning the designation later might lead to the wrongful conclusion that it was to come after the completion of the bull offering. The repetition of verse 6 in verse 11a marks the end of this parenthetical unit and the resumption of the main sequence of events (Milgrom 1991, 1063).

There are no stylistic clues for subdividing the remainder of the main body (vv. 11-28), as there is a virtually unbroken chain of typical prose sentences. Only the contents themselves reveal a logical progression. First there is the sin offering for the priestly house, the incense for the inner sanctuary, and the sin offering for the people. The final offering makes atonement for the sanctuary, the tent of meeting, and the altar (vv. 11-19; Exod 30:10). These offerings precede the release of the scapegoat (vv. 20-22). The remainder concerns the cleansing of the main participants, from the priest's ritual bathing (vv. 23-24) to the disposal of the remains of the animals sacrificed and the washing of the priest's assistants (vv. 25-28).

There is a noticeable shift with verse 29. The speaker now addresses the audience in the plural. All before had been instructions that Moses was to pass on to Aaron. The author maintains this new mode of addressing the people through verse 31. The dual reference to a "statute" forms an inclusio within verses 29-31. The main character in verses 32-33 is the high priest (as in the main law), which seems to confirm the isolation of verses 29-31. However, there is a fuller repetition of the beginning of verse 29 at the beginning of verse 34, suggesting a larger inclusio around verses 29-34a; verse 34a summarizes verses 32-33. The narrative ending (v. 34b) speaks of the fulfillment of the prescriptions in verses 6-28 at that time, without reference to the annual observances in verses 29-34a. It is logical to conclude that verses 29-34a constitute a secondary appendix, presented in two parts. These two parts might come from different scribal hands (cf. 23:26-32).

The narrative ending is most like those in chapters 8–10. This strengthens the link between this atonement ceremony and the events in those chapters. The translation in the NRSV is misleading. The subject is "he," most likely to be Aaron, not Moses. Aaron is fulfilling instructions from the Lord that Moses passed on to him (v. 2). Aaron's execution of these commands resolves his anguish at the end of chapter 10. Moses had encouraged him to eat his portion of a typical sin offering, but these instructions call for a special sin offering that is destroyed outside the camp. Aaron completes these instructions, and so he will feel worthy to fulfill his priestly duties again.

Exegetical Analysis

Preparing to Enter the (Most) Holy Place (16:1-5)

The preceding analysis substantiates the impression of the introductory note that the priests originally performed this ritual in response to special circumstances, and only later did it become an annual ceremony. Several situations might precipitate the entrance of the high priest into the Holy Place; however, the inclusion of offerings for the people shows that this extends beyond the events in chapter 10 (v. 5). The offering of unholy fire was a priestly offense; there would be no reason for the people to petition for forgiveness. Verses 2-5 apply to any time that the high priest would want to enter the central sanctuary. The broader context suggests that these atonement rituals apply to all of chapters 10–15.

This law stipulates that even Aaron cannot go "inside the curtain" without making special preparations. The ark rests behind the curtain (Exod 26:33; 40:3, 21), and only the descendants of Aaron may enter past it (Num 18:6-7). Most rituals are performed in front of the curtain (Lev 4:6, 17). The curtain obstructs everyone's view of the ark. On this occasion, smoke from the incense temporarily serves the same function as the curtain, obstructing the view between the priest and the presence of the Lord over the ark (vv. 12-13). What is unusual is the designation of the sacred area as "the sanctuary" or "the holy place" (vv. 2-3, 16, 17, 20,

23, 27; both expressions render the same Hebrew term). Other texts designate this inner chamber as the holy of holies (Exod 26:31-35; Milgrom 1991, 1063; Hartley 1992, 226).

Another sort of uncertainty revolves around the designation "mercy seat" (Exod 25:17-22). This rendering comes from the LXX translators, who apparently envision this as a throne from which the Lord extends mercy to his subjects. The Hebrew term for "mercy seat" (kappōreth) might come from the root that underlies "make atonement" (kippēr), but some interpreters relate it to a word for "cover." It is unclear whether this term designates the "cover" or "lid" on the ark, or the place from which the Lord administers mercy. There is further disagreement about whether the ark (or the lid of the ark) was thought to serve as the seat on which the Lord sat, or the footstool on which he rested his feet as he sat on his throne. Either conception would fit.

The linen garments that Aaron wears are not the typical priestly garments (vv. 23-24; Exod 28). Many commentators assert that linen garments are plain in comparison to the usual priestly vestments, probably suggesting that the priests are assuming a stance that aligns them more closely with the rest of the people. On the other hand, some point out that descriptions of angels often have them wearing white linen; so perhaps these garments are meant to convey that the priest is entering a realm of special holiness.

Performance of the Atonement Process (16:6-28)

There seems to be a simple progression in the offerings. The priest presents the sin offering for himself and his family (vv. 6, 11-14), and then the first goat as a sin offering for the people (vv. 15-19). An assistant then releases the second goat into the wilderness (vv. 20-22). Following a changing of vestments, the priest offers two burnt offerings (vv. 23-24). Finally, the priest and his assistants dispose of the remains of the offerings (vv. 25-28).

A more careful scrutiny raises several questions. The most significant concerns the nuances of "make atonement" (Heb. kippēr). This verb appears fifteen times in this chapter in four different constructions. The most consistent is the construction "make atonement in" (kippēr be-). The object of this construction is the location where the priest makes an atoning offering (vv. 17, 27). There are then three different Hebrew constructions that are translated "make atonement for." Two of these constructions have consistent uses: *kippēr ʾet* occurs with parts of the sanctuary as its object (vv. 20, 33), and *kippēr baʿad* is used when the object is a person (vv. 6, 11, 17, 24). Thus, in this chapter, the first construction relates where the ritual takes place, the second connotes inanimate objects that receive atonement, and the third identifies persons that receive atonement.

There is one puzzle arising with these constructions. The priest "[makes] atonement for himself and for his house" with the first sin offering (vv. 6, 11), and this extends to "all the assembly of Israel" with the second sin offering (v. 17). He will "[make] atonement for himself and for the people" a little later, when he offers the two burnt offerings (v. 24). This is one of the few times where atonement results from a burnt offering (cf. 1:4; 14:20), and it is puzzling here because the text indicates that the preceding sin offerings had already provided atonement for all these people. It is most likely that the burnt offerings mark the conclusion of the sacrificial portion of the atonement process.

The fourth construction (*kippēr ʿal*) is more ambiguous. The writer uses this construction in three ways: "make atonement over" (v. 10), "make atonement for" (v. 16), and "make atonement [on behalf of]" (v. 18). In these two verses, this construction has the same force that *kippēr ʾet* carries in the summary statements (with places as the object). However, in the summary section itself, this construction (*kippēr ʿal*) carries the same force that *kippēr baʿad* has in the main section (with persons as the object; vv. 30, 33, 34). There have been some attempts to explain these variations on the basis of multiple authors, but no reconstruction has been able to build a consensus of opinion.

A deeper issue involves the need to make atonement for the sanctuary. Verses 16, 30, and 33 reveal the issue most clearly. Verse 33 summarizes who the beneficiaries of the atonement are, listing the sanctuary, the tent of meeting, the altar, the priests, and the people. The previous verses identify the justification for atonement—the "uncleannesses" and "sins" of the people. This has sparked a considerable discussion regarding why the sins of the people defile the sanctuary. Why does this defilement exist after the people have presented their offerings to receive forgiveness? One explanation is that the usual offerings for forgiveness transferred the offense from the offender to the sanctuary. A variation on this suggests that an offense defiled the offender and the sanctuary at the same time, and the usual offerings cleansed the offender but not the sanctuary. In both of these views, a second offering (this ceremony) is needed to remove the "stain" of the offenses from the sanctuary. A third view holds that the usual offerings provided forgiveness and atonement for lesser offenses (unintentional sins or unavoidable impurities), but this ceremony is necessary to grant forgiveness and atonement for intentional sins (Num 15:27-31).

These views attempt to account for three aspects of this ceremony that set it apart: the priest's entrance "behind the curtain," the release of the scapegoat, and the fact that this ceremony is performed only once a year. The repetition in verses 6 and 11 is related to the first aspect. The priest presents a sin offering to make atonement for himself, so that he is worthy to enter the innermost sanctuary. He takes blood from his sin offering and the people's sin offering with him. The text describes the slaughtering of the two animals and the collection and sprinkling of their blood separately, but the priest does not make separate entries to perform these rites. The redactor tries to convey this fact by bracketing the designations of the goats between a duplicative reference to the priest's sin offering in verses 6 and 11.

This still leaves the question of why the priest needs to enter the most holy place. Originally, it might have been to seek atonement for offenses committed by the sanctuary priests. Verse 1 points to the sin of Nadab and Abihu as the reason for this offering. The references to "iniquities," "transgressions," and "sins" of the people of Israel appear to be late additions (cf. Exod 34:7; Job 14:16-17; Pss 32:1-2; 51:1-2; Isa 43:24-25; 59:12). But even if ritual sin by the priests had been the full scope of the case at some time, this does not change the basic notion underlying these rites: human sin pollutes the Lord's sanctuary. Removal of this pollution comes in stages, as the purification process moves from the "holy place" to the broader tent of meeting and then out to the altar (vv. 15-19). The release of the scapegoat represents the complete expulsion of the effects of the sin away from the community (vv. 20-22). The present wording of the law reflects the belief that any sin or impurity results in this pollution and the need for its removal (v. 16).

The magnitude of the release of the scapegoat is surprising. This ritual is unusual because it promises atonement through the preservation of the life of the sacrificial animal. The blood of the sin offerings "makes atonement" on behalf of the people and the sanctuary (v. 19), but the living goat carries the sins away from the community (v. 22). There is no indication about what makes this so. Some suggest it is the placement of both hands, rather than just one (1:4), on the goat; but it is possible that the priest uses two hands because of his dual role as representative for his own family and representative for the people. Others believe the confession endows the rite with its special function, but there is little evidence that confession alone would make such an important difference.

Equally puzzling are the references here to "Azazel" (vv. 8, 10, 26). The term is unattested outside this chapter or in ancient Near Eastern texts. Many interpret this as the proper name for a desert demon, but this raises other problems. In a religion that so staunchly rejects the notion of other deities, it seems odd to lend viability to one here. It is also curious that the goat would be sent to a demon. There is no hint that the demon is threatening the community. Some assert that the goat is returning sins to their place of origin, but it is unlikely that they would think of one demon in the wilderness as the source of all their sins. Some early translators thought that the name derived from a Hebrew phrase meaning "goat that goes away." Others associated the term with a place, rendering the expression as "a rocky precipice" or "hardest of the mountains" (cf. v. 22). A recent suggestion translates it as an abstract noun, meaning "(for) entire removal." The problem with these proposals is that Azazel does not stand as a rival to the Lord, as suggested by verses 7-10. This leads back to the first proposal and its unorthodox doctrine in a text that many believe to be heavily redacted (Hartley 1992, 237-38).

Perhaps, though, this focuses attention on the wrong aspect of these rituals. The introduction places the most significance on the priest's entrance into the most holy portion of the sanctuary, where the Lord dwells. The sense of privilege and intimacy with the divine that this communicates overshadows the significance of the release of the scapegoat. That is just one of many rites that highlights the mercy on the Lord's part that allow these rites to serve as a means for removing spiritual impurities and sin.

The cleansing rites in verses 23-28 reinforce this sense of special privilege. The high priest removes his linen garments, bathes, and then dresses again in his usual priestly vestments. Some compare this to the belief that handling the Scriptures "defiles the hands." The priest has come so close to what is truly holy that he must honor the experience by removing any trace of it from his person. The destruction of the remains of the offerings and the washing of the priestly attendants substantiate this perspective.

Establishment of Yom Kippur (16:29-34)

The concluding paragraph calls for this to be an annual ceremony. Several features argue for attributing this section to a redactor. This might reflect the transformation of a local, occasional ritual into a national ceremony. In any case, the canonical text presents several important ideas. The most critical is that any misdeed or impurity necessitates the cleansing of the person and the sanctuary. Verses 29-31 demand that every individual participate in this ceremony. The ceremony provides atonement "for you" (pl.), but the call to recognize this day is directed to individuals, to "the citizen [and] the alien" alike (v. 29). The remaining verses emphasize the corporate perspective on this ceremony, as it concerns "all the people of the assembly" (v. 33).

The language points the reader toward a broader perspective. Just as the release of the goat to the wilderness and the disposal of sacrificial items outside the camp remind of the world beyond the sanctuary, so the calls for a community-wide Sabbath and time of self-denial show that this ceremony concerns more than just the priests and the sanctuary (vv. 29, 31). These calls surround the divine promise of cleansing (v. 30), exposing the more significant implications of this cleansing ceremony. Subsequent passages emphasize the self-denial in this ceremony (Lev 23:27-32; Num 29:7), as part of a larger exposition of the responsibilities and benefits of being the Lord's people.

Theological and Ethical Analysis

This chapter exposes the depth and the breadth of the effects of sin, while at the same time revealing the corresponding mercy and grace of the Lord. The sins of God's people contaminate the innermost and holiest parts of the sanctuary. Symbolically this means that their misdeeds and impurities are affronts against the very core of who the Lord is. What the people do reflects on the Lord's character. Their actions bring dishonor to their God. Their actions connect the source of life with the things of death.

The acceptance of this ceremony as a means of atonement reveals the Lord's great mercy. This cleansing of the sanctuary is required only once a year. The sins and impurities "pile up"—apparently—in the sanctuary for a year, illustrating the Lord's willingness to bear this burden. The rites that "make atonement" for the priests and the people are relatively minor, considering the enormity of what they accomplish. Offerings that otherwise atone for one person's single offense make atonement here for all the sins of the entire nation for a whole year. The use of the scapegoat in this peculiar way hardly seems to warrant the results that it brings. This highlights the magnitude of the Lord's mercy in accepting these small gestures as cleansing for such pervasive defilement.

There is a hint of how enormous this purification is in verse 31. "It is a sabbath of complete rest to you." The reference to the Sabbath points back to the initial creation story. That account concludes with God resting and consecrating the Sabbath (Gen 2:1-3). By making this connection between Yom Kippur and the Sabbath, the text implies that this ceremony works to restore the original order and harmony of creation itself. With this ceremony, the world is made new.

The evidence for scribal redaction prompts some to dismiss its theological significance. This is to favor the intent of a reconstructed text over the intent of the current text. Some consider the actions of priests to have more serious consequences for the community relationship with the Lord than does anyone else's actions. The current form of the text implies that any person's sins are as damaging to that relationship as any sins that the priests might commit. Therefore, it is the responsibility of each and every member of the community to honor the Lord in order to maintain the whole community's healthy relationship with the Lord. Each person's actions affect the Lord's willingness to dwell among the group.

Such a perspective is not popular in a modern, individualistic worldview, but one finds it throughout Scripture. Just as the sins of individuals threaten the health of the group and contaminate the sanctuary in which the Lord resides, so Paul warns Christians about the effects that the impure behavior of individual Christians will have on "the temple of God" (1 Cor 3:16-17; 2 Cor 6:14–7:1). It is fair in some sense to hold clergy to a higher standard, but this does not mean that the offenses of laypersons have a lesser impact on the life of the believing community. This chapter implies that atonement is a matter of concern for the whole community, not just the priests.

While the threat to the nation's relationship with the Lord includes the sins of laypersons, the text maintains the central importance played by the priests in restoring that relationship. It is crucial that the priest first mend the relationship between himself and the Lord before he turns his attention to other matters. He is not in a position to cleanse the sanctuary or mend the people's relationship with the Lord unless he first mends his own relationship with the Lord. Clergy need to identify with nonclergy, and they are just as vulnerable to sinful actions as anyone else, yet they need to remember and honor their role as mediators by mending their own relationship with the Lord before attempting to address the Lord's relationship with others.

LEVITICUS 17–27

Many researchers of the Pentateuch conclude that Lev 17–27 stand apart from other groups of laws (some do not include chap.

27 in this block). Source critics typically designate this the "Holiness Code" ("H") because of the repetition of formulas such as "You shall be holy, for I the LORD your God am holy" (19:2; cf. 20:7-8, 26) and "I am the LORD; I sanctify you" (20:8; cf. 21:15, 23). The language, style, and structure of individual units distinguish these chapters from the preceding sacrifice and purity laws (but see 11:44-45), but the two halves of the book are complementary. The second half assumes the sacrifice and purity laws of the first half, and the significance of those laws is minimized without the holiness laws of the second half.

The material within this block of eleven chapters falls into three pieces. The first consists of chapters 17–22, with a core in chapters 18–20. The theme of personal holiness permeates these chapters, but this holiness is grounded in the exodus event and manifested primarily in ethical behavior. The surrounding chapters throw a different light on offerings and the purity of priests, placing more attention on day-to-day matters that might affect their cultic status. These chapters show how the principles and concepts underlying cultic holiness also are the bedrock on which rules for daily living stand. The next piece in this block extends from chapter 23 to chapter 26. Here the dominant theme is sacred time. This is derived primarily from the theme of the Sabbath, which has its own ties to creation and the exodus. These three together provide the motivation and structure for lives lived in holiness. The final piece is chapter 27, which deals with gifts and voluntary offerings to the Lord. The latter points back to the beginning of the book, suggesting the interconnectedness of the whole; but it also exemplifies the devotion and integrity that the people need to show in fulfilling the commands of the Lord.

LEVITICUS 17

Chapter 17 serves as a hinge or bridge in the book. It has to do with the proper consumption or sacrificial use of animals, but like chapter 16, it broadens the reader's perspective on this, pointing from the sanctuary out into other areas of life in the Israelite community. The laws reflect the fundamental principle that behavior in areas outside the cult is founded on ideas derived from the cult. The language and style here share some aspects with the preceding chapters, but more with those following. This overlap also reflects the intent to link the cultic ideas of the first sixteen chapters with concerns about everyday moral and ethical behavior in the later chapters.

Literary Analysis

Narrative introductions in 17:1 and 18:1 demarcate this as a self-contained piece. The call to address the priests and the people (v. 2) introduces five units (vv. 3-7, 8-9, 10-12, 13-14, 15-16). A unique secondary call in verse 8a joins the first two units, which deal specifically with sacrifices. The first four units begin with the same formula, "(If) anyone of the house/people of Israel" (vv. 3, 8, 10, 13). The second, third, and fourth units complement this with the phrase, "or of the aliens who reside among them." The threatened punishment for violators in all four units is that they will be "cut off" (vv. 4, 9, 10, 14). The fifth unit varies from this pattern, identifying referents as "all persons, citizens or aliens," and requiring ritual washing of offenders, lest they "bear their guilt."

Other characteristics further subdivide certain units. The notice that offenders will be "cut off" concludes the second and fourth units (vv. 9 and 14). In the first and third units, the same threat stands at the end of a primary law, but explanatory clauses follow. The explanatory portion in the first unit is introduced by "in order that" (v. 5), and it concludes with the statement that this is to be "a statute forever" (cf. 7:34, 36; 16:29, 31, 34). The third unit consists of a warning explained by two causal clauses (introduced by "for"; v. 11), and then a reiteration of the warning in the form of a prohibition (v. 12). This highlights the rationale (v. 11) for the unit's prohibition (vv. 10, 12). The fourth unit also carries a double causal clause, linking it to the rationale in the preceding unit. The final unit contains the only example in this chapter of the typical transition, "but if." Thus, it falls into two parts, giving a primary command (v. 15) and its corollary (v. 16).

The resulting picture is a logical progression of laws on the consumption of meat. The first unit requires the people to bring all sacrifices of well-being to the tent of meeting (vv. 3-7). The second unit expands on the first to include all offerings (vv. 8-9). The third unit provides the underlying principle for the prohibition against consuming blood (vv. 10-12). This derives from sacrifice, but it applies to sacrificial and nonsacrificial consumption alike. This opens the way to the fourth unit, concerning the disposal of blood before consuming an animal killed in a hunt (vv. 13-14). The final unit applies the same principle to animals that have died naturally (vv. 15-16). Thus, verses 10-12 function as a pivot in the flow of the chapter. Two units regarding animals slaughtered in sacrifice precede those verses, and two units regarding animals that die in noncultic contexts follow them.

Exegetical Analysis

Restricting Sacrifices to the Tent of Meeting (17:3-7, 8-9)

The primary law of the first unit appears to restrict the killing of species used in sacrifice to sacrifice alone (vv. 3-4). This would eliminate the slaughter of these animals for food in a noncultic setting. Based solely on these verses, some scholars conclude that noncultic slaughter was once considered tantamount to murder ("bloodshed"), and that killing an animal was acceptable only if its blood was offered properly to the Lord (Brichto 1976, 45-50; Milgrom 1991, 707-13). They link this to Gen 9:4-5 to argue that, after the flood, the Lord modified the originally vegetarian diet for humans, but that the modification allowed only for the consumption of animals devoted to sacrificial use. That would make this law a step between strict vegetarianism and the omnivorous diet permitted in Deut 12.

The stated reason for the primary law casts this in a different light. It expresses concern that the people might offer sacrifices to other deities. The text mentions only "sacrifices of well-being," which the worshipers, the priests, and the Lord consume. Such meals demonstrate fellowship among the participants. The concern of the law is that the people would be associating themselves with other deities by consuming their offerings (cf. Rom 14). This law demands instead that they make sure that they share such an offering only with the Lord.

The interpretation that this law forbids foreign sacrifices still leaves unexplained the designation of ritual slaughter as "bloodshed." One would have to conclude that sacrificing an animal to another deity is considered murder. In other words, "bloodshed" is defined generally as taking life for inappropriate reasons, and in this case what is inappropriate is that the flesh of the slain animal is shared with another god. This interpretation makes this law consistent with the law on "profane slaughter" in Deut 12. To be fair, there is no other reference to the slaughter of animals in foreign worship as "bloodshed," but neither are there references to profane slaughter as "bloodshed." In any interpretation, what is clear is that this text restricts the offering of sacrifices of well-being to the tent of meeting.

The next law extends this restriction to all offerings. The closing phrase of verse 8 ("burnt offering or sacrifice") is a merism, a formula that mentions the extremes of a group and thereby implies the whole group. The laws on consumption of offerings begin with burnt offerings and conclude with sacrifices of well-being, so this expression implies those two and all in between them. This unit also extends this prohibition to include "aliens" living among the Israelites (v. 8). Concerns about influences to worship foreign deities lie behind this as well.

The Basic Principle Regarding Blood (17:10-12)

This unit states in simple but profound terms the basic principle underlying these prescriptions regarding blood. The first and third parts (vv. 10 and 12) state the prohibition: no one shall consume the blood of an animal (cf. 3:17; 7:26-27). The use of "eat" (rather than "drink") shows that the writer is talking about the blood in meat as well as blood by itself. This law also applies to native Israelites and aliens alike (cf. Acts 15:20, 29). The modification of the clause regarding "cutting off" the offender reflects the seriousness of this offense. The Lord will ensure that the guilty person is "cut off from his people" (see v. 10b).

The rationale in verse 11 has attracted much scholarly attention. The text begins by stating the main principle: the "life" (*nepeš*) of a creature is in its blood. This is not something inherent in blood, but it is because the Lord has "given" to blood the function of atonement in sacrifices. The particular wording here reveals the dual aspects to atonement. It is clear from earlier references that the Israelites associate atonement with purification (16:30). Here, the writer uses the expression "make atonement for your lives" (*nĕp̱āšôt*), an expression used only twice elsewhere, and both times in reference to the payment of a ransom (Exod 30:11-16; Num 31:48-54). The blood of offerings not only purifies the guilty person, the "life" of the animal that is in the blood serves as a ransom for the "lives" of the worshipers.

The final clause brings the two preceding thoughts together, but the precise meaning of the clause is uncertain. The crucial point is the force of the preposition *beth* with "life" ("For, *as* life, it is the blood that makes atonement," emphasis added). There are three proposals regarding how this phrase explains the atoning function of the blood in sacrifice. Either the blood makes atonement "as life" (as the NRSV suggests), or the blood makes atonement "by the price of the life (of the animal)," or the blood makes atonement "by means of the life (of the animal)." The first seems unlikely; it equates life and blood in general, but blood can also have a contaminating effect. The second option assumes that the middle clause of the verse limits atonement to ransom, excluding any notion of purification. This leaves the third option, which says that the presence of "life" in blood is why the Lord assigns an atoning function to sacrificial blood. This understanding allows for the dual function of blood in sacrifice, involving both ransom and purification.

Some interpret the link between blood in sacrifice and the prohibition against the consumption of blood in a narrow sense, saying that the writer is returning his attention in verse 11 to sacrifices of well-being alone. The problem is that verse 11 mentions atonement, but atonement is not associated with sacrifices of well-being, except in Ezek 45:15, 17. On this basis, some argue that this passage is later than most in Leviticus on sacrifice and perhaps applicable only as a later reflection on the meaning of blood in sacrifice. It is more common to read the rationale in verse 11 in a broader sense. First, while the only sacrificial meat eaten by the general population is that of the sacrifice of well-being, one cannot forget that the priests eat the flesh of other offerings. Further, other passages assume that people can eat nonsacrificial meat, but the prohibition of blood still applies. It seems then that there is a general principle against consuming the blood in the flesh, and this principle derives from the sacrificial function of blood. The Lord has assigned to blood the sole function of atonement in sacrificial offerings; therefore, it cannot be consumed (and give "life") in any other way.

Consumption of Nonsacrificial Animals (17:13-16)

The two remaining laws extend this principle to meat eaten in noncultic contexts. The first concerns the blood of an animal killed while hunting. The hunter must bury the blood, apparently to honor the life that was in the blood. The primary concern is that no one eats the blood (v. 14). To consume it is to ignore the connection between life and blood. The warning about being "cut off" stands at the end of another double "for"-clause, as in verses 10-12. This links the sacrificial application of the principle in verse 11 to the nonsacrificial realm here.

The final law derives from the basic principle already proposed. The law considers the possibility that someone might eat the meat of an animal that dies naturally. There is no mention of draining the blood before preparing the food, probably because the blood has dried; nevertheless, eating this meat yields only temporary defilement, not divine retribution and exclusion from the community. Why does this not dishonor the "life" of the animal? The most plausible explanation is that the nonfluidity of the blood means the "life" has completely left the animal, so one cannot expect the eater to dispose of it in a way that honors the "life." Instead, the blood now is in a state that merely causes ritual defilement, and so the person must undergo the usual cleansings prompted by contact with a carcass (11:25, 28, 40).

Theological and Ethical Analysis

The primary principle in this chapter is the sacredness of life. Blood carries life, and because life is sacred, humans must treat blood with the utmost respect. Using blood appropriately honors the life within the creature and, beyond that, it honors the giver of life: the Lord. Eating the meat of an animal requires one to distinguish between the creature as common and the life within it as sacred. Among other things, this reinforces the notion that persons are not to see the creature as the source of life and so honor it, but instead they are to see the divine source of the life implanted in the creature. One must discern between what is "alive" and what is "life." (In recognizing this distinction, one might see some justification in translating the Hebrew term for "life" [*nepheš*] with the Greek term for "soul" [*psuchē*].) Something that is "alive" has "life" in it, and people are to honor that "life"; but the same creature, devoid of "life," is no longer "alive," and people can use it for common purposes. On the other hand, the sacredness of blood is not inherent to blood, but derives from the "life" that is in it. Blood defiles once it is devoid of "life," becoming like other substances that the body expels.

The heart of this chapter establishes strict limits on the use of blood, based on the ideas that there is life in the blood and that the Lord is the source of life. The Lord restricts the use of blood by humans to sacrifice, ordaining that the life in the blood of certain creatures can atone for the impure lives of sinful humans. The blood rituals that effect atonement entail purification from sin and the substitution of one creature's life for the lives of others. The accompanying laws represent practical implications of such a narrow restriction. Any other use of "life" (carried in blood) brings divine wrath. Humans give credit for life to no other being but the Lord by being careful to use blood only in ways that the Lord ordains.

The application of these principles to noncultic settings in this chapter has implications on two levels. First, it points more broadly to the fact that theological ideas are not limited to the cultic arena in their significance. One central purpose of the cult is to provide a theological lens through which people interpret the physical things and events around them. In this case, one can see how the sacredness accorded to blood in a cultic context is also to be assumed outside that context. On the other hand, this lens does not eliminate the line between the cultic sphere and the noncultic sphere. People manipulate blood for sacrifice in cult; they dispose of it in a respectful manner outside of cult. In both contexts, they honor the life in the blood and honor the Lord in turn. The way in which they show this varies depending on the context.

These principles also touch on ideas that are involved in modern moral debates about life-and-death matters. This text upholds the importance of life and that life is to be honored. Unfortunately, recognition of this principle does not absolutely determine the answers to many of the questions posed by modern readers. For example, some apply the honoring of life to human diet and call for strict vegetarianism, yet it is clear that this passage does not completely prohibit the eating of meat. Many link the call to honor life to the issue of capital punishment, yet the related passage in Gen 9 demands capital punishment in cases of murder. Others apply the principle of honoring life to debates over abortion, but this passage does not answer the question of when the life of a fetus is distinguishable from its mother's life. One has to go to other texts for that. So, while these laws show that believers are to apply the principle of honoring life beyond the context of the cult, they do not make clear what that application should be, except in regard to the consumption of blood.

LEVITICUS 18

The main part of this chapter is a catalog of incestuous liaisons. Chapter 20 supplements this with punishments for such relationships. Both chapters point to Israel's neighbors as the instigators of these behaviors, so these regulations appear at first blush to function as ethnic boundary markers. This is a common phenomenon, but it is not certain in the case of Israel whether the laws are concerned more with ethnic purity or with religious purity.

Literary Analysis

A typical combination of narrative heading and discourse heading opens the chapter (vv. 1-2a), which then consists of three units. The verbs are plural throughout the first unit (vv. 2b-5), which breaks naturally into two subunits. The first subunit (vv. 2b-4) begins and ends with the divine self-declaration "I am the Lord your God" (also v. 30b). Within this subunit, each clause ends with a verb. The second subunit (v. 5) concludes with a shortened self-declaration, "I am the Lord." Exhortations about keeping the Lord's "statutes and ordinances" balance the two parts.

The second unit opens in verse 6 with the introductory formula "None of you" (cf. 17:3, 8, 10, 13; 20:2, 9). The verb in verse 6 is plural, and the verse concludes with the shorter self-declaration formula. This creates a link between the "statutes and ordinances" in verse 5 and the regulations introduced in verse 6. Verse 6 introduces the topic of incest, which continues through verse 18. The subsequent verses (19-23) concern other sexual taboos. The verbs in verses 7-23 are consistently singular. This gives the clear impression that verse 6 stands as the introduction to verses 7-23, constituting a two-part catalog of prohibitions against illicit sexual unions.

There is a general consistency in this catalog through verse 18. Each entry begins "You shall not uncover the nakedness of" some close female relative. Verse 19 reverts to the language of verse 6 at the beginning, but then it expands the scope for consideration to include all women. Verses 20 and 23 warn against "sexual relations." Relations with a kinsman's wife are "defilement" (vv. 24-30); with an animal, "perversion." It is not immediately clear that verse 21 concerns sexual relations. This item alone concludes with a divine self-declaration. Perhaps it has been inserted in anticipation of chapter 20 (20:2-5). Verse 22 stands alone in identifying an act as an "abomination" (vv. 26-27). For reasons such as these, some contend that verses 19-23 were not originally united with the primary catalog of verses 7-18.

The third and final unit (vv. 24-30) is framed by the prohibition "Do not defile yourselves." The verb "defile" dominates this brief unit. It shares several features with the first (vv. 2b-5), creating a frame around the longer middle unit. The verbs throughout these units are plural. In both units the Lord warns the Israelites to avoid the practices of other nations, and in both he calls for them to follow "my statutes and my ordinances" (vv. 4-5, 26). The concluding self-declaration formula creates an inclusio with verse 2b. There is a greatly expanded use of the first person by the Lord in these units. This is not unprecedented in Leviticus (7:34; 11:44-45), but the prevalence of it is. This style continues through chapter 26. Many consider it a distinguishing stylistic feature of H.

Exegetical Analysis

A Call to Be Different (18:2-5)

The instructions on personal morality begin by emphasizing the need to be distinctive. The juxtaposing references to Egypt and Canaan point to past and present influences, respectively (v. 3). Interpreters confirm this impression by citing evidence of Egyptian and Canaanite practices that ran counter to the standards espoused in this chapter. Egyptian pharaohs, for example, could marry their closest relatives. Hittite laws do not prohibit all types of bestiality. There is evidence that child sacrifice (v. 21) was a part of the religious practices among the Canaanites. Interpreters do not know, however, how prevalent these practices were. This might represent natural inclinations to attribute unsavory behavior to foreigners when reinforcing a call for moral behavior. There are linguistic connections between this chapter and the curse on Canaan (Gen 9:18-27). Perhaps that story promoted a conceptual link in the Israelite mind between Canaanites (and Egyptians; Gen 10:6) and illicit sexual behavior.

The divine self-declaration formula contributes to this call for distinctiveness. This formula carries three main implications in Leviticus. The first is a link to the exodus, along with a call for holiness (e.g., 11:44-45; 19:2, 36; 22:2, 9, 16, 32-33; cf. Exod 20:2). These two overlap, because the Lord brought them from Egypt to "sanctify them." These references to holiness justify the label for this block ("Holiness Code"). A corollary implication is that the people will emulate the Lord's character in their own lives. They will be holy as he is holy.

This passage identifies Israel's distinctiveness in terms of the Lord's "statutes and ordinances." These exist in contrast to the statutes and ordinances of other peoples. The Lord's statutes and ordinances lead one to life ("by doing so one shall live"), implying that the contrasting statutes and ordinances of others lead to death. This connection between the Lord's "statutes and ordinances," personal morality, and the theme of "life" is not unique to Leviticus or the Holiness Code. One finds the same combination in Deuteronomic works (Deut 4:1, 5, 8, 14, 45; 5:1, 31; 6:1, 20; 26:16-17; 30:16), and some passages directly link the exodus event to personal ethics and morality (e.g., Deut 24:17-22). The Deuteronomists join these ideas to the Davidic Covenant (1 Kgs 2:3; 9:4-5; cf. 11:11), and they attribute the fall of the northern kingdom to the "customs" [= "statutes"] of other nations (2 Kgs 17:8; cf. Lev 20:3). So, there are similar categories for conceptualizing these ideas in these different groups, but there are differences as well. In contrast to the Holiness Code, there are few examples in Deuteronomic texts of the self-declaration formula (Deut 29:6; Judg 6:10) or calls for holiness (Deut 14:2, 21). Instead, the focus there shifts to the Shema and its exhortation to "love the LORD your God with all your heart." There is ample reason to trace these associations in D and H back to the Decalogue. A consensus about the direction and the timing/sequence of developments beyond that initial impetus remains elusive, though.

Inappropriate Sexual Relations (18:6-23)

The central catalog that delineates incestuous relationships proceeds from a male perspective (vv. 7-18). It identifies eleven women among a man's close relatives with whom he may not have sexual relations: mother, any other wife to his father (polygamy was permissible), sister, granddaughter, half-sister, aunts (3), daughter-in-law, brother's wife, the daughter or granddaughter of a current wife, and the sister of a current wife. The introductory statement in verse 6 classifies these females together under the category "anyone near of kin" ("flesh of his flesh"; cf. Gen 2:23).

There is a growing consensus that the phrase "uncover the nakedness" is a euphemism for sexual relations (Milgrom 2000a,

1532). This might entail the mere exposure of a woman, neutralizing the suggestion that it is a lesser sin if the couple does not engage in intercourse. A more significant matter is the omission of a man's daughter from this catalog. Some argue that such a prohibition is not necessary; however, there are examples of such unions from among Israel's neighbors. Others contend that the prohibition against having a woman and her daughter at the same time covers the topic of any daughter (v. 17), but this does not address what might be allowed if one's wife has died. Others argue that "near of kin" in verse 6 implies daughters (21:1-3). The obvious objection is that the same should apply to one's mother, yet the text specifically mentions her. So, while there is no clear explanation for this omission, it is certain that relations with one's daughter were forbidden.

Two other matters present more serious difficulties. One is that there are examples of some of these prohibited unions existing in Israel. Abraham married his father's daughter (v. 11), Jacob married two sisters at the same time (v. 18), and Judah fathered children through his daughter-in-law (v. 15). Certainly the latter was unwitting on Judah's part, but he did declare Tamar to be more "righteous" than himself, even though she was acting in violation of this statute. This affair highlights another apparent inconsistency, since the rules of levirate marriage seem to contradict the prohibition against relations with one's sister-in-law (v. 18; see Deut 25:5-10). The only "justification" for some of these unions is that they existed prior to the giving of these laws, yet one would expect to hear divine disapproval for inherently inappropriate relations. Most of the later examples occur within the royal family, suggesting some leeway there in the application of these regulations (2 Sam 13:11-13; 16:22; 1 Kgs 2:13-18). Unfortunately, the texts do not mention any divine evaluations of the liaisons. There are prophetic texts that speak metaphorically of the Lord marrying two sisters (Jer 3:6-10; Ezek 23:1-49), which at some level undercuts the prohibition against such arrangements here.

The other difficult matter is the specification of a practical rationale for these prohibitions. The most plausible explanations are social. Unions such as these foment rivalry and strife among the members of one's extended family. Verse 18 explicitly refers to this possibility, and Jacob's marriage to Leah and Rachel exemplifies the kind of long-term strife these unions could engender. But this does not explain all these prohibitions. The introductory lines in verse 6 and the motive clauses in many of the prohibitions indicate that these illicit unions would constitute an affront against the honor of another member of one's extended family. For example, to sleep with the wife of one's uncle is an affront against that uncle (v. 14). A man's wife is a part of him. This is a manifestation of the principle initiated in the Garden Narrative, where Adam says the woman is "flesh of my flesh" (Gen 2:23). The wording here is slightly different, but the idea is the same. To assume intimate relations with another man's wife is to stain his honor. The same principle holds in regard to a man's other close relatives (21:1-3). There is a sense of corporate oneness that binds these individuals together in the minds of the people. To intrude upon the private things of a member of that conceptual unity is to defile the dignity of all the persons in it.

Verses 19-23 present their own set of questions. It is curious that the first regulation essentially repeats the purity law in 15:19-24. The second constitutes adultery, which is treated in other laws; or, if the law is speaking about a union with a kinsman's wife after the kinsman has died, then it is saying that one must honor his kinsman's sphere of relations even after his death. It is also surprising to find a prohibition against the worship of Molech in this group (v. 21), because there is no known connection between that religion and sexual behavior. It could be because this religion involves child sacrifice, which the writer regards as a dishonoring of the family unit akin to illicit sex. The most likely explanation derives from chapter 20, which speaks of the worship of Molech as if it were the epitome of foreign religions. Some speculate that Molech worship was so common that many considered it native to Israel (1 Kgs 11:7), but Baal worship could also have this status. Perhaps its inclusion emphasizes that this truly is a foreign thing, just as many of these sexual relations represent foreign practices. The same might be true of the prohibitions against homosexuality and bestiality; however, there are other considerations at work in those cases.

Warning against Sexual Defilement (18:24-30)

This unit repeats some of the ideas dealt with in the opening unit (vv. 2-5). One significant addition is the repetition of "defile," which creates a link between these "statutes and ordinances" and chapters 11–16. The Israelites are to remember that the Lord is calling them to uphold special standards in order to maintain their relationship with him. The use of "abominations" (vv. 26, 27, 30) identifies these as foreign practices, but such contrasts are not merely for the sake of ethnic distinctiveness. These verses call for native Israelites and aliens alike to abide by these guidelines. This call for personal morality within a particular geographical region indicates that the land ultimately belongs to the Lord. The people show honor to the Lord by upholding these standards.

The language of the land "vomiting out" those who break these statutes furthers the idea that the land is the Lord's. Higher standards exist for the inhabitants of this land than for those inhabiting other lands. The Lord lives within this land, and the people who live there must be holy to honor him. This warning foreshadows exile. If the Israelites commit the same sins as their predecessors, they can expect the same fate (Deut 9:4-7). In this sense, this text justifies the future exile on the basis of parallels between the sins of Israel and the sins of previous inhabitants of the land (2 Kgs 17:7-18).

Theological and Ethical Analysis

The dominant principles in chapter 18 are the need to be distinctive and the standards of sexual purity. The two work together in the sense that the people maintain their distinctiveness by adhering to strict regulations regarding sexual behavior. These regulations do not prohibit unions with those outside one's ethnic group; instead, they control unions according to particular moral standards. This applies to all the laws in this block. These laws define the people of the Lord by their adherence to moral standards, not by ethnic descent. This presents an unchanging challenge to the people of God in every generation about how they are to be distinctive. It sets that call within the framework of morality and religious ethics. The prophets contend that this framework is more crucial than cultic practices; in other words, they give priority to this portion of Leviticus over the first sixteen chapters of the book. It is more accurate to say that legislating cultic practices and personal morality and ethics in one book demonstrates that they are indelibly intertwined as complementary manifestations of a single religion.

The standards that this text promotes derive from ideas rooted in creation. God set up social relations and works to honor and protect them. These relationships are foundational to "life." To abide by these guidelines is to participate in the things of life. These regulations expand on the notion that a man and woman become "one" in marriage (Gen 2:23-24), identifying how far this "one-ness" extends. Those forbidden to a man are already one with that man, or with another man that is closely related. By honoring each group that is "one," the people promote life, in the broadest sense of that term.

Though the text does not explicitly state the circumstances of these illicit unions, it is likely that virtually all cases of incest would involve the abuse of a man's power—either physical or psychological/social—over a woman. The absence of any exception clause denies a man the possibility of contending that his actions could be condoned by virtue of the (extremely dubious) claim that the union was consensual; even if that were to be true, it would not alter the fact that it is a defiling act. The act itself might be confined to individuals within a single (extended) family unit, but its effects reach beyond those circumscribed social boundaries. The androcentric perspective evident in these prescriptions might lead some to assume that there is an implicit concern for how an illicit union would affect the man, who is almost certainly the perpetrator. That is to miss the essence of the implicit effect of such unions. The primary effect of an incestuous union is the permanent scarring it inflicts on the personhood of the woman, which in turn negatively impacts the entire community in a fundamental way.

Another aspect of these laws that is particularly troublesome for Western readers is the prohibition against homosexuality (v. 22). Many today see homosexuality in a different light than the other forbidden unions in this chapter. All agree that it is wrong for a man to have sexual relations with his mother, his daughter-in-law, his half-sister, and so on. These involve a choice by a man from among several possible female partners. Many today believe homosexuality reflects genetics, not a choice, and so some argue that this text does not concern those born to be homosexual, but only heterosexuals who deny their genetic sexuality and engage in homosexual relations with other heterosexuals, or those who impose homosexuality on children. Others contend that this prohibition concerns only homosexual acts that were part of foreign worship rituals, because the framework of the chapter warns of foreign influences. Still others argue that this prohibition derives from an ancient assumption that sexual relations are solely for procreation, but that such an assumption does not hold in the modern world. A major hurdle for these explanations is that the other cases in this chapter do not involve such nuanced interpretations. Instead, the controlling assumption regarding sexual relations seems to be that they reflect and support social alignments. The text forbids violations of a core social unit, a unit radiating out from one man. It is likely that they would proscribe homosexuality for related reasons.

The guidelines this chapter considers are not the only matters that threaten the socioreligious integrity of the group. These come first because they make the point of distinctiveness. Just as the people maintain the distinctiveness of their family units through sexual relations, so they maintain their distinctive relationship with the Lord in other aspects of their lives. Some of these are taken up in the next chapter. Those matters (justice, charity, respect for the infirm and foreigners, and so forth) are just as crucial as sexual relations in promoting true life in their community.

LEVITICUS 19

The biblical call for holiness resounds in Lev 19. The presentation of holiness is like a computer-generated montage of tiny photographs that come together to create another picture. Each seemingly random piece contributes to the overall picture of holiness. This chapter is important for three specific reasons. One is that it pushes holiness beyond the realm of sanctuary and cult to the everyday world of common people. Second, it draws no distinction between "ritual purity" and "ethical purity." Both are equally indicative of a person's devotion to God. Third, an extension of these is the citation of verse 18 by Jesus (Matt 22:34-40). His linking of this verse with the Shema succinctly captures the underlying spirit of this whole passage.

Literary Analysis

The introductory section is unique in identifying the addressees as "all the congregation" (v. 2a). The adjoining call to be holy like the Lord sets the tone for the chapter (v. 2b). This includes an expansion of the self-declaration formula ("You shall be holy, for I the Lord your God am holy"). A few stylistic features demarcate the balance of the chapter into eighteen units plus a concluding exhortation (v. 37). Fourteen units and the closing exhortation conclude with the self-declaration formula. The four remaining units distinguish themselves by other means (vv. 5-8, 19, 20-22, 29). The verbs in verses 5-8 and 20-22 are third-person impersonal verbs, which do not work syntactically with the self-declaration formula. Verse 19b contains singular verbs in between a general exhortation that uses plural forms (v. 19a) and a longer unit that uses third-person impersonal forms (vv. 20-22). Verse 29 also distinguishes itself by using singular verbs.

Most of these units appear to be arranged haphazardly, with the noticeable exception of the four units in verses 11-18. The verbs in these units vacillate between singular and plural, but all four conclude with the shorter formula, "I am the LORD." All four deal with community ethics, and there is a general progression in the mention of one's fellow citizens, moving from "companion" (vv. 11-12; "to one another," NRSV) to "neighbor" (vv. 13-14) to "neighbor" and "people" (vv. 15-16; NRSV translates two different Hebrew words as "neighbor" here) to "anyone of your kin" and the three acquaintances of the preceding units (vv. 17-18).

It is helpful to consider these observations in conjunction with the opening clause of verse 19 (cf. v. 37; 18:4-5, 26; 20:22; 25:18). This brief exhortation splits the contents of the chapter into two parts, consisting of eight units and ten units. One cannot be certain whether the "statutes"-clause of verse 19a functions as the conclusion of what precedes it or as the heading to what follows. In either case, verse 19a is a structural divider for the chapter, creating parallel halves of a common whole. The resulting bifurcated sequence of units is as follows:

v. 3	parents, Sabbaths	v. 19b	mixing of crops
v. 4	idols	vv. 20-22	defiling a slave woman
vv. 5-8	fellowship offerings	vv. 23-25	new fruit trees
vv. 9-10	gleanings	vv. 26-28	foreign piety
vv. 11-12	theft, deception	v. 29	prostituting daughter
vv. 13-14	fraud, handicaps	v. 30	sabbaths, sanctuary
vv. 15-16	injustice, slander	v. 31	mediums and wizards
vv. 17-18	grudges	v. 32	honoring the elderly
		vv. 33-34	treatment of foreigners
		vv. 35-36	dishonest business

Several items in the first half of the chapter have close thematic parallels in the second half. The clearest are the two clauses on the sabbaths (vv. 3, 30). There have been attempts to identify other parallels. For example, some see a connection between gleanings (vv. 9-10) and harvesting from fruit trees (vv. 23-25). Others see an intentional connection between deceptive acts (vv. 11-12) and dishonest practices (vv. 35-36). Any claims about intentionality are subjective. For example, some see a connection between the admonitions regarding parents and the elderly (vv. 3, 32), but the repetition of the clause "you shall fear your God" (vv. 14, 32) suggests that the compilers saw a closer connection between the elderly and the physically infirm. The similarity between "you shall love your neighbor as yourself" (v. 18) and "you shall love the alien as yourself" (v. 34) provokes further reflection on attitudes toward aliens (v. 10). Taken together, these observations suggest that the compilers noticed the motivations in the first half of the chapter, and on that basis they incorporated the teachings of the second half.

This supports the view that the exhortations in verses 19a and 37 frame the second half of the chapter. This makes the four units in verses 11-18 the concluding segment of an existing collection of statutes, a collection that the compilers now supplement with verses 19-36. They cement the two groups together by continuing to use the self-declaration formulas. It is likely that the same compilers are responsible for chapter 26 (cf. 19:3, 30; 26:2).

Still, it seems futile to search for an organizing principle for the chapter. What sets this collection apart is the admonition to "be holy, for I the LORD your God am holy" (v. 2) and the repetition of the self-declaration formula. Most of the chapter consists of previously independent laws that have been brought together under this call to imitate the Lord's holiness. The haphazard arrangement might reflect the fact that, in life, choices about holiness do not present themselves in any logical order or according to rigid categories.

Exegetical Analysis

A Call to Holiness (19:2-37)

The compilers take the theme of distinctiveness and define it in diverse ways in this chapter. Chapters 18 and 20 show the depth of detail possible in applying the principle of distinctiveness, while this chapter reveals the breadth of that principle. The Lord calls on the Israelites to emulate divine holiness. Some take this too far in one direction and read verse 2 as a demand that the people become as holy as the Lord, and then they discuss how such a call is inherently impossible. No one can be as holy as the Lord. That does not reflect the tone of this admonition. The tone derives from the self-declaration formula, which is embedded in the call for holiness. This formula evokes thoughts of the Decalogue (Exod 20:2). There the formula continues into a reference about the Lord's works in the exodus. Every repetition of this formula reminds the Israelites that these demands come from a God who has done mighty deeds on their behalf in faithfulness to an ancient covenant. A key implication is that a call to be holy does not merely involve physical separation from unholy objects and people, but it involves the avoidance of the activities of "death" and a participation in the activities of "life" (Milgrom 2000a, 1604; cf. Rom 12:21).

The connection between the Decalogue and the self-declaration formula makes the inclusion of parts of the Decalogue seem quite natural (vv. 3-4, 11-12). The goal in including these with other laws is to show the breadth of holiness. The people are not to restrict holiness to the sanctuary and the cult, nor are they to restrict their application of "holiness" laws to the Decalogue. Honoring one's parents and properly consuming a sacrifice of well-being serve equally as manifestations of holiness (vv. 3, 5-8). Honoring the Lord's name and doing business honestly reflect the common desire to exhibit divine-like holiness (vv. 12, 35-36). Each command constitutes either a holy response to the actions of the Lord or reflects the holy character of the Lord, or both.

Some of the connections between holiness and the topics included here are more obvious than others. The most natural are those that forbid idolatry or recourse to foreign worship practices, or those that promote typical biblical worship. Dietary laws and laws about sexual purity also are not surprising. On the other hand, it might be difficult to recognize what leaving grain for aliens has to do with holiness. The most likely places to search for underlying assumptions are in the stories of creation and the exodus. For example, a rationale for the prohibition against eating a tree's fruit for the first three years is not immediately obvious. The text goes on to explain, however, that the fourth year's fruit is "set apart for rejoicing in the LORD" (v. 24). The underlying principle is that the fruit manifests the Lord's life-giving power. Eating the fruit is a participation in divine (holy) activity, the giving and sustaining of life. Leaving part of the harvest for the poor and the alien exemplifies this principle. Persons with access to the things of life pass them on to those who do not enjoy such access, in imitation of what the Lord does in creation. Reverence for parents also grows out of recognition of the created order of things (v. 3). Parents are every person's link back to the first parents, the original recipients of life from the Lord. Showing respect to every person, regardless of physical perfection or age, is to "fear your God" (vv. 14, 32). It acknowledges the high status placed on humans in creation (Gen 1:26-27); it honors what is divine or holy about the life God has created.

The final two units base business ethics and the treatment of aliens on the exodus (vv. 33-36). The Israelites are to show kindness to aliens as the Lord showed kindness to them when they were aliens in Egypt. The connection between the exodus and honesty in business is less obvious. A likely explanation comes from the Jubilee laws, which forbid ruling over an Israelite "with harshness" (25:43, 46, 53). Exodus 1:13-14 uses the same language to describe Egyptian treatment of the Israelites. The Israelites will be distinctive by being different from their Egyptian overlords.

The central section brings together these ideas of holiness derived from creation and the exodus (vv. 11-18). It starts with allusions to the Decalogue, the first laws that the Lord revealed to Moses following the exodus. The people are to receive the current commands with the same attitude as that with which they received those earliest commands (cf. Deut 5:22-29). The commission of these sins is to "[profane] the name of your God" (v. 12), the name that the Lord "made known" in the exodus (Exod 6:6-8; 7:5, 17; 9:14-16). The command for impartiality (v. 15) rests primarily on the creation principle that every person is made in God's image (Gen 1:26-27). The directive not to "profit by the blood of your neighbor" probably refers to the shedding of innocent blood following an unfair accusation (v. 16), but it might also include an allusion to the first murder (Gen 4:8-13). The possibility of an allusion to the Cain story increases as one moves into verses 17-18. Cain hated his brother and "incurred guilt" when he killed Abel, just as one who hates his kin will "incur guilt" for hating him rather than reproving him (Gen 4:13; 1 John 3:11-12). These allusions look back to creation and the earliest sins to show that holiness is the remedy for sin; it replaces death with life, curse with blessing.

Finally, this collection of statutes and ordinances is more exemplary than exhaustive. It does not include all the commandments of the Decalogue, though each is a manifestation of holiness. The collection does not mention all offerings that priests might consume, but it implies that holiness involves the proper presentation of every sacrifice. It does not mention every form of idolatry and foreign worship, but it is clear that the Israelites are not to tolerate any of them. It does not detail every injustice or unethical act, but it is clear that holiness involves only what is just and righteous.

Theological and Ethical Analysis

Addressing these laws to "all the congregation" reminds the readers that they are a religious community (v. 2). The redactors seek to bring this idea into sharpest focus. Members of this community are to be "holy" like God. A basic definition of holiness involves ideas of separation and distinctive behavior, but these commonly evoke images of a cloistered life and the avoidance of activities of a common person's life. Holiness in these teachings has to do with ritual and piety, to be sure, but it is just as concerned with a person's loving attitude toward family and neighbors. Holiness involves someone's behavior toward the poor and the handicapped, and even toward foreigners with whom they are unfamiliar. Holiness involves how people in business treat their employees and their customers.

This view of holiness assumes that there is a creator God who has delivered individuals from the control of death and slavery and brought them into the realm of life and righteousness. This attitude assumes that the readers will respond to God's "holiness" by imitating the righteousness manifested to them. This is the attitude of Paul in Romans concerning righteousness. This is the attitude promoted by Jesus in the Sermon on the Mount, when he speaks of righteousness that exceeds current notions of righteousness and identifies Lev 19:18 as the second most important command. Thus, their message is ultimately a call to embrace the original spirit of the Old Testament laws.

Chapters 18–20 form a cohesive block, so readers should naturally consider them together. Chapters 18 and 20 portray sexual offenses as unsavory foreign behavior. The sinful behavior of this chapter is not so "shocking," so that it might have caught the people off guard to hear laws about matters such as business ethics in this context. Holiness is not just about such things as sexual boundaries, it is about justice and kindness and honesty. It is just as despicable to defraud a friend as it is to sleep with one's daughter-in-law. It is just as important to ease the plight of the poor as it is to honor the sexual privileges of one's father or brother.

This point of view understands holiness as a matter of the heart, not simply a matter of external actions. This comes through most clearly in verse 17, which forbids hatred of kin "in your heart." Similarly, to "revile the deaf or put a stumbling block before the blind" reflects a calloused heart toward the physically infirm (v. 14). Concerns about leaving portions of a harvest for the poor betray the fact that those who have material goods often feel less than charitable in their hearts toward those who do not. The parallel commands to "love the alien as yourself" and "love your neighbor as yourself" might be surprising because they come in the broader context of warnings about the dangers of foreign influences. These laws actually counterbalance the general stereotyping that attributes unsavory behavior to foreigners.

These ideas about holiness provide an interesting test case for contemporary American Christians. Two of the primary passages concerning homosexuality stand in chapters 18 and 20, framing this chapter on holiness. Many speak out against homosexuality as an unholy state on the basis of those passages. Leviticus 19 challenges the same Christians to be just as vocal about treating aliens like citizens (19:34). The general context suggests that the violation of one of these commands defiles the believer as much as violation of any other command defiles. All derive from the same foundation, "I am the LORD your God."

LEVITICUS 20

Leviticus 20 demonstrates the belief that immorality is a community-wide threat in a religious context. These commands call for the removal of offenders from the community by the community. Failure to do so threatens the "life" that such a community is trying to promote. But such a stance also raises important questions for a community of believers about competing loyalties and priorities.

Literary Analysis

The literary structure of this chapter parallels that of chapter 18. Following a dual heading (vv. 1-2a), there are three main units. The opening unit (vv. 2b-8) finds its correspondence in the third (vv. 22-27). These two address the threat of foreign influences that can corrupt the people of Israel. The opening clause of the first unit parallels the opening clauses to each unit in chapter 17. Verses 4 and 6 introduce secondary cases. Each case carries the dual threat that the Lord will "set his face against" the offenders and "cut them off from among their people." Verses 7-8 constitute a lengthy conclusion to this unit. They contain dual exhortations for holiness (11:44-45; 19:2; 21:8, 23) and dual examples of the self-declaration formula. Verse 8 reinforces these with a call to "keep my statutes" (18:4-5, 26). Verses 22-27 form a loose inclusio with the opening unit. There is a loose chiastic structure to the whole chapter, as this unit begins with a call to "keep all my statutes" (v. 22, cf. v. 8) and concludes with a command to stone "medium[s] and wizard[s]" (v. 27, cf. vv. 2, 6). The self-declaration formula appears only in these units.

The final unit contains a hodgepodge of ideas, though. It mentions the possibility of the land "vomiting out" the people (cf. 18:24-30), but it also contains the only instance in Leviticus of the phrase "a land flowing with milk and honey" (v. 24). Verse 25 evokes thoughts of the ending of chapter 11. Finally, while verse 27 contains elements that can form an inclusio with verses 2 and 6, it also seems like an afterthought. Two formulas in it are characteristic of the central unit in the chapter, which suggests that it previously stood with those prohibitions.

The main unit extends from verses 9-21. A primary introductory formula ushers in the opening case, a statute against cursing one's parents. There follows a series of twelve cases (see below on vv. 18-19), each introduced as a subordinate case. There are several recurring formulas in these cases, usually coming in pairs. The clause "he/they shall be put to death" is in seven of the first eight cases (vv. 9-16). A corresponding clause in five cases states "his/their blood is upon him/them" (cf. v. 27). One case in the midst of these calls for the burning of the offenders (v. 14). The remaining cases share the formula "they shall be subject to punishment" (vv. 17-21). Preceding the first two instances of that formula is the warning "they shall be cut off"; completing the latter two instances is the warning "they shall be childless."

Exegetical Analysis

Rejection of Foreign Worship Practices (20:2-8)

This law cites two examples of foreign worship practices. The first involves child sacrifice to "Molech." There is some debate as to whether this is the personal name of a foreign deity (also Milcom) or the designation of a type of foreign sacrifice. The name is unattested outside the Bible. The mention of "mediums and wizards" probably reflects ancestor worship (v. 6), a common feature in many ancient Near Eastern societies. It is possible that Molech-worship is also to be linked to ancestor worship. The severity of the punishment betrays the gravity of these offenses. The execution of the punishment is to be a cooperative effort, because such practices offend the honor of the people and of the Lord. These activities dishonor the home and name of the Lord, which the Israelites ought to regard as a dishonoring of their own homes and names. This should broaden their view of the Lord's presence beyond the confines of the sanctuary. The entire land is the Lord's home. "Ritual purity" is important not only in the sanctuary but it also extends to other areas of life. Consulting with mediums and wizards was something the people probably did "in the privacy of their own homes," which they might have felt was separate from the sanctuary. These regulations show that such distinctions are untenable.

The concluding verses make it impossible to miss this point (vv. 7-8). They carry forward and round off the appeal to "be holy" that dominates chapter 19. Verse 8 extends this one step further by declaring that the Lord makes the people holy. The Lord has sanctified them by delivering them from slavery, so that they could live holy lives in their own land (Ps 105:43-45). These verses anticipate verses 22-26. This implies that holiness is the ultimate state in which a human can live, the deepest desire within the heart of every human.

It is common to question why concerns about foreign worship introduce a series of statutes regarding sexual misconduct. One obvious link is the characterization of those that engage in these practices as "prostituting themselves." The parallels between a relationship with the Lord and marriage are obvious. Examples exist in Deuteronomic texts (Deut 26:16-19), but they are more pronounced in prophetic writings. There is also a more direct and personal consideration at work. Participation in foreign religious rituals compromises the solidarity of an extended family group, just as illicit sexual behavior does. The specific practices condemned here probably promoted the interests of one family over the broader community. These chapters promote the idea that loyalty to the Lord supersedes the divisive interests of individual families.

Punishment for Illicit Sexual Activity (20:9-21)

These ordinances cover the same topics as the central part of chapter 18, with a few minor variations. The most noticeable are the first two (vv. 9-10). One is the negative counterpart to the first ordinance in chapter 19. Many interpreters contend that all the cases of sexual misconduct that follow in this list derive from this law. This law exhorts the people to maintain the honor of their families, and the subsequent regulations give some of the specifics about what this involves. The second ordinance descends most directly from the Decalogue. Other passages consider permutations on this offense (e.g., Deut 22:13-29). This illustrates that these regulations are not exhaustive; other situations would warrant similar responses. As one other variation, this list forbids a man from marrying his wife's mother (v. 14), while only the catalog in chapter 18 forbids a man from marrying his wife's sister.

There is a general progression in the punishments that the respective offenses evoke, showing that these constitute different degrees of wrongdoing. The statutes in verses 9-16 call for the execution of the guilty parties. These offenders threaten genuine "life" in the community, and so "their blood is upon them" (v. 13); those who kill them will not be guilty of "shedding innocent blood." The next cases call for the expulsion of the perpetrators (vv. 17-19). The remainder result in childlessness (vv. 20-21), but it is not necessary that these individuals leave the community. The final case is strange, because it establishes childlessness as the consequence that follows when a man sleeps with his brother's wife, even though the levirate law requires a man to father children through his brother's wife, if his brother dies childless (Deut 25:5-10).

A Call to Be Separate (20:22-27)

This concluding unit presents all that comes before as directly opposite to what the Israelites see around them. They are to keep the Lord's "statutes" (*ḥuqqōt*) rather than following the "practices" (*ḥuqqōt*) of those being driven from the land (vv. 22-23). The Lord's statutes lead to life, while the statutes of other nations result in death. This explains the shift to clean/unclean animals in verses 25-26. The purity laws assume the associations between "clean" and "life" and between "unclean" and "death." Adopting the "practices of the nation[s] I am driving out" (v. 23) will yield the same result as consuming what is unclean. Both are abominations, and both lead to death.

The antithesis of these abominations is holiness. The Lord expects holiness of all the people of Israel, not just the priests. These laws define holiness in terms of what people do on a daily basis, away from the sanctuary and the home of God. They present the belief that the Lord's home is not restricted to a sanctuary.

This is consistent with other texts that speak of the Lord's home in terms of the whole land of Israel.

Theological and Ethical Analysis

A major portion of this chapter speaks of sexual improprieties, yet the primary concern is with community integrity. There is far less about sex with persons outside one's family than there is about incestuous relationships, yet the laws call on the broader community to take the punitive action. This infers that some of what happens inside a family has ramifications for life beyond the family. This explains why the main section begins with a law about cursing one's parents. By the same token, these laws appeal for loyalty to the Lord above all others. The community is to stand united against the splintering effects of the activities prohibited here. This is clearest in the opening unit, where the text forbids Molech worship. This betrays the possibility that individuals might side with idolaters among their family members against the Lord, perhaps in the name of family unity. These laws call on individuals to choose the Lord over their (apostate) family members.

The sexual unions that the main body of statutes and ordinances forbids amount to selfish acts by individuals that damage the social dynamics of the broader group. These acts disrupt the life of the family, which in turn threatens the integrity of the community. Despite these obvious adverse effects, the temptation to participate in such unions can still be strong. Overcoming this temptation involves not only the submission of an individual's will to the will of God but also recognition of the benefits that come from subordinating personal desires to the needs of the broader community.

These regulations carry on from the previous chapters the emphasis on being a "separate people." This amounts to an ancient example of a struggle that believers commonly face, a struggle to strike a balance between life in a geographic community and life in a religious community. These regulations call for individuals to adhere to a certain set of moral values to the point of removing "corrupting elements" from within the religious community. Besides the difficulties posed when these "corrupting elements" arise from one's own family, there are similarly difficult choices faced when members of one's geographic community subscribe to opposing moral values. They believe in the moral rightness of their values, but the Israelites must maintain their own values over against those of the broader culture. Such a struggle is never easy, and it never ends. It is a necessary consequence of being set apart and being holy as the Lord is holy.

LEVITICUS 21

The preceding laws call for the people to maintain the holiness of the entire land, but there is still the understanding that additional restrictions give the sanctuary a higher standard of holiness. Within the sanctuary, there is an "extra special" area governed by its own restrictions (chap. 16). The five messages in chapters 21–22 show how the same sort of "graded holiness" applies to priests and high priests in comparison with the rest of the people, as they fulfill their official responsibilities (Jenson 1992, 36-39).

Literary Analysis

The narrator divides this chapter into two events. Verse 1a introduces a message that Moses is to convey to Aaron and his sons (vv. 1b-15). The wording of the initial clause is rare for Leviticus, occurring only here and in 16:2. Verse 16 introduces a second, shorter message that Moses is to pass on to Aaron alone (vv. 17-23).

The concluding self-declaration formulas in verses 8 and 15, coupled with "when" at the beginning of verse 9, appear to split the first message into two parts (vv. 1-8, 9-15). Verse 9 clearly goes with verses 1b-7, however, so most commentators regard verse 9 as a supplementary. Also, many regard verse 8 as a parenetic interpolation addressed to the congregation. These considerations point to a more accurate division into verses 1-9 and verses 10-15. The first part delimits restrictions regarding priestly participation in ceremonies for the dead and regarding marriage. The second part deals with restrictions that apply to the high priest alone. The syntax of verses 10-15 confirms the unity of this part. The composer places the negative particle with the verb at the end of each clause, except in verses 12 and 15. There, the same prohibition ("he may not profane") places the verb first in an explanatory clause.

The longer self-declaration formulas set the tone of the first message, placing the focus on the holiness of priests. Frequent use of "defile" and "profane" reinforces this theme. The second message concludes with the same theme of holiness, but it focuses entirely on physical blemishes that would compromise a priest's worthiness to fulfill his duties. It is likely that this list of blemishes derives from the list of blemishes on sacrificial animals in 22:21-25.

Verse 24 concludes these addresses by reporting "Thus Moses spoke." The narrator uses the same summarizing construction at the end of chapter 23, where its function is clear; and it forms part of a longer conclusion at the end of chapter 24, where again it is a logical component. It is difficult to give a rationale for such a summary at the end of chapter 21, though. The text reports that Moses delivered these words "to Aaron and to his sons and to all the people of Israel." This triad corresponds to 17:1-2 or 22:18, but not 21:1. Moreover, this summary gives a wrongful impression of finality, because chapter 22 clearly continues the themes of chapter 21. It would make more sense to place the summary at the end of chapter 22, but perhaps the presence of a spoken summary there precluded that placement. These two chapters stand together, clearly separate from the festival regulations in chapter 23.

Exegetical Analysis

Special Standards for the Priests (21:1-9) and the High Priest (21:10-15)

The text identifies two areas requiring special restrictions for the priests. The first involves priestly participation in ceremonies for the dead (vv. 1b-6). Many commentators believe that these laws address concerns about associations with the "cult of the dead," that is, a variety of customs for honoring one's ancestors in ways that would compete with the worship of the Lord. The acts in verse 5 probably represent the most common customs. Forbidding priests from such activities would discourage the general population from regarding these rites as part of the Lord worship. There are also concerns here about contact with death. Contact rendered the priests unclean for a week, preventing them from fulfilling their priestly duties (Ezek 44:15-27).

Verse 4 requires some explanation. A very literal translation reads "He shall not defile himself, a master/husband among his peoples, to profane himself." The meaning of the noun phrase in the middle is unclear. Many commentators understand this verse to prohibit a priest from burying his own wife. "Wife" is missing from the list in verse 2, which is limited to immediate blood relatives. Others read "master among his peoples" as a reference to any man's social obligations when someone of his community dies. Thus, verses 1b and 4 form a frame around verses 2-3. The frame gives the general rule, while the inner verses mention the few exceptions. Still others assume that a priest in neighboring nations served as "master" of those around him. Officiating at ceremonies for the dead was a powerful way to lay claim to this role. From this perspective, this law discourages the Israelites from confusing their priests with neighboring priests.

There is some curiosity regarding the designation of offerings in verse 6 as "the food of their God" (cf. 21:8, 17, 21, 22; 22:25). There are indications that Israel's neighbors thought of sacrifices as food for gods, but the Old Testament writers consistently reject this notion for sacrifices offered to the Lord. Perhaps the cult of the dead involved food offerings to one's ancestors, and these laws make it clear that Israelite offerings should go to the Lord alone.

The second area of special restrictions entails marriage laws. Verse 7 prohibits a priest's marriage to a woman who is not a virgin or a widow, and verse 9 calls for the harshest of punishments on a prostituting daughter. The same term is translated "defiled" and "profanes" in verses 7 and 9, and it serves elsewhere as the direct opposite to "holy" (10:10; Ezek 22:26; 42:20). Allowing a priest to marry a widow shows that the ultimate criterion of this holiness is not virginity. Instead, the predominant notion is that a priest's marriage should embody the uncompromised singularity of the covenant relationship between God and Israel. The special restrictions on the wives and daughters in priestly families reflect their unique holiness as priests, and this reinforces the call for the singular commitment of the people to God ("You shall be holy, for I the LORD your God am holy").

Special rules for the high priest follow in verses 10-15. These move the priest one step farther away from the rights of a commoner. First, they prohibit him from engaging in typical acts of grieving (disheveling his hair, tearing his robes), which is a step removed from disfiguring himself (v. 5). Further, these rules deny the high priest any exceptions for close relatives, nor may he leave the sanctuary to attend funeral ceremonies. There is but one high priest; if he defiles himself or leaves the sanctuary, there is no one else who can stand for the people before the Lord. Second, the high priest has additional restrictions that require him to marry "a virgin of his own kin" (v. 14). The writer adds the category of "widow" to the earlier list of forbidden women.

One lesser question involves the absence of the designation "high priest." The text simply mentions the ceremonial distinctions of the high priest (anointment, vestments). Interpreters argue about what this says about the date of the law's composition. As with so many other issues of this sort, there is too little evidence and too much subjectivity involved to reach a truly "educated" conclusion.

Priests and Physical Blemishes (21:16-24)

This message begins by reiterating that the primary concern is a priest's worthiness to stand as a representative for worshipers before the Lord. This flows into a list of twelve physical imperfections that would disqualify a priest from performing priestly duties. Later rabbis took these twelve to be categories and derived a fuller list of 142 defiling blemishes (Milgrom 2000a, 1825). These could be abnormalities from birth or the result of diseases or injuries (24:19-20). It is uncertain what precise conditions some of the Hebrew terms designate. For example, the "blind" (v. 19) might include someone who is blind in one eye only. The root of the term for "dwarf" (v. 20) refers to something that is very fine or crushed, such as powder (16:12); so here it might refer to someone who is exceptionally thin or whose skin is shriveled and thin. About half of these terms appear only here and in 22:21-25. These abnormalities prevent the individuals from officiating at rituals, but they do not exclude them from priestly benefits. There is no implication that these indicate moral flaws or divine punishment.

Theological and Ethical Analysis

Modern readers might have negative reactions initially to these laws, but they bring up practical issues that believers of every generation face. First, the basic principles for priests have their application in Christianity as well. Christian teachings that speak of Jesus as a "high priest" are sure to emphasize that he was holy enough to lay claim to such a designation (Heb 4–10). Similarly, people always place higher expectations on religious leaders than on "average" constituents. Even among groups that speak of "the priesthood of all believers" (1 Pet 2:5-9) and resist hierarchical structures, there is a sense that leaders are to uphold higher standards. This chapter is in line with that way of thinking. Priests, pastors, and ministers should not be surprised when they find their own words and actions more carefully scrutinized.

The sentiments of the closing section are patently unfair in a world that frowns on discrimination based on physical characteristics. Some of these blemishes are the result of birth defects. They are part of how God made these individuals. These are blemishes; as such, they do not represent punishment for sin. At the same time, they do change the status of the individuals so that they are restricted from performing priestly functions, just like all the lay Israelites. They would "profane" the sanctuary if they approached to officiate over a worship ritual.

For the Israelite, this reflects the notion that there are different "grades" of holiness. The foundational principle is that the Lord expects the best from humans when they worship. These guidelines parallel rules about animals used in sacrifice (22:21-25). People may eat animals that are clean, yet are not worthy as offerings to the Lord. Similarly, there are things that one might do or say that would not constitute sin, yet they would still disqualify one from serving in worship and within the confines of a sanctuary. Such distinctions promote the notion of the holiness—the otherness—of God in the physical world. The present-day rejection of gradations based on physical blemishes derives from prophetic notions about God's acceptance of the blemished (Isa 56:3-8; Jer 31:7-9; cf. Luke 14:7-24). From a canonical perspective, this should not be seen as a dilution of the divine demand for holiness but as a manifestation of divine mercy.

LEVITICUS 22

The messages in this chapter complement the messages on holiness and priests in chapter 21 by addressing the topic of holiness and offerings. There are verbal ties between chapters 21 and 22 and the preceding chapters on holiness. A couple of particular elements produce a sense of completion of matters that began in chapter 17, so that many commentators speak of chapters 17–22 as a cohesive block. But the connections do not end there. References to defiling discharges, leprous diseases, and unclean animals push the reader further back into the book, and additional regulations about priests eating portions of offerings reach back as far as chapter 7. The result is a sense of unity to the whole book, something that defies absolute demarcations into sources and redaction layers from distinct historical periods.

Literary Analysis

Narrative introductions in verses 1, 17, and 26 break this chapter into three messages. The first message Moses is to deliver "to Aaron and his sons," who are then to act on behalf of "the people of Israel." The second one Moses is to pass on to the same priests and "all the people of Israel," and the third implies the same, broad audience.

Several terms associated with holiness appear throughout the first message ("holy," "sanctify," "profane," and "unclean"). The self-declaration formula, which contributes to the holiness theme, appears five times in this message. The final two instances carry the complementary phrase, "I sanctify them" (vv. 9, 16). Formulaic features divide the first message into four units (vv. 2, 3, 4-9, 10-16). Each of the first two units concludes with the short self-declaration formula. A typical introductory construction ushers in the third unit. Following another self-declaration clause (v. 8), a longer summary statement and self-declaration formula bring the unit to a close (v. 9). The fourth unit consists of a simple prohibition, followed by a fourfold series of secondary cases (vv. 11, 12, 13, 14). This unit too concludes with an extended self-declaration clause.

There are fewer literary clues to the structure of the second message (vv. 18-25). The introductory formula of the main address matches the unit introductions in chapter 17, and proper handling of sacrifices of well-being is a central concern to both passages (17:3-8; 22:21). The only other structural indicator is the introductory "when" in verse 21 that divides the message into two units (vv. 18-20, 21-25). This message contains no direct references to holiness. Besides the similarities to the opening of chapter 17, the main verbal connections are between this message and 21:17-23. The absence of other links to the preceding chapters suggests that this is the older message of the two.

The main body of the third and final message comprises verses 27-30. The double use of "when" in verses 27 and 29 demarcates two related units. The reference to an "acceptable . . . offering by fire" evokes the episode in chapter 10, and verse 29 contains only the second reference to a thanksgiving offering in the entire book (7:12-15).

Verses 31-33 stand as a lengthy conclusion to this short address, but they actually function as a conclusion to a string of messages. The admonition to "keep my commandments and observe them" has parallels in 18:26, 19:37, and 20:22. The Lord's expressed concern that the people not "profane my holy name" points back to the opening units of the last two chapters (21:6; 22:2). The expanded self-declaration clause ties this conclusion to 21:8 and 15. This is one of three occurrences of the formula in as many verses. On the whole, this conclusion brings together chapters 21–22 as a unified collection of messages, which round out a block of messages extending back at least to chapter 18.

Exegetical Analysis

Proper Treatment of Offerings (22:1-16)

The regulations in this chapter follow naturally on those in chapter 21. Those lay out criteria that do not disqualify individuals from eating from sacrificial offerings (priests with blemishes, 21:23), while this chapter indicates what criteria do disqualify individuals from eating. The order for the priests to "deal carefully" with these items (v. 2) involves a word derived from the root for "Nazirite" (Num 6). There is no indication, however, of what the priests would do to designate these foods as "sacred donations," except that they were scrupulous about who could eat them.

The first extended unit lists the primary categories of defiling things that would preclude a priest from eating. The main section summarizes the laws in chapters 11 and 13–15 (vv. 4-7). Verse 8 is a terse supplement, incorporating the situations envisioned in 17:15-16, a unit that itself might be a secondary addition. This list proceeds in descending order according to how long the defilements persist. These restrictions spell out a practical implication arising from the defilement laws. The primary goal is to maintain distance—spatially and symbolically—between the sacred and the defiled.

There is uncertainty about whether these "sacred donations" were presented and eaten exclusively within the sanctuary precinct. It is likely that individuals could present them to priests located anywhere in the nation. Excavations have yielded examples of pottery inscribed with the designation "holy" or "holy to the LORD," suggesting that their contents might have been for this purpose. The nature of the offering, rather than where it rests, is most significant in this regard. The NRSV translation of verse 9 implies that the death of the one eating—and the act of eating—occurs "in the sanctuary," but the Hebrew is ambiguous on this point. It reads "so that they may not incur guilt and die in the sanctuary for having profaned it." It could be, however, that the offending priest eats the sacred donation away from the sanctuary but dies the next time he enters. The possibility that sacred donations might be kept away from the sanctuary would explain how a layperson might eat from them unintentionally (v. 14). It is conceivable that the concern is about a layperson "unintentionally" eating the donation before he gets it to the priest; or it might be that the priests had laypersons as dinner guests at the sanctuary, but then failed to advise them as to which items were sacred. In any case, it is the responsibility of the priests to ensure that only ritually qualified individuals participate in the consumption of these foods (vv. 2, 15-16). Their failure in this regard makes them culpable for the sins of others.

The biblical text is unclear about when it might be possible for a layperson to eat from food designated for a priest. The details in verses 10-13 only partially clarify this issue. A priest was responsible for feeding any servants under his charge, so verse 10 distinguishes between those who are still socially independent (the "bound or hired servant") and those that are part of the priestly family by birth or purchase. Only the latter may eat of the sacred donations. A priest's daughter acquires the status of a layperson when she marries a nonpriestly husband, but she returns to her previous status when legal obligations no longer bind her to persons (husband or children) outside her birth family (see above on 21:7-9).

The final portion of this message places the blame for an unintentional breach of these rules more on the priests than on the offenders (vv. 14-16). This is not a matter of culpability for the actions of others; rather, it is a matter of responsibly fulfilling one's priestly responsibilities. The laypersons, for their part, are to respect the boundaries between sacred and profane, and when they do not it requires compensation with interest. Unscrupulous priests might see an opportunity in verse 14 to get more food (through the requirement for compensation), but they are to remember the more pressing need to maintain the distinction between sacred and profane.

There is also uncertainty about the precise meaning of the final clause (v. 16). Does the Lord sanctify the donations, the priests, or the people? All are possible antecedents of "them." The first two interpretations can be supported by appeal to the same construction in 21:23b. Justification for the final interpretation ("I sanctify [the people]") comes from passages that expand on the self-declaration formula (as in vv. 31-33). In any of these interpretations, the concern is that the priests could undermine the sanctifying work of the Lord. Also, the final clause affirms that it is the Lord who sanctifies, so that the people will not assume that their own actions (the eating of sacred food) make them holy.

Unacceptable Offerings (22:17-25)

The second message of chapter 22 is a bit curious, because it addresses details that fit more naturally earlier in the book. Its contents are assumed or anticipated as early as chapter 1, when the prescriptions for a burnt offering call for the use of animals "without blemish" that will be "for acceptance in your behalf before the LORD" (1:3). The current message specifies what "without blemish" might entail, listing a dozen conditions that would disqualify an offering (cf. 21:18-20). It refers five times to worthy offerings as "acceptable/accepted in your behalf" (the next message includes two more examples). This does not denote what is just satisfactory, however, but what "brings a smile" to the recipient. The first unit involves the burnt offering, while the second moves to sacrifices of well-being (chap. 3). These are the first two types of animal sacrifice that the opening section of the book considers, so it is reasonable to assume that the same principles intend to apply to the remaining animal sacrifices as well (chaps. 4–6; cf. chap. 17).

These rules apply to "votive" or "freewill" offerings. Both come at the initiative of the worshiper. The first refers to items that the worshiper pledges on one occasion and then brings later (chap. 27), and the second occurs all at one time. These are offerings that the worshiper has volunteered to bring forward. An underlying concern is that participants might excuse the use of a less-than-acceptable animal. The final case hints at this most clearly (v. 25). It envisions the possibility that a foreigner might wish to bring an offering (1 Kgs 8:41-43). A foreigner might not be aware of the specific guidelines for Israelite offerings, yet the priests must not confuse the generosity of the gesture with the acceptability of the offering. The purity of the offering is the true test of the sincerity of the gesture. Some expand the application of these requirements to noncultic life (e.g., those who believe that the ending of v. 24 prohibits castration of any animals); but this ignores the specifics of the context.

This directs attention to one other question: Do the compilers mean to prohibit "profane slaughter"? This denotes the consumption of animals in noncultic settings. It is most likely that the current statutes do not intend to apply to that. They do not prohibit the possession of blemished animals; they only consider their use in a cultic context. This infers that there were blemished animals, and the Israelites must have used them in some productive way. Not to consume them would be a waste of resources, and to consume them in a noncultic setting would not destroy the sacred-profane dichotomy that this text seeks to sustain. This is consistent with the passages that do allow for profane slaughter, such as Deut 12. That text specifically prohibits the eating of "votive gifts" and "freewill offerings" and "donations" ("offering" in Lev 22:12), but it allows for the consumption of nonsacred meat away from the sanctuary (Deut 12:13-27).

Acceptable Offerings (22:26-33)

The final message of the chapter concerns three details of animal sacrifice. The first two involve the sacrifice of young livestock. If there is a connection between the need to wait until the animal is a week old and the law of human circumcision (12:2-3), that connection is not obvious. Similarly, there is no clear correspondence between the restriction in verse 28 and the prohibition against boiling a kid in its mother's milk. The stipulation that a thanksgiving offering should be eaten on the day one offers it is consistent with the instructions in 7:11-18.

Theological and Ethical Analysis

This chapter revisits theological matters that have already been addressed in Leviticus, but the concluding remarks of both messages reiterate and sharpen a couple of key aspects. The reminder at the end of the first message (vv. 15-16) is that the priests' primary responsibility is to distinguish between sacred and profane, between clean and unclean (11:46-47; 13:59; 14:57; 20:25). This is a distinction between the things of life and the things of death; a failure by the priests threatens the life of God's people. The priests might be tempted to satisfy their immediate and physical desires, but they would be doing so at the expense of the long-term and spiritual needs of their constituents. This is a common sort of dilemma. The stakes are higher here, because it touches on the people's sanctification. Their sanctification qualifies them to fulfill the nation's role as a blessing to all the families of the earth. Their defilement hinders them in this role, furthering death rather than life on earth. Their defilement "profanes [the LORD's] holy name" in the earth (see vv. 2, 32). It undermines the divine reputation among other peoples, so that they are disinclined to look to the Lord for life. This text is another reminder of that ultimate responsibility of the Israelite people and their priests.

The words of the Lord attach two significant claims to the self-declaration formula at the end of the chapter. The first is the sanctification clause (v. 32; cf. 20:8; 21:8, 15, 23; 22:9, 16). The second is the exodus clause, which reaches back to 11:45, but then is more common in this latter portion of the book (19:36; 25:38, 42, 55; 26:13, 45). Related to this are the separation statements in 20:24 and 26. Some assert that these are equal claims, meaning that the Lord views the exodus as the event when the Israelites were separated from all other peoples to be sanctified. This discounts the ongoing work of sanctification in which the priests involve themselves, so others counter this and say that they are complementary divine actions. First the Lord delivered Israel from Egypt, and now the Lord acts to sanctify them through laws and cultic ritual. There is probably some overlap intended in this. Sanctification involves transformation from death to life, and a part of this involves deliverance from forces and powers that bring "death" in a physical sense or in a spiritual sense (see Rom 5–8). The exodus is a physical illustration of this, but it is not the only deliverance that the Lord provides. Any transition from death to life is deliverance (= salvation). The concluding remarks show that deliverance/salvation is not just a one-time event, it is an ongoing and never-ending rejuvenation. It can involve specific events of physical separation from situations that bring death, but it also involves the maintaining of essential distinctions between what is clean and unclean, between what is holy and profane.

LEVITICUS 23

Leviticus 23 shifts the focus from the holiness of the people to the holiness of time. There is little said about holiness, except in the repetition of the expression "holy convocation." The addressees are "the people of Israel," and that will be the case for the remainder of the book. These laws do not stipulate what the people must do to become holy or to remain holy; instead, they call on a holy people to incorporate regular reminders of the Lord into their lives. The goal is to maintain a zeal for holiness and devotion to the Lord. These laws establish a rhythm to their lives that resonates with God's creative and holy work in the world. That rhythm is based on a combination of agricultural seasons, the Sabbath, and the exodus. There are two festivals anchored in the first month (March–April), and three in the seventh month (September–October). Other considerations influence the length and the themes of these festivals.

Literary Analysis

This is one of five texts in the Pentateuch that delineates significant portions of the religious calendar (Exod 23:14-17; 34:18, 21-24; Num 28:1–29:40; Deut 16:1-17). Other texts describe events for only one festival (Exod 12:1-28; 12:43–13:16; Lev 16:1-34). There are divergent theories about which texts came first and which were later elaborations. Space allows for only a few preliminary observations.

The narrator divides these instructions into five speech units (vv. 2b-8, 10-22, 24-25, 27-32, 34-43). There is a general consistency in the style and structure of these units, with a few notable exceptions. Each unit begins by establishing the date(s) that the people are to observe each respective festival. The second unit varies from this slightly, because the writer coordinates this date directly with the date in the first unit. Each festival carries the designation "holy convocation." There is at least one prohibition against doing work during all or part of each festival. There is at least one directive to "present the LORD's offerings by fire" within each unit.

This last characteristic is an important witness to a complex literary linkage between this chapter and Num 28–29. That passage covers the same festivals, but it gives more details about the offerings that accompany them. Of the five texts that describe the annual festivals, these are the only two that refer to them as "holy convocations"; the only two passages that include the Festival of Trumpets and the Day of Atonement in the list of national festivals; and the only passages that mention drink offerings in connection with these festivals.

The instructions in Lev 23 omit most of the details about the offerings. The text refers to these generically as "the LORD's offerings by fire." The writer of Lev 23 gives details about the offerings for a particular festival only when the details do not appear in Numbers (vv. 10-14; Num 28:26) or where the details differ from those in Numbers (vv. 15-21).

These observations confirm recent proposals that a redactor has constructed Lev 23 out of the instructions in Num 28–29 (Knohl 1995, 8-45; Milgrom 2000a, 1345; Milgrom 2000b, 2054-56). There is a consensus that the Numbers passage is from the Priestly source. Older theories give priority of composition to Lev 23, but this was based on the assumption that the Holiness Code always precedes the Priestly source. It is more likely, however, that a writer would summarize existing instructions, rather than give generic instructions about ritual offerings that later writers would flesh out. Thus, it is more likely that Num 28–29 predate Lev 23. The designation of these festivals as "appointed festivals of the LORD" (v. 37) is found only in this chapter and in one passage in Ezra (vv. 2, 4, 37, 44; Ezra 3:5). If the development were from Lev 23 to Num 28–29, one would expect to find this designation in Numbers as well.

There is evidence of secondary accretions in Lev 23. First, there is a dual introduction in verses 2b and 4, and a dual conclusion in verses 37-38 and 44. Both introductions and both conclusions mention "the appointed festivals of the Lord," but verse 2b also includes "my appointed festivals." The subject of verse 3 (the Sabbath) is not an annual celebration, like the other holy days in this chapter. This raises suspicions about verses 2b-3. Verses 37-38 confirm these suspicions, as the text states that these "appointed festivals" do not include "the sabbaths of the LORD." It seems that a redactor has added verses 2b-3 before the original introduction in verse 4. Verse 4 forms an inclusio with verses

37-38, suggesting that verses 39-43 are also secondary. The narrative summary in verse 44 mentions "appointed festivals" again, forming an additional bracket with verse 2b that encompasses verses 3 and 39-43. Verses 39-43 come after a summary statement in verses 37-38, and they speak about the same festival that verses 34-36 prescribe. Verses 40 + 42-43 provide details that one finds in none of the other festival texts in the Pentateuch. These observations expose verses 2b-3, and 39-43 as secondary additions. There is less certainty that these verses were introduced at the same time as verse 44, which has parallels elsewhere in the book (21:24; 24:23).

Verse 22 stands out for a couple of reasons. The speech unit in which it stands (vv. 9-22) divides naturally into two parts, each of which concludes by referring to the instructions as "a statute forever" (vv. 14, 21). What is more, verse 22 repeats Lev 19:9 + 10b, almost verbatim, including the closing self-declaration formula. The most logical conclusion is that 23:4-38 (excluding v. 22) originally constituted an abbreviated and supplemented rendition of Num 28–29. A redactor has shaped these instructions to stand with chapters 17–22. The duplications from chapter 19 and the self-declaration formula (also in v. 43) show that this redactor is incorporating existing Holiness Code phraseology in these additions.

Exegetical Analysis

Sabbath, Passover, and the Festival of Unleavened Bread (23:2-8)

The current form of the chapter begins the calendar with the Sabbath (v. 3). This sets a special tone for what follows, indicating the importance of the number seven and of days of rest. The writer designates the seventh day as "a sabbath of complete rest." The latter term is an abstract noun derived from the root for Sabbath, so one might translate this "a Sabbath of Sabbath-ness." There is a double reference to this as a "sabbath to the LORD," implying something that extends beyond the weekly Sabbath. This is the basis for the priests' schema of time, a schema that they play out in regard to Sabbath years and Jubilee years. It is related to the Sabbath of creation, but it stands closer to the Sabbath texts of the Decalogue, with their links to creation and the exodus. Only three other texts carry this construction (Exod 16:23, 25; 31:15; 35:2). All three include language of "Sabbath-ness" or about the Sabbath as "holy," and Exod 31:13 includes a reference to the exodus as an event of sanctification (cf. Lev 22:32). It is surprising, then, that the only direct reference to holiness is "holy convocation," which appears only here and in Num 28–29 (and Exod 12:16). An indirect reference to holiness is in the self-declaration formula, which enters late in the chapter's development.

There is speculation that the Festival of Unleavened Bread originated as part of an agricultural festival, but the biblical rationale for it always ties it to the exodus and Passover (vv. 5-8; Exod 12–13; Num 28:16-25). The Passover falls on a Sabbath ("the first day"), and the following Sabbath marks the culmination of the festival. This double-Sabbath celebration creates a connection between the Sabbath of creation and the exodus.

The term for "festival" (v. 6) refers to a pilgrimage (*hag*; cf. the Islamic *hajj*). Other festival texts use the term to designate three annual festivals (Unleavened Bread, Weeks, and Booths), but only the first and last receive the label here. This corresponds precisely to the usage in Numbers (Num 28:17; 29:12). It is likely that this originally implied a brief journey to a local sanctuary, but eventually celebrations were limited to the Jerusalem Temple.

First Fruits and the Festival of Weeks (23:9-22)

This unit falls into two parts (vv. 9-14, 15-22), creating a parallel with the preceding unit. Just as Passover initiates a festival period of seven days that culminates in a day of rest, so the celebration of first fruits initiates a period of seven weeks that culminates in a festival and a day of rest. The text identifies the offering of first fruits with "the day after the sabbath" (v. 15), but it does not specify which Sabbath this is. There are at least four interpretations. First, some argue that the text is purposefully ambiguous, because the date of the gathering of first fruits would fluctuate from year to year and from region to region. The assumption is that this is the first Sabbath after the harvest begins, and the presentation of the first fruits would come the following day. Second, some link the presentation of first fruits with the day after Passover, on the basis of Joshua's actions in Josh 5:10-12 (LXX). This requires an overlap, however, between the Festival of Unleavened Bread and the presentation of first fruits. Third, the reference to Passover might imply the Festival of Unleavened Bread as well, and so some interpreters place the date on the day after the end of that festival (the 22nd of the month). A fourth view is that the Israelites were to allow one week to pass after the first festival, and then they would present the first fruits on the day after the next Sabbath (the 29th of the month).

The Festival of Weeks is coordinated with the presentation of first fruits. Both fall on Sundays, being the first and fiftieth days in the people's calculations. This timing derives from agricultural considerations, but the exact nature of those considerations is unclear. The presentation of first fruits marks the beginning of grain harvest season, so many hold that the Festival of Weeks marks the end of harvest. Some associate the first feast with the barley harvest and the second with the wheat harvest. There is speculation that ties this festival to the giving of the laws at Sinai (Exod 19:1), so some wonder if covenant renewal was a part of this celebration.

This is the longest unit in the chapter because it includes detailed instructions about the offerings that the people are to make at these celebrations. The first set of instructions (vv. 10b-13) has no counterpart in Num 28:26-31, which lumps together the offerings of the beginning and the end of the seven weeks. The second set of instructions (vv. 17-19) calls for slightly different offerings than those in Num 28:27-31.

The Festival of Trumpets (23:23-25)

The Festival of Trumpets falls at the midpoint of the year, but it is difficult to find a rationale for it. Trumpet blasts can have either encouraging or discouraging functions. They serve as an alarm of impending battle (Josh 6:5, 20; Amos 2:2), and they announce times of celebration (2 Sam 6:15; Ps 98:6). The trumpet blasts that call the people to move forward through the wilderness combine these two notions (Num 10:1-10). The trumpet blasts on this particular feast day function as "commemoration." As such, they could intend to remind the Lord of divine promises, or to remind the people of what the Lord has done for them. It could be a reminder to both of their mutual obligations to each other (Num 10:10). It might serve as a "first volley" for the festivals that are to follow shortly, calling the people to prepare their hearts for the upcoming season of worship (Isa 18:3-7).

The Day of Atonement (23:26-32)

This unit omits any introductory instruction to address "the people of Israel." The language of the unit is closest to that in Num 29:7-11 and Lev 16:29-34a. Neither of these reflects some of the central details of 16:1-28. Two or three characteristics set this short message apart from its parallels. There is a greater emphasis here on self-denial in relation to Yom Kippur. This is in contrast to the other festivals, which encourage worshipers to celebrate the things the Lord has provided. This passage contains a warning against those who do not participate. It uses the language of the Lord "cutting off" those who do not practice self-denial (cf. 7:21, 25, 27; 17:4, 9, 10, 14). It is the only instance in this chapter that mentions consequences for those who labor on such a day (v. 30). This unit closes with a clarification regarding the precise extent of the day. One wonders when this would have been a disputed matter in the history of Israel.

The Festival of Booths (23:33-43)

This final unit falls into three parts (vv. 34-36, 37-38, 39-43). The first gives a summary of the instructions from Num 29:12-38. The two texts agree in giving the eighth day the designation of a "solemn assembly" (v. 36; Num 29:35). Deuteronomy alone applies this designation to the Passover (Deut 16:8). The Hebrew root of the term implies binding or restricting, so this day might have involved special restrictions on the people's activities.

The second part of the unit functions as a summary of verses 4-36. The list of offerings matches the list in Num 29:39, which functions as the summary to all of Num 28–29. That summary mentions "your votive offerings and your freewill offerings" as exceptions, as does this text; but this one also excludes "sabbaths of the LORD" and "gifts." The latter is a term rarely used, while the former is in verse 3. The fact that votive and freewill offerings are in the final message in chapter 22 contributes to the impression that this is looking backward beyond the present group of festivals in reverse order to the topics that immediately precede it in the book.

The final portion of the unit furnishes a second set of instructions regarding the Festival of Booths, giving detailed instructions about the booths themselves. Baruch Levine asserts that the first set of instructions involves worship at the sanctuary, while these involve activities in local communities; but the call to "rejoice before the LORD" in verse 40 suggests a gathering in the sanctuary as well. These instructions draw a direct line from the Festival of Booths to the exodus. At one level this creates another layer of inclusio with the opening of the chapter, because the Passover commemorates the exodus. Tradition associates the Festival of Booths with the receiving of the laws at Sinai and the sojourn in the wilderness (Deut 31:10-13; cf. Neh 8:13-18). Some note that the festival falls at the end of the dry season, and so observances might have included prayers for renewed rains. This fits well in the wilderness motif, when the people were in need of water on several occasions (cf. John 7:37-38).

Theological and Ethical Analysis

The main pillars of sacred time for the Israelites are the exodus and creation, corresponding to times of harvest, in the first and the seventh months. Harvests remind them of the Lord's continuing blessings, blessings that began in creation. The Israelite festivals show how Israel in particular is tied to the life-giving blessings of the Lord that creation manifests. These laws predicate the harvest festivals on the Lord's salvific acts. The offering of the first fruits and the Festival of Weeks follow immediately after Passover and the Festival of Unleavened Bread. Passover and the Festival of Unleavened Bread are paired, setting the stage in the calendar for the pairing of two harvest festivals (first fruit and Weeks). Just as Passover and Unleavened Bread work together to celebrate the Lord's deliverance of the people from Egypt, so do the harvest festivals work together to celebrate how the Lord brought Israel to the land to enjoy its blessings. The Festival of Unleavened Bread marks the end of the old time of slavery and forced residence outside the promised land, and the offering of first fruits marks the beginning of the new time, when the Israelites take possession of their own inheritances as a blessing from the Lord.

The remaining festivals repeat this combination in a slightly different mode. Here the Festival of Booths, with its basis in the grape harvest, comes immediately after the Day of Atonement, a time when the people are delivered from the enslavement to their own sinful actions. They receive atonement and sanctification and again are able to enjoy the blessings that the Lord provides through creation. Just before the Day of Atonement is the Festival of Trumpets, when the trumpet blasts probably echo trumpet blasts that announced the Lord's victory over the Egyptians and trumpet blasts that celebrate the Lord's agricultural blessings.

The Sabbath represents the completion and perfection of creation (Gen 2:1-3; Exod 20:8-11). It is more than a coincidence that the celebration of the harvests is tied to a Sabbath (vv. 11, 15), that one harvest festival concludes after seven weeks of Sabbaths (vv. 15-16), and that the other spans two Sabbaths (vv. 34-36, 39). At the same time, the Sabbath commemorates the exodus from Egypt (Exod 31:12-17; Deut 5:12-15). The exodus ushers in a more figurative Sabbath, what other writers refer to as "a sabbath-rest" (Heb 4:9; cf. Deut 12:8-11; Ps 95:8-11). The Passover-Unleavened Bread festival reminds the people of this as historical event and initial sanctification, while the Day of Atonement brings this into the arena of cultic atonement and ongoing sanctification. Both bring one back to the notion of rest and contentment that the Lord provides. The fact that the Sabbath clause is probably one of the latest layers in the development of this chapter does not undermine this significance; that layer simply makes explicit what would have been implicit to any Israelite who observed the Sabbath. It emphasizes the particularly Israelite nature of these festivals.

Verse 22 serves a similarly important function in the final form of the chapter. It reiterates a principle that is in chapter 19, namely, do to others as the Lord has done to you. It calls on the people to include generosity and concern for the poor in their harvest celebrations. A natural way to acknowledge the Lord's blessings is to share those blessings with others. Other texts show how this principle should flow out of the worshipers' experiences with the Lord as creator-provider and as deliverer (Deut 24:17-22). Genuine celebratory worship motivates the same thoughtfulness for others that the Lord affords to his worshipers.

LEVITICUS 24

Leviticus 24 consists of two short messages and a brief narrative squeezed between the lengthier calendar of festivals and the rules for sabbatical years. There are semantic links betweenthis chapter and the Sabbath law in Exod 31:12-17. These links sufficiently justify the placement of this chapter. The first part concerns cultic items that are to be prepared "regularly," as in Num 28:1-15. Those are described there just before the offerings of the annual festivals, which have been the subject of Lev 23. The second part of the chapter deals with a case of blasphemy against the Lord's name, providing a concrete example of a general principle from chapter 22 (22:2, 32), as well as demonstrating a concrete application of a legal principle (*lex talionis*).

Literary Analysis

The first literary unit contains a two-part message concerning the lamps and the table of bread in the sanctuary (vv. 2-4, 5-9). The first part begins with a directive to "command" the people, yet most of the instructions are for Aaron. In fact, the second part of the message shifts from addressing the people (plural) to addressing Moses (singular). The only other instance of "command" as a directive in Leviticus is in a heading to laws addressed to Aaron and his sons (6:9 [6:2]), but one also finds it in the heading of the instructions on "regular" offerings in Num 28:2. It is likely that the latter has influenced this reading, but the bulk of verses 2-3 corresponds almost verbatim with Exod 27:20-21. The compiler probably includes these offerings with the annual festivals because that is the case in Num 28–29, but the details come from elsewhere. Each instruction is "a statute forever" (vv. 3, 9 NOAB). The second also bears the designation of "a covenant forever" (cf. Gen 9:16; 17:1-22; Ezek 37:24-27). Both instructions involve items that are to be set up "before the LORD regularly," the first on a daily basis and the second every Sabbath (vv. 2, 3, 4, 8). Both involve items that are "set up" or "arranged" (vv. 3, 4, 8; the noun for "rows" in vv. 6-7 comes from the same root).

The text conveys the divine response to blasphemy chiastically:

A —"The LORD said to Moses" (24:13)
    B —order to stone the blasphemer (24:14)
        C —"speak to the people of Israel" (24:15a)
            D —prohibition against cursing God (24:15b)
                E —application to alien and citizen alike
                  (24:16)
                    F —response to the killing of a human
                      (24:17)
                        G —response to the killing of an ani-
                        mal (24:18)
                          H —talion response to injuries
                          (24:19-20)
                      G' —response to the killing of an
                      animal (24:21a)
                  F' —response to the killing of a human
                    (24:21b)
                E' —application to alien and citizen alike
                  (24:22a)
             D' —"I am the LORD your God" (24:22b)
        C' —"Moses spoke thus to the people of Israel"
        (24:23a)
    B' —stoning of the blasphemer (24:23b)
A' —"as the LORD had commanded Moses" (24:23c)

The second unit places a short message on personal injury within a brief narrative about blasphemy (vv. 10-23). The blasphemy event necessitates an addition to the beginning of the message itself in verse 14, an addition that is unusual among the messages in Leviticus. The instructions proper begin in verse 15b with the common introduction "anyone who." Variations and related issues are then introduced with "anyone who" or "one who." This yields an initial case (v. 15b) and six subordinate cases (vv. 16-21). The concluding statement about equal application of these laws to aliens and citizens ends with the self-declaration formula, reminding the reader that this concerns personal holiness.

The structural focus of this chiasmus is the declaration of the talion principle in verses 19-20. This principle dominates the message, and a balancing of phrases in the chiastic structure reinforces it. There is a coordinated use of "give" in the fulcrum of verses 19-20. "Anyone who maims" reads, more literally, "When a man gives an injury." Corresponding to this, the concluding clause reads, "Just as he gives an injury to a man, thus it shall be given to him." These clauses surround the triple iteration of the talion principle. The next two levels of the chiasmus involve the killing of an animal and the killing of a human, respectively. Both iterations of the response to the killing of an animal call the offender to "make restitution" (vv. 18, 21a), but there is a balanced alternation from longer to shorter phrases in the other instructions. The Hebrew gives a longer designation for "human being" and "animal" in verses 17 and 18 than in verse 21 ("[the soul of] a man/animal" become "a man/animal"). Likewise, the ending of verse 17 declares that the manslayer "shall [surely] be put to death," while the corresponding clause in verse 21b states he "shall be put to death." The same alternation is found in verse 16, regarding blasphemy. The final clause contains the phrase "aliens as well as citizens," which has a direct correspondence in verse 22. The first and last clauses of verse 14 correspond almost exactly to the report of the execution in the middle of verse 23. The final clause of verse 23 rounds off the unit by mentioning "the LORD" and "Moses" again, pointing back to verse 13.

These features bring a sense of completion and closure to this event, implying that order has been restored to a world jeopardized by sin. The dominant syntactic structure in these laws is the *lex talionis* form. The balance in these corresponding phrases throughout the literary unit mimics the balance in the legal formulation. The writer has chosen a narrative style that reinforces the legal principle that lies at the heart of the unit.

The narrative flow of this unit is similar to three other stories, all in the book of Numbers (Num 9:6-14; 15:32-36; 27:1-11). All four are situations for which the Lord has not yet provided instructions. The cumulative response probably sets a precedent for responding to other situations for which a specific law does not already exist. In each case, Moses consults the Lord, he reports the Lord's response to the people, and then the people carry out the instructions. An underlying principle in this is that they see the Lord as the ultimate legal authority for the nation.

Exegetical Analysis

The Lamp and the Table (24:2-9)

It is difficult to interpret how this message fits into the bigger picture of Tabernacle instructions. Verses 2-3 reiterate a command that the Lord gives to Moses in Exod 27:20-21. An old explanation of this duplication says that the command in Exodus was forecasting that Moses would later pass on the command to the Israelites, and then this passage is the actual proclamation of the command. A modern critical reading is concerned with the literary sources and relative dates for the two passages. Most conclude that a priestly writer composed the Exodus passage and then repeated it here. Israel Knohl and Jacob Milgrom argue that both entries derive from a writer associated with the Holiness Code, and that the Exodus passage is a secondary interpolation (Milgrom 2000b, 2084-91; Knohl 1995, 119-21).

Verse 4 speaks of "lamps on the lampstand." This almost certainly constitutes a secondary redaction. It might betray an attempt to bring the reference to "a light" in verse 2 in line with the instructions in Exod 25:31-39 (cf. 37:17-24), which describe a "lampstand" that holds seven "lamps." Milgrom reconciles these by translating "light/lamps" as "flame(s)" in verse 2 and its parallel in Exod 27:20 (Milgrom 2000b, 2087-88); to be consistent, however, one should do the same in verse 4. Perhaps there were conflicting traditions about the number of lamps in the sanctuary (cf. Num 8:1-4; 1 Kgs 7:48-50; 2 Chr 4:7-8). Exodus 40:22-25 mentions the table and the lampstand side by side, and that Moses set up those items in fulfillment of the Lord's commands. This raises the question of the need for this commandment in this context. The main concern of this passage is not the original installation of holy items, but their maintenance in the years to come. Again, these instructions complement the instructions in chapter 23, addressing certain daily and weekly requirements, just as those instructions address certain requirements of the annual festivals (Num 28–29).

The designation of "the curtain of the covenant" in verse 3 is unique. The fuller reading in Exod 27:21 identifies it as "the curtain that is before the covenant." The term for "covenant" is related to the word for "testimony" or "witness" (Exod 26:33; 40:3, 21), but this passage uses it as an elliptical reference to the ark (Lev 16:13; Num 1:53; 17:4). The term probably is an allusion to mutual pledges of fidelity that the Lord and the people make in establishing their covenant (Josh 24:22). Other phrases designate specific stipulations, which are associated with the tablets in the ark (Exod 34:28; Deut 9:9). The daily burning of these lamps serves as a constant reminder of the covenant.

There is general consensus that "you" in verses 5-9 refers to Moses, since this individual must enter the sanctuary, and verses 8-9 mention Aaron in the third person. There is a similar consensus that the number of loaves (12) represents the tribes of Israel. This number points to the covenantal significance of this bread, complementing the reference to it as "a covenant forever" (v. 8). The bread is a "sign" of the covenant between the tribes and the Lord. This is one of two connections between this passage and Exod 31:12-17. There it is the Sabbath that is a "sign" of a "perpetual covenant" between the Lord and the people. This text implies that the bread connotes the people's dedication to the Sabbath, which speaks to their commitment to the covenant. This connection to the Sabbath explains the placement of these instructions immediately after the festivals in chapter 23. The "token offering" of frankincense speaks to this as well. This designation derives from the root for "remember," so the bread offering is a commemoration or reminder. Like the Sabbath, this weekly offering reminds the Lord and the people of Israel of their covenantal obligations to one another. Roy Gane (2005) offers the intriguing observation that this brings together the symbolism of the Lord's time of rest (the Sabbath) with God's place of rest (the Tabernacle). There are other references to "eternal" covenants between the Lord and the Israelites, but this seems to be the most pertinent to the present context.

Blasphemy and the Talion Law (24:10-23)

This episode takes an existing legal principle (*lex talionis*) and shows how it applies to a new situation. There is strong evidence that the principle was widely accepted in the ancient Near East long before Israel emerged. Two other texts explicitly verbalize this principle (Exod 21:23-25; Deut 19:21), and it is possible that one or both of these predates the present text.

The talion principle expresses a right and an obligation. "This principle does not imply that punishment was carried out by inflicting bodily injury in kind, but that punishment for harm to a person is to be commensurate with the harm done, not greater, as revenge dictates, nor less, as indulgence desires" (Hartley 1992, lxii). Persons have the right to retaliate proportionately to an offense, but only to a degree that equals the original offense. To go farther is to escalate the situation, when the goal is to prevent the matter from expanding. The offended party can choose to retaliate to a less-than-equitable degree, but that runs into the matter of obligation. In this case, the obligation is covenantal. The offending party has cursed the Lord, and the Lord calls on his covenant partners to retaliate. How they actually respond is a reflection of the strength of their sense of obligation to the covenant.

The Hebrew term translated "maim" and "injury" in verse 19 is translated "blemish" in chapters 21–22. The "injury" is a permanent disfigurement or damage to the body. It renders the victim "profane" and unfit to enter the sanctuary. The core notion of the talion law is that the response should be equitable to the offense. If the injury prevents the victim from participating in the cult, then an equitable response has the same effect. The determination of what is equitable depends on what has been lost. If it is possible to restore what was lost, then that is done, as the command to "make restitution" implies (vv. 18, 21). Otherwise, an equitable loss is imposed on the perpetrator.

The text elaborates on the principle of reciprocity in two directions. These are inferred to be whatever prompts Moses to consult the Lord. It could be that the guilty man's mixed heritage provokes the inquiry. This law applies to anyone who blasphemes the Lord (vv. 16, 22). The Hebrew text is more explicit about this than the NRSV, stating, "Anyone who curses *his* God shall bear the sin" (v. 15, emphasis added). Some take this as a general warning against cursing any deity, implying that each god responds to blasphemy as he sees fit; the text then goes on to specify how the Lord chooses to respond. It is more likely that "his God" refers solely to the Lord, and that it is stating that no one can blaspheme the Lord without suffering serious repercussions (Num 35:30-34). This text applies this principle to anyone who has implicitly or explicitly made the Lord "his God" by residing in the land.

Many interpreters portray the guilty person as a foreigner, as if such a person has no obligations to Israel and Israel's God. But this man is living among the Israelites, his mother is Israelite, and he is seeking protection and sustenance among Israelites and from their God. It is not certain that they consider him an "alien," much less a "foreigner." The fact that only the man's mother is Israelite probably explains why the text gives only her name and lineage. In any case, the law is stated broadly enough to show that it could apply to natives or aliens.

The second possibility is that this text intends to clarify the gravity of the sin of either blasphemy or cursing, or both. Unfortunately, there is hardly any mention of blasphemy in ancient Near Eastern texts, and only one refers to the sort of punishment one might expect for blasphemy (Milgrom 2000b, 2120). This text implies that "cursing the LORD" is a graver offense than murder. The chiastic center of this directive concerns injury. The seriousness of the offenses increases as one moves out from that center, from injury to the killing of an animal to homicide. Cursing God is one degree beyond that.

The writer uses two verbs to denote the man's offense: he "blaspheme[s] the Name [of the LORD]" and he "curses [his God]." Both expressions appear in the narrative (v. 11) and in the law (vv. 15-16). The first verb normally carries a neutral connotation of "mention" or "utter" (Num 1:17; 1 Chr 16:41). It conveys a derogatory meaning here because of its association with "curse." In verse 11 the two verbs form a compound predicate, "he blasphemed . . . in a curse" (Levine 1989, 166). In verses 15-16 it is the parallelism between the verb for "blaspheme" and the verb for "curse" that gives the former its derogatory nuance. The latter term derives from a root that connotes that something is "insignificant" or "light." One finds it most often as the opposite to "bless" (Gen 27:12; Ps 109:17, 28; Zech 8:13), but its most direct antithesis is "honor," which derives from a root meaning "heavy" or "important" (1 Sam 2:30; Isa 9:1 [8:23]). A clear example of this antithesis is evident in the juxtaposition between "*honor* your father and your mother" (Exod 20:12 emphasis added; Deut 5:16 emphasis added) and "all who *curse* father or mother shall be put to death" (Lev 20:9 emphasis added).

There is a less direct connection with Exod 31:12-17. That passage demands that anyone who "profanes" the Sabbath "shall be put to death." This passage demands that anyone who "curses" God "shall be put to death." Both are about respecting that which is holy, and both call for the death of those who do not do so. The Lord's dual warning that the people are not to "profane my holy name" brings these ideas into close proximity (22:2, 32). This text complements these ideas.

The first expression is a major impetus for the Jewish practice of prohibiting the voicing of the divine name. The verb often connotes the mention of a name; the negative connotation ("blaspheme") derives from the broader context. Early rabbis deduced from this passage a general prohibition against any use of the divine name. Different groups began to use substitutes for the divine name, the most common being "the Name" and "the LORD" (*ădōnay*). The former comes directly out of this passage. The latter became the norm in early translations of the Bible. The name "Jehovah" emerged in the Middle Ages from a mixing of the consonants of the divine name (Y-H-W-H) and the vowels of ʾădōnay.

The structure of the passage infers that blasphemy is an offense more severe than murder. Sociological considerations show that the Israelites conceived of "murder" more broadly than the physical termination of someone's life. Death occurred when someone's name was "blotted out." Individuals continued to live, in some sense, as long as their memory was kept alive. This is why they made the exceptional allowance for levirate marriage. Under normal circumstances, such a union would have rendered a man and woman unclean, but not to produce an heir is to blot out a man's name (Ruth 4:10; cf. 2 Sam 14:1-11). The offender in the present episode blasphemes against the "Name" of the Lord. This verbal act is equivalent to a denial of the life that is associated with the Lord (cf. Matt 5:21-22; 1 John 3:11-15). It is tantamount to murder.

Another intriguing issue is the command for the people to "lay their hands on" the head of the blasphemer (v. 14). Interpreters regard the same gesture in sacrifices as a sign of identification with the animal that is to die or a transferring of guilt to that animal (1:4; 16:21). Those placing their hands on the man are not guilty of the sin in this case, however, so it is natural to look to another explanation. Some propose that it is not appropriate to think in terms of guilt. Those who heard the blasphemy carry "pollution," and this act transfers that pollution from them back onto its source. The weakness in this proposal is that there is no instruction for purification. Others propose that the gesture serves as "sworn testimony" to identify the guilty party.

Theological and Ethical Analysis

The subjects of this chapter are extensions to the theme of Sabbath. Every week ends with a Sabbath, and so every week ends with a reminder of the first Sabbath. Every Sabbath reminds the Lord's people of the blessing of everyday things. The presence of the bread is a reminder of how the Lord has blessed them. Every week begins with light shining in darkness, just as the first day of creation began with God commanding light to shine in darkness. Every day begins this way, reminding the people that the Lord creates light out of darkness and life out of death.

The ideas associated with Sabbath are part of a bigger picture of the Lord and holiness. The Sabbath is a time to remember that the Lord is holy and the Lord sanctifies (Exod 31:12-17; Lev 23:2, 32). Holiness and life go hand in hand, just as sin and death go hand in hand. The goal of these laws is that the people "may have life, and have it abundantly" (John 10:10). The blasphemer speaks against the Lord, threatening the life that is in those who hear the blasphemy. To profane the Sabbath is to diminish its sanctifying nature, thereby threatening its life-giving role. To blaspheme the name of the Lord is to deny the life-giving power that is inherent to the Lord.

This chapter is first about maintaining a covenant relationship. It is about acknowledging what is holy in life and then providing constant reminders of that holiness. The initial command here is that the people are to provide oil for the lamps. The perpetuation of these reminders requires popular participation. This chapter is about restoring holiness to a world jeopardized by sin. Previous chapters deal with cultic measures that play a role in this restoration; this chapter presents pertinent legal procedures and principles.

It is common for moderns to separate legal issues from religious or cultic issues, separating "cultic law" from "civil law" or "ethical law." Several commentators react to this particular law and wonder if there were parallel judicial systems in Israel, one for civil disputes and one for religious disputes. It is likely that the Israelites did not recognize such distinctions. Biblical law encompasses both areas, because both fit under the common umbrella of holiness and divine authority. Offenses of both types threaten separation from the Lord. Adjudication in all cases has the same goal of reconciliation with the Lord. Civil offenses and religious offenses both carry a spiritual meaning, so all are subsumed within a common collection of laws, and all are adjudicated within a common legal system. This passage reaffirms that the Lord is the ultimate legal authority. The nature of a case might alter which human "specialists" are involved, but they all operate under the Lord's authority.

The structure of the legal narrative shows that cursing the Lord constitutes something more serious than murder. Murder is an affront against a life, but this cursing of the Lord is an affront against the source of life. To mention the "name" of the Lord is to recall all that the Lord is and does. It is to recall the Lord's essence (Exod 34:5-7) and the Lord's mighty acts (Exod 9:16; Ps 105:1-2). To curse the Lord is to deny the Lord's essence and power, and it is to refute the reality of the Lord's loving and holy acts. It is to take the light out of day; it is to take the breath out of life.

This passage also reminds the Israelites that they should regard an affront against the Lord as an affront against themselves. The first part of the chapter contains reminders that they are in covenant relationship with the Lord (vv. 3, 8). The Lord reminds them of this when he says, "I am the LORD your God." The Lord calls on "the whole congregation" to respond to this verbal attack against their God, because it is an attack against them as well. It is a direct threat to their identity as a people, a direct threat to their lives.

All of this speaks to a corporate understanding of religion and spiritual well-being. Breaking a law has spiritual implications for everyone in the religious community. Previous passages speak of sin as something that defiles the land (18:24-30). The same principle explains why succeeding laws demand harsh punishment for crimes like murder (Num 35:30-34). These offenses threaten the holiness of the land and the life of the people. Private offenses have public implications; individual sins corrupt corporately. The legal principle of talion addresses these concerns. It is not fundamentally about retaliation and getting even; it is about repairing a broken relationship and restoring holiness that the offense has destroyed. The talion response appreciates the magnitude of the offense, but it holds up the well-being of the broader community as its ultimate goal.

Leviticus 25

The compiler now takes the theme of Sabbath and applies it to the lineage-based landholding structure of the nation. This land tenure policy supports the economic power base of Israel's traditional clans and families. Many regard the policy merely as a utopian ideal, but the reader should consider this assessment in conjunction with the following chapter. The Sabbath-based potentialities here give way to imposed Sabbaths in 26:34-35. This implies that chapter 25 intends to present an idealized program, but not an impossible one. The program depends on the righteousness and holiness of the people for its realization. There is no evidence that the Israelites ever observed Jubilee; but in light of chapter 26, this fact stands as an indictment, and as an inducement to each generation to strive for ever-greater righteousness and holiness.

Literary Analysis

The introductory reference to Mount Sinai points the reader ahead to the summary in 26:46 (cf. 7:37-38; 27:34). The narrator is presenting the two chapters together as a literary unit. A combination of literary markers and contextual clues demarcates six units in chapter 25, split into two sets. Each set begins with the simple introductory particle "when"/"if" (vv. 2b, 25). The result is two units that establish a fifty-year calendar regarding general use of the land (vv. 2b-24), followed by four units prescribing measures to redeem property in order to maintain the lineage-based land tenure system (vv. 25-54; cf. 27:16-25).

The first unit lays out guidelines regarding sabbatical years and Jubilee years (vv. 2b-17). The heading introduces the general premise (v. 2b), and verse 3 depicts typical years as times of sowing, pruning, and gathering "their yield." Verses 4-7 call for a Sabbath year, when they suspend these typical activities, but the land still provides "its yield" (v. 7). Verses 8-12 supply corresponding ideas for the Jubilee year, a sort of Sabbath of Sabbath years. Verse 12 clearly stands as the conclusion to this subunit, beginning with the explicative "for" and concluding with terms that parallel those at the end of verse 7. A third subunit begins in verse 13 (cf. v. 4), and the repetition of the call to return to one's family property marks what follows as an expansion of verse 10b. The subordinate introduction in verse 14 and the concluding self-declaration formula in verse 17 are linked to injunctions against "cheating" in both verses, revealing the subunit's theme.

Verses 18-24 stand as a transitional unit. The opening exhortation to "observe my statutes and faithfully keep my ordinances" shows that this unit probably comes from an early redactor (cf. 18:4-5, 26; 19:37; 20:22). The repetition of "eat" and "sow" and "gather" and "produce" suggests reflection on the preceding unit, while verses 23-24 open the door to the next unit.

The balance of the chapter consists of four units with similar introductions (vv. 25-34, 35-37, 39-46, 47-54). Three of the four begin with the same clause, "If any of your kin fall into difficulty" (the NRSV translation for v. 39 is different, but the Hebrew underlying it is the same). The introduction to the final unit includes an additional clause: "If resident aliens among you prosper" (v. 47). Two concluding statements constructed around the self-declaration formula (vv. 38 and 55) divide these units into two pairs. Both base the directives in this section on the exodus, supplementing that theme with the notion of Israelites as the Lord's "servants" (26:13, 45).

Within verses 25-34 there are two pairs of balanced subunits. Verse 25 is presented in the second-person singular (in Hebrew), but the remaining verses address the hearers in the third-person impersonal form. The initial phrases in verses 26 and 29 are identical in Hebrew, while identical phrases in verses 28 and 30 introduce antithetical alternatives ("And if it/there is not"). It is likely that verses 32-34 constitute a separate subcategory, although there are no clear markers that separate these verses from what precedes. Verses 35-37 contain no subunits; but the following verse constitutes a concluding motive clause, constructed as an extended self-declaration formula (cf. v. 55). The next unit breaks into two subunits (vv. 39-43, 44-46), with a lengthy rationale in verses 42-43 concluding the first subunit. This subunit addresses the audience in the singular voice, and the second shifts to the plural voice. The conclusion of the first subunit anticipates the final line of the unit ("not rule ... with harshness," vv. 43, 46) and the conclusion of the entire chapter ("they are my servants," vv. 42, 55; cf. vv. 17, 36). The final unit presents a primary case in verses 47-50, and this is followed by three subordinate cases (vv. 51, 52-53, and 54). This unit is like verses 25-34 in that the writer addresses the audience in the singular in the first verse, but then shifts to the third-person impersonal tone in the remaining verses.

There is a logical progression in these four units, concerning increasingly desperate financial straits. The exact nature of the crisis in each case is disputed, but it appears to progress in the following ways: the first case considers someone who sells land to stay out of debt (vv. 25-34); the next considers persons who have no land left to sell, but who can survive by leasing land from another Israelite (vv. 35-38); the third envisions debt enslavement to a fellow Israelite (vv. 39-46); and the final unit envisions the most desperate situation, that of debt enslavement to a non-Israelite (vv. 47-55).

Exegetical Analysis

The Sabbath Principle Applied to the Land (25:2b-24)

The only references to actual observances of sabbatical years for the land come from Second Temple Judah (e.g., Neh 10:31). The oldest legislation implies a staggered rotation of fallow fields (Exod 23:10-11), while the present laws apply the sabbatical year to the entire land at once. The language for this derives from Lev 23, which in turn probably derives from Exod 31:12-17. There is more speculation about the relation of this legislation to Deut 15:1-18, which calls for septennial remission of debts and manumission of Hebrew slaves (cf. Exod 21:1-11; Jer 34:8-22). Older explanations see these as separate problems, with Deuteronomy calling for release from monetary debt and this legislation calling for release from land debt. More recent reconstructions posit a sequence in the development of rival legal codes. Firm conclusions are elusive, primarily because there is little evidence that Israel ever observed the Jubilee year, which is emphasized only here.

The first half of this chapter takes the principle of Sabbaths (chap. 23) and expands it to apply to years and the long-term ebb and flow of agricultural life. The Sabbath represents a weekly time to reflect on what the Lord provides. The weekly cessation of work poses a risk in an agricultural society, but the overall risk is rather minimal. The imposition of a Sabbath year multiplies that risk, so the rationale in Exodus gives way here to a statement about what the people will consume during a sabbatical year (v. 20).

The second paragraph applies the earlier "sabbath of weeks" (Pentecost) to call for a year of Jubilee (vv. 8-12). The term "Jubilee" comes from the Hebrew term *yōbēl*. This relatively rare term is associated with a ram's horn, referring to the blowing of trumpets to announce the beginning of this special year (v. 9; Josh 6:6-13). Martin Noth suggests that this is an ancient designation, replaced in the monarchic period with the more common shofar. This is part of a larger discussion of the practicality of the Jubilee year. Some contend that it was an agrarian tradition that was increasingly ignored as Israel became more urbanized. Early rabbis spoke of the Jubilee year as an institution that was obsolete by the time Israel returned from exile, and some modern critics agree. Interestingly, others assert that the Jubilee year was an innovation of exilic or post-exilic thought, even if the people living then never actually observed it. For the latter, post-exilic readers would consider this a utopian program, while proponents of the former view assume that the post-exilic community read it and "longed for the good old days."

There were general parallels to the Jubilee year in ancient Near Eastern culture. The closest was the Assyrian practice of *andurarum* (cf. Hebrew *dĕrōr*, v. 10; Isa 61:1). This was an occasional decree by a king, announcing a release from financial burdens for loyal subjects, intending to relieve them of widespread financial hardship. Biblical legislation differs in that it ties the Jubilee to the calendar, and because a nonroyal authority ordains it.

The text is unclear regarding a few technical points. The most significant is the coordination between sabbatical years and the Jubilee year. Some conclude that the Jubilee year falls immediately after the seventh sabbatical year, resulting in two consecutive years without planting or harvest. This contributes to the charge that the legislation is utopian. Such considerations lead to three other proposals: (1) the Jubilee "year" is not a full year, but a period of forty-nine days that corrects differences between lunar and solar calendars; (2) the Jubilee year and sabbatical years are based on competing calendars, so the forty-ninth and fiftieth years overlap by six months; and (3) every seventh sabbatical year is given the special designation of "Jubilee year," so the two are actually one and the same year (Hartley 1992, 434-36).

Verses 13-17 are informative of the Israelite understanding of property and ownership. The law considers only arable land, and its value is determined by its annual productivity. They viewed the value of land strictly in terms of what it could produce. This paragraph interprets "cheating" in terms of a buyer undervaluing the crop potential of a field and a seller overvaluing that potential. This basic understanding of property values explains why there is less concern about the redemption of houses in a city (vv. 29-31). This understanding reinforces the implicit promise that the Lord will personally bless the land so that it maintains an adequate productivity level to compensate for each sabbatical year.

This promise serves as the backbone to the parenetic unit in verses 18-24 (especially v. 21). There is no other instruction about tithing or setting aside annually. The people are to trust that the Lord will provide an overabundance during the sixth year, just as he had provided an overabundance of manna every sixth day in the wilderness (Exod 16:22-30). This passage intimates a restoration of the world as it was first created, when God ordered the earth to produce its fruit and then "blessed" and "hallowed" the Sabbath (Gen 1:29; 2:3). Still, like the manna in the wilderness, this is linked to the people's adherence to the Lord's "statutes and ordinances" (v. 18; cf. Exod 16:27-30).

The broader context of Leviticus suggests that "statutes and ordinances" refer to all the laws in this half of the book, but the immediate context associates them with the instructions of this chapter. The promise of blessings in the sixth year is tied to the Lord's ownership of the land, which is associated directly with the self-declaration clause in verses 38 and 55. The target audience in this passage would be prospering landholders. They are concerned about the loss of a year's produce and income, and they are inclined to see themselves—rather than the Lord—as the ultimate owners of the land. They acknowledge divine ownership by accepting their status as "aliens and tenants," and they acknowledge that status when they "provide for the redemption of the land" (v. 24) according to the guidelines in verses 25-55. They are the ones best able to serve as redeemers, and they are the ones most tempted not to do so (Ruth 4:6).

Redemption of Property (25:25-55)

The basic premise of these four laws is that individuals who own land might "fall into difficulty," but the "fall" can occur to varying degrees. The verb connotes "collapse," probably in reference to agricultural ruin precipitated by a calamitous event. The person at risk is "anyone of your kin" (literally, "your brother"). This designation is relational and relative. It is relational in that it appeals to an individual's sense of personal obligation. The breadth of those feelings is relative, depending on the situation. These four laws progress according to the severity to which a situation threatens a man's standing in his clan, within his tribe, or within the nation. The first involves "anyone...[who] sells a piece of property" because of hardship (v. 25). This can alter a man's ability to contribute to the stability of his clan, so the law appeals to clan brothers ("next of kin") to provide assistance. The second law considers "any...[who] become dependent on you" (v. 35). The Hebrew literally reads "his hand trembles with you." Such a man cannot maintain his place in the clan, so he becomes the "son" of another clan member, or he migrates to another clan or tribal region. The third law considers a more severe situation: "If any . . . sell themselves to you" (v. 39). Such individuals have effectively lost their place in the lineage system. They become "servants of" an Israelite and are no longer "children of" an Israelite. The final stage of destitution involves "any...[who] sell themselves to an alien" (v. 47). The text literally describes the alien as one whose "hand prospers" while "your kin fall into difficulty." The needy person is now a "servant of" a non-Israelite. This portion of the law goes to such lengths to identify possible redeemers—brothers, uncles, cousins, or "anyone of their family" (vv. 48-49). This is a final appeal to their sense of covenant obligation. Every Israelite should be concerned, but it is left first to clan and tribe brothers to preserve the person's "name" in the nation (Deut 25:7, 9; Ruth 4:10).

The fluid social standing of impoverished individuals reveals part of the radical nature of the Jubilee laws. These individuals are at risk of losing their name. The Jubilee laws mandate the restoration of their name in the fiftieth year, even though they do nothing to earn their restored status. The Jubilee laws are radical because they negate social imbalances caused by disastrous events. This discourages wealthy clan members from being callous about the financial hardships of clan members. There is no long-term benefit to looking the other way when there is a need.

These laws stand as supplements to existing redemption laws/customs. The only issues addressed involve the calculation of the redemption price and a few exceptions to the general rule of land tenure (vv. 29-34). The price is tied to two factors: what one can expect the land to produce and the number of years until the next Jubilee. The first exception involves residences whose value is not tied to agricultural production. The exception to that exception entails the homes of Levites, which are the only property they can own; their value is not determined by what they can produce. But all of this assumes an existing set of customs/laws regarding redemption, with concerns about mutual obligations among landowners.

There are questions about some of the details involved in redemption, but these are not unique to this passage. One basic question is the fate of redeemed land. The redeemer pays what the traditional owner could not pay, but he does so from a defensive posture (for the sake of the clan). The right of redemption is always available; the exercise of this right depends on the redeemer's willingness to provide the money for redemption. But the text is unclear about what happens with the property. The primary concern is that the property remains in the same clan. There is no indication, however, that the redeemer hands the property back to the traditional owner (consider Boaz in Ruth 4). The first scenario in this group of four laws envisions someone who sells some property but still retains other property. The text mentions unredeemed property in the final sentence (v. 28), and that property is restored to its previous owner. The fourth scenario implies the same idea, only in regard to persons rather than land. The second and third scenarios make no mention of redemption or restoration of property, because the destitute persons and their property never leave clan hands. Perhaps this implies that the clan is overseeing the distribution of property within its own territory.

Land could be bought and sold outside one's clan. That land did not revert to the clan in the Jubilee year, if the sale did not take place under duress. The natural ebb and flow in the life of a lineage could result in shifting clan strengths and necessitate the transfer of landholdings. One would expect the clan to have a say in that process, but there could be many circumstances in which a clan would approve such a transaction. For example, Num 36:4 refers to land lost through marriage, and a different law addresses that case. The present passage only addresses cases related to impoverishment.

Theological and Ethical Analysis

The legislation for sabbatical and Jubilee years is an outgrowth of ideas associated with creation, exodus, and Sabbath. The Lord lays claim to the land of Israel on the basis of God's authority as creator. It is the Lord's claim over Israel that the pharaoh of the exodus rejects, because he does not "fear the LORD God" (Exod 9:29-30; cf. Lev 25:17, 36, 43). In effect, he rejects the Lord's claim to be creator. It is on the basis of this claim that the Lord demands holiness, manifested in ethical behavior (Exod 19:4-6; Deut 10:12-20). The people of Israel are the Lord's "servants" on the basis of the salvific acts of the exodus (vv. 38, 42, 55). The culminating act of the exodus was the giving of this land to Israel as a home. This is the starting point of this chapter (v. 2), and that theme is widespread in the laws. This passage reminds the people that the land still does not belong to them. It calls on them to recognize the Lord's ownership through submission to a divine structuring of time (Sabbath) and territory (ancestral property).

The structuring of time according to the Sabbath principle is not merely the division of time into sevens; it requires a faith-based cessation of human effort that is otherwise expended to sustain life. The people work the land to enjoy the blessings of life that the Lord has to offer, but it is easy to lose sight of the Lord's role in this and attribute blessings to their own work. This Sabbath-based calendar stands as a corrective to that skewed picture, reminding the people that the Lord is the sustainer of life. These laws point back to creation, when God made life out of a "formless void" and ordered creation to produce in a world over which humans "have dominion" ("rule," in this chapter). God capped off creation by blessing and hallowing the Sabbath (Gen 2:3). The people honor God when they incorporate "Sabbath time" into their lives and hallow Sabbath years (25:10). This requires the faith that the Lord will continue to provide for them (v. 21).

The Jubilee principle shows how this perspective works in conjunction with the redemption laws to promote healing in a wounded world. There is no discussion of what causes individuals to "fall into difficulty"; instead, the text offers a solution to that reality. The redemption laws call for people to lend a hand to those who have fallen, and the principle of Jubilee reminds them that they do so in view of their common status before the Lord. An implicit example of this entails the warnings against those who would "rule with harshness" (vv. 43, 46, 53). God gave humans "dominion" (Gen 1:26, 28). The Egyptians embodied the abuse of this role, treating the Israelites "with harshness" ("ruthlessly"— Exod 1:13-14). The Lord delivered the people from this corrupt dominion, and they should strive to rule as God originally intended (cf. Ezek 34:4).

Many draw inspiration from the imagery of sabbatical years and Jubilee to conceive of a renewed and perfected existence with God. The utopian-like ideals associated with the Jubilee laws are not very different from the stylized images of Israel in Ezek 47–48. Post-exilic Isaiah announces his commission to "proclaim liberty" (Isa 61:1; cf. Luke 4:18-19), echoing the summons of the Jubilee year (25:10). The imagery of believers as "servants" living under a divine landowner is common in Jesus' parables. Other visualizations of God's rule incorporate ideas associated with the Jubilee. These rest on the premise that the culmination of history will be a return to the beginning, a time before human sin defiled the earth and brought in death. They also stem from the recognition that the creator is the great deliverer, who frees people from slavery and death, so that they might be free to live as the Lord intended (Isa 45:1-7, 11-13).

The ideas in this chapter are not entirely utopian dreams about what might be someday in a transformed future; they have concrete realities in the here and now. These laws function as a call for improvements. They appeal to the reader to incorporate the things of sabbatical and Jubilee years into life today. This involves an acceptance that the Lord is the true landowner. Believers are "aliens and tenants," not owners (vv. 23, 42, 55). These instructions speak of sharing Sabbath blessings with slaves and laborers (v. 7). They call on believers to elevate their estimation of the status of others and lower their estimation of their own status. They promote a worldview that overturns the conceptual foundations for the usual systems of privilege and self-advancement of the strong at the expense of the weak and vulnerable.

LEVITICUS 26

It was common in the ancient Near East to conclude a treaty or code of laws with a section of blessings and curses. Treaties and law codes often operated in a setting where the human participants might not be able to reward or punish their coparticipants for their adherence to or deviations from the terms of their agreements, so it was natural for them to look to higher authorities to oversee them. Leviticus 26 fits this genre well, even though the terms "blessings" and "curses" never come up. The closest biblical parallels appear in Exod 23:20-33 and Deut 27–28. Both share a few verbal links to Lev 26. The section in Exod 23 is preceded by laws on the festivals and the Sabbath, so that text might have influenced the general arrangement of Lev 23–26.

Literary Analysis

The only narrated portion of this chapter comes in verse 46, where the phrase "on Mount Sinai" forms a link with 25:1. This link supplements key verbal connections that bind together the direct address in these two chapters. One connection involves the "sabbaths" for the land in 25:2-7 and 26:34-35, 43. This forms a bracket around the entire message portions of these two chapters. Running parallel to this are clauses appended to the self-declaration formulas. One is the reference to the Israelites as former slaves to the Egyptians in 26:13. This is the converse to the Lord's claim to a master-servant relationship with the Israelites in 25:55. More significant is the repeated mention of the covenant formulas in conjunction with the self-declaration formula (25:38; 26:12, 45; cf. Exod 6:7; Deut 26:16-19). These are the only passages in Leviticus that make this connection. This suggests a unity to these two chapters, but unity should not be regarded as a sign of their isolation from the rest of the book. The triad of "statutes and ordinances and laws" in the narrative conclusion encompasses all the laws of the book (7:37-38; 11:46-47; 12:7; 13:59; etc.). The more direct narrative links with the beginning of chapter 25 indicate that chapters 25 and 26 work together to conclude the book.

The text consistently refers to the addressees with plural forms, and transitions are indicated mostly by shifts in the subject matter. Verses 1-2 stand somewhat isolated from the rest of the chapter. Both conclude with the self-declaration formula, which forms a connection with verses 13 and 44-45 (and 25:17, 38, 55); but the vocabulary within the remainder of verses 1-2 does not cohere well with what precedes or what follows. Only the term "sabbaths" has ties to the surrounding block, and "my sanctuary" evokes memories of Exod 25–40; but the other terms are unusual within the Holiness/Priestly corpus. Verses 3-13 stand together, beginning with the conditional particle "if" and concluding with an extended self-declaration statement (v. 13). Within these verses there is an alternation between what "you" (the people) will do and what the Lord will do. This culminates in the covenant formula, "I...will be your God, and you shall be my people" (v. 12).

The conclusion expands the self-declaration formula in a unique way regarding their enslavement in Egypt.

Verses 3-13 do stand as the positive half of a contrast; the negative counterpart begins in verse 14 with "but if." This contrasting section extends through verse 33, consisting of five conditional statements, each beginning with "(but) if" (vv. 14-17, 18-20, 21-22, 23-26, 27-33). Each statement uses a protasis-apodosis construction to juxtapose what the people might do with what the Lord would do in response ("But if you... then I..."). The first statement has a double protasis (vv. 14-15), and the fifth statement contains an extended juxtaposition ("you" in vv. 27, 29, 33b; "I" in vv. 28 and 30-33a). The initial protasis presents the possibility "if you will not obey me, and do not observe all these commandments, if you spurn my statutes, and abhor my ordinances." Subsequent protases condense this to "if... you will not obey me." These stand in contrast to the hope that the people will "follow my statutes and keep my commandments" (v. 3).

There are several contrasts between the contents of these two sections, some more specific than others. The two sections follow different arrangements. The negative tone of the latter section crescendos through variations on a few key clauses. The Lord's initial threat to "set my face against you" (v. 17) gives way to a pledge to punish the people "sevenfold" for their sins (vv. 18, 21, 24, 28). The third, fourth, and fifth parts each preface the people's disobedience with the idea that they will "continue hostile" (vv. 21, 23, 27). In the fourth case the Lord responds to their "hostile" attitude with God's own "hostile" actions (v. 24), and in the final case the Lord is "hostile... [with] fury" (v. 28). This progression reflects the Lord's growing frustration with their obstinate disobedience.

The double occasion of the particle "then" in verse 34 denotes a definite shift in thought. Now the subject is "the land," rather than "you" or "I," as the topic of sabbaths for the land resurfaces. The preceding section describes destruction and devastation (vv. 14-33), and this section describes what will/can happen in the wake of such destruction. This section extends to the end of the direct address (v. 45), but there are two or three parts to it. The opening phrase of verse 36 signals a transition from the land back to the people. The same opening phrase in verse 39 might signal another shift, or it might constitute the closing of a bracket around verses 36-39. Several phrases and coordinating particles in verses 40-42 are difficult to translate with certainty, as the text gradually shifts attention away from the people and over to the Lord. In any case, the writer recapitulates verses 34-42 in verses 43-45, moving from "sabbath years" for the land (vv. 34b and 41b) to "mak[ing] amends" (vv. 41b and 43b) to "remember[ing] the covenant" (vv. 42 and 44-45). This recapitulation includes a double iteration of the self-declaration formula. This formula creates a balance with verse 13, but the extended phrasing points the reader back to 25:38 and 55.

Exegetical Analysis

Undivided Cultic Worship (26:1-2)

These two verses stand as an unexpected transition. Particularly surprising is the absence of a narrated introduction. Some regard this paragraph as the conclusion to chapter 25, but it is difficult to see how these verses function with that chapter alone. A few view the stylistic differences as clues that this unit substitutes for a narrated introduction. More attractive is the proposal that these verses envision all the preceding laws under this umbrella call for obedience. The mention of idols and images echoes the Decalogue, the sanctuary is the main topic in Exod 25–40 and Lev 1–16, and the Sabbath is a unifying element in much of Lev 17–25.

The literary sources of this exhortation are complex. The directive to "keep my sabbaths and reverence my sanctuary" (v. 2) repeats 19:30. Its message resonates with several passages in the intervening chapters, but this does not explain its placement here. The first verse does not sound so familiar. The terms for "idols" and "images" are more common in Deuteronomy, the Historical Books, and Isaiah, but they also occur in Exodus–Numbers. The term for "figured stones" occurs only three other places in the Old Testament (Num 33:52; translated "images" in Ezek 8:12, and "setting" in Prov 25:11). The strongest ties are to the Decalogue

(Exod 20:4-5; Deut 5:8-9) and perhaps a few phrases in Exod 23:24. This suggests a wide swath of legal material, hinting at the interconnectedness of it all.

Promised Blessings for Obedience (26:3-13)

The use of "my statutes and . . . my commandments" in verse 3 (cf. vv. 14-15) constitutes a departure from the norm in Leviticus. Previous examples stand in summary introductions and conclusions, where they probably reflect the hand of a compiler who is referring to adjoining collections of instructions. Here the phrase stands in the main law. This indicates that the writer associates verses 3-13 with the preceding passages that contain these terms as summarizing labels, going back at least to chapter 18.

There have been varying enumerations of the list of blessings that flows from this premise of obedience. The repetition of "I will give" and "I will look with favor" suggests four categories of promises (vv. 4, 6, 9, 11). These correspond to the ancestral promises of land, blessings (which included possession of their enemies' gates), and offspring, plus the promises "I am with you" (Gen 28:15 NOAB) and "I will dwell among the Israelites" (Exod 29:45-46). Others break this unit into smaller pieces, consisting of a series of dual and triple clauses. There is a promise of agricultural prosperity, followed by a prediction that there will be no time to rest between seasonal harvests (cf. Amos 9:13-15). The word for "overtake" in verses 4-5 is the same word translated "prosper" in 25:26, 47, 49, suggesting that this promise addresses the uncertainty envisioned there. This prediction gives way to two promises of domestic peace and security in the land (v. 6; 25:18-19). The prediction of secure borders achieved through lopsided military victories is common fare in this genre (vv. 7-8; Deut 28:7). The thought then moves forward to a promise that this blessed state will continue into future generations (vv. 9-10), and then the list culminates with the ultimate promise: the Lord will dwell among them (vv. 11-12).

The language of verses 9-12 is reminiscent of the promises to Abraham in Gen 17:4-8 ("fruitful," "establish [= maintain] my covenant," "I will be their God"), but this also applies to the covenant with Noah (Gen 9:1-17), and the latter plus the covenant formula (v. 12) are important components of the exodus event (Exod 6:2-8), which leads up to the Sinai Covenant. The Lord's promise to "walk among" them (v. 12) is part of a wide-ranging motif in the Old Testament, reaching all the way back to Gen 3:8. This desire for relationship is the ultimate goal in this covenant. The full elaboration of the self-declaration formula in verse 13 points to the strong thematic triangle between the ancestral promises, the Sinai Covenant, and the exodus-conquest motif (cf. Deut 8:17-20). In any case, these blessings come together to paint a picture in which the fulfillment of the promises to the ancestors is indelibly tied to the fulfillment of the Sinaitic covenant obligations.

The closest parallel to this passage comes in Ezek 34:25-30. This is the concluding section of a prophecy that blames the exile on the corruption of Israel's "shepherds." One of the accusations Ezekiel levels against these leaders is that they ruled "with force and harshness" (see Ezek 34:4), in direct contradiction to Lev 25:43, 46. The final paragraph envisions a time following exile when the Lord will enter into this covenant relationship anew. Ezekiel speaks of the expulsion of "wild animals," people living "securely," the sending of rain so that the "trees of the field will yield their fruit," and so forth. That passage is different, however, in its inclusion of "my servant David" as the one true shepherd and prince. It is likely that Ezekiel is expanding on Lev 26:3-13.

Warnings of Consequences for Disobedience (26:14-33)

The section delineating the consequences of disobedience is much longer than its positive counterpart. The five scenarios increase in severity, in tandem with the Lord's growing frustration over the people's obstinacy. The first scenario warns of disease and foreign domination (vv. 16-17), predicting that others will eat what the people have sown. These probably were common features among "curses" in law codes and treaties (Deut 28:22, 30, 39; Amos 5:11; Hag 1:6). The second scenario speaks of unremitting drought, resulting in a reversal of the prosperity promised earlier (vv. 4, 19-20; cf. Deut 28:23; Ezek 7:24; 33:28). The third scenario shows the results when this situation lingers, and those in more exposed settings die while wild animals ascend in strength (v. 6 and Ezek 33:27). The fourth scenario envisions foreign invasions with devastating sieges, as the people seek refuge in their cities, only to encounter disease and starvation (cf. Jeremiah's frequent "sword, famine, and pestilence"; Deut 28:38-39). The final scenario depicts the utter desperation of the final stages of a siege. Parents are reduced to eating their own children (2 Kgs 6:24-31), and the most precious places are desecrated. The writer reflects the Lord's bitterness in this section, speaking of "the carcasses of your idols" and "your sanctuaries" (vv. 30-31). There would be no reference to such installations if the people were abiding by the covenant; and there is a definite irony in referring to the "carcasses" of idols, as if the Lord is ridiculing the notion that these statues were ever actually alive. The threat to "scatter [the people] among the nations" has parallels in Deut 4:27 and Jer 9:16, as well as in several passages from Ezekiel (12:15; 20:23; 22:15; 29:12; 30:23, 26). The closing mention of "desolation" and "waste" is a common refrain in prophetic depictions of a land that has been conquered and depopulated (Jer 49:19; Ezek 29:9-10; 36:4). A part of post-exilic Isaiah's Jubilee oracle responds to this (Isa 61:4; cf. 58:12).

Anguish and Hope in Exile (26:34-45)

This final section progresses through three phases (vv. 34-42), followed by a recapitulation (vv. 43-45). The first phase speaks of the land enjoying the "rest" that it deserves (vv. 34-35). The verb for "shall rest" is *šābat*, from which the noun "Sabbath" is derived. The people should have been giving the land "Sabbaths" over the years (chaps. 23 and 25), but the presence of desolation and exile implies their negligence. The Chronicler provides the only appropriation of the rare expression "the land shall enjoy its sabbath years" (vv. 34, 43a), speaking of the exile as the fulfillment of Jeremiah's "seventy years," during which time the land would be "a ruin and a waste" (2 Chr 36:21; Jer 25:11; so Lev 26:31, 33). The Chronicler understood these "seventy years" as a derivative from the Sabbath principle. The ten "Sabbaths" of the exile are to make up for the "Sabbath years" that the people have not been observing. On this basis, it is probably better to read here "the land shall satisfy its sabbath years." Through exile, the people pay compensation to the land for their prior neglect of the land.

The second part of this section describes the fate of the exiles. They are "in the lands of their enemies," and constantly fear for their lives. This part might extend into verse 39. That depends on the meaning of the double expression, "[they] shall languish...because of [their] iniquities." The root meaning of "languish" connotes something that rots or is putrid (Ps 38:5; Zech 14:12), but many interpreters balk at the closing reference to "the iniquities of their ancestors." The Septuagint excises the final clause as an addition, because the people should not "languish" over the sins of others. Ezekiel uses this expression as the culmination of times of suffering for past wrongs, so it is tempting to interpret it as an expression of remorse or regret (Ezek 4:17; 24:23; 33:10). This verse would then represent the first step toward the repentance that follows in verses 40-42.

In any case, the final phase consists of the people's contrition and the Lord's mercy. This act of confession goes beyond that of individual guilt (5:5) or national guilt on an annual basis (16:21). It is somewhat surprising, then, that there is no mention of sacrifices here. This tone continues, as the text calls for something physical, circumcision, and demands the humility of the circumcised heart (cf. Deut 10:16; 30:6; Jer 9:26; Ezek 44:7, 9). This is a requirement for which there is no visible proof, which might explain the unspecified nature of the final part of contrition, when the people are to "make amends for their iniquity" (v. 41). The verb here is the same as that used in verse 34 for "enjoy its sabbath[s]." The notion of "satisfy" fits better here as well, but in the sense of "make satisfaction" for something (i.e., pay back or compensate for a wrong done). The text is completely ambiguous, however, about how the nation would "make amends."

The description of the Lord's reactions invites parallels with the Lord's salvific acts in previous events. The Lord promises to "remember my covenant" (vv. 42, 45; cf. Gen 9:15-16). The same statement explains God's actions in the exodus (Exod 2:24; 6:5). This would provide encouragement to exiles, as they would view a return from exile as a new exodus event. There are a couple of curious aspects to the reference to covenant here, though. The first reference is to the Abrahamic Covenant and the second reference is to the Sinai Covenant. It would be easy to attribute this to competing redactors, but it is more appropriate to see here a statement about the exodus as a fulfillment of God's promises to the ancestors (again, cf. Deut 8:18). This supports the notion that the Sinai Covenant is an extension or partner of the ancestral covenant. A second curiosity is the order of the references to the patriarchs. Other references start with Abraham and proceed forward chronologically. This one reverses the order and then adds "I will remember the land." The context suggests that "the land" here is Israel; but it could be that this intends to reflect the Genesis narrative in reverse, with "the land" referring to God's existing covenant with the whole earth (Gen 9:11-13). This perspective evokes a reminder that the covenant with the patriarchs entails a promise for the blessing of all the earth.

Finally, this closing section presents an intriguing contrast regarding divine retribution. The movement from Israel's sins to the Lord's punishment is extended by repeated references to the people's sins. The writer separates the acts of confession and penitence with a reminder that the people "continued hostile" to the Lord, and so "I . . . continued hostile to them" (vv. 40b-41a). This suggests a quid pro quo mentality in the Lord's dealings with his people. There is a different perspective on this in the recapitulation portion (vv. 43-45). The people have "spurned" the Lord's instructions and "abhorred" the Lord's laws, but the Lord promises not to "spurn" and "abhor" them while they are in exile. They have broken the covenant, but the Lord will "remember" the covenant. At the immediate level, this highlights the magnitude of their sins and the magnitude of the Lord's forgiveness, driving home the need for true contrition. At a broader level, this shows how the covenant involves more than a single generation. Exile comes as the culmination of multigenerational sin, but renewal reaches back even farther to encompass the entire history of the covenant relationship.

Theological and Ethical Analysis

The perspective of this chapter raises some "big picture" issues. For example, there are numerous connections between Leviticus and Ezekiel, but the multigenerational perspective on sin and punishment here seems to run contrary to the doctrine of individual culpability in Ezek 18. This contrast is heightened by Ezekiel's use of language from Leviticus in his list of sins that the Lord punishes (e.g., "cheat" in Lev 25:13-17; Ezek 18:7, 12, 16). The doctrine of individual culpability does not preclude Ezekiel from writing elsewhere about the corporate nature of the covenant in ways that parallel Leviticus (Ezek 34:25-31). What does run consistently between the two is the belief that the perpetuation of the covenant is dependent on the will of the Lord alone. The people "break" the covenant, and the Lord "maintains" the covenant.

Another "big picture" issue is the presence of parallels between this chapter and the closing sections of Deuteronomy. Deuteronomy calls for a public reading of the laws during the Feast of Booths in each sabbatical year (Deut 31:10). Leviticus makes no mention of this ceremony. Instead, Leviticus points to the Sabbath and a Sabbath-based rhythm of life as the mechanism for encouraging obedience. The absence of a narrative division between chapters 25 and 26 suggests a strong conceptual bond between the two chapters. Adherence to a conceptual framework based in Sabbath (chap. 25) is foundational to bringing one's life into line with the world as the Lord created and structured it, and resistance to the "statutes and ordinances and laws" of the Lord threatens expulsion from that world (i.e., the land; chap. 26).

This text also reaches back to Genesis. The language echoes that of the covenants with Abraham (Gen 17:4-8) and with Noah (Gen 9:1-15), but in some sense it supersedes them. This description of the land of the people who obey the Lord's commands paints in broad strokes a picture of the world moving toward its original, pristine state, a state that it enjoyed before there was a need for a chosen people and covenants. It is not perfect, but it is the best that any land can expect to become in the current age.

The terms of repentance are consistent with this supracovenant ideal (vv. 40-41). They anticipate confession of all sins, even those of one's ancestors, and unspecified (nonsacrificial) measures to compensate for their sins. They anticipate circumcision of the heart in a covenant whose identity is bound to circumcision (Gen 17). All this points to an undoing of what has gone wrong and a return to a former idyllic time.

In the face of these "big picture" issues, the reader must not lose sight of the immediate goal of this concluding chapter: to motivate obedience to the laws of the Lord. Typical for this genre, more is said here about punitive measures than positive inducements. The writer has realistic expectations. The human participants in this covenant will falter, even in the face of increasingly severe attempts by the Lord to correct their course. What is remarkable is the corresponding expectation of the Lord's faithfulness to the covenant. This stands in contrast to the usual bodies of blessings and curses that one finds in ancient Near Eastern treaties and law codes. Those involve straightforward matters of reward and punishment. The people live in a world that views life as a constant struggle between good and evil, an unending cycle of plenty and want, where gods rule like powerful warlords over disposable peasants. The view of life envisioned by Leviticus is more linear, considering the possibility of something different and better. A core element in this worldview is that there is a God who works to maintain a personal covenant relationship with God's people. This God is driven by a desire to walk and live among these people, not just rule over them. This God creates and maintains life for them and desires life with them. Humans access this life through obedience to this God's "statutes and ordinances and laws." Most remarkably, this God believes that such obedience is possible, that people can become better, that they can move beyond an unending struggle between good and evil to a place of good only. In the end, it is the author of this text who comes across as the realist about human life, and it is the Lord who is the idealist. Such optimism for humanity is part of the essence of "the LORD your God, who brought you out of the land of Egypt."

LEVITICUS 27

The final chapter of the book is a puzzle, simply because of its placement. It gives guidelines to priests for assessing the value of items that a layperson might donate to the cult. In some sense this amounts to rules for "supplementary income" for the priests. The text offers no rationale or motivation for bringing these gifts, it merely provides a means for assessing their financial value. Many regard this as an appendix, perhaps secondarily attached to the book. It presupposes the legislation of chapter 25, because it mentions the Jubilee year. Because the narrator has joined chapters 25 and 26, this chapter might have seemed out of order any place else. Jacob Milgrom cites four general explanations that scholars have offered, and the one he adopts has the most to commend it. He notes that the book begins with instructions for voluntary offerings. It makes some sense, then, to conclude the book with instructions regarding voluntary gifts for the sanctuary. It also complements the Sabbath year and Jubilee year instructions by bringing up ways that the people can honor the Lord at times other than those required by the religious calendar (Milgrom 2000b, 2408-9; cf. Hartley 1992, 479). The main theme in the chapter is that it is important to pay what one has vowed to the Lord. This serves as an implicit reminder to be zealous to fulfill all of one's covenant obligations.

Literary Analysis

The narrator brackets this final chapter in typical style. There is a common heading to introduce direct address (v. 1). The spoken heading identifies the recipients as "the people of Israel" (v. 2a; cf. the headings in chapters 23–26). The chapter summary places the giving of these instructions "on Mount Sinai," consistent with the narrative statements of the previous two chapters (27:34; cf. 25:1; 26:46). This summary identifies the contents of this chapter as "commandments," suggesting that these complement the "statutes and ordinances and laws" of the preceding chapters (26:46).

The bulk of the chapter consists of a string of "casuistic beads."

Virtually every verse begins with the conditional particle "(but) if." Each constitutes a separate case that the priests must evaluate. A combination of stylistic clues and contents points to a division into three groups:

Explicit Vows (vv. 2b-13)
    For a male (v. 3)
    For a female (v. 4)
    For persons between five and twenty years of age (v. 5)
    For infants less than five years of age (v. 6)
    For persons over sixty years of age (v. 7)
    For the destitute (v. 8)
    For sacrificial animals (vv. 9-10)
    For nonsacrificial animals (vv. 11-13)
Consecrating property (vv. 14-25)
    Houses (vv. 14-15)
    Inherited property (vv. 16-21)
    Purchased property (vv. 22-25)
Restricted items (vv. 26-33)
    Firstlings (vv. 26-27)
    Items devoted to destruction (vv. 28-29)
    Tithes (vv. 30-33)

The opening phrases in verses 2b and 14 mark those as primary cases ("When/If a person"). In between these, the initial subject and the type of action performed combine to call for a general distinction between verses 2b-8 ("a person [who] makes an explicit vow") and verses 9-13 ("an animal that may [not] be brought"). All are living things that are vowed to the Lord, and the distinction is between humans and all other living creatures. The second unit deals with different properties that one can "consecrate to the Lord" (vv. 14-25). Corresponding pairs of introductory phrases divide the final unit into the three subunits (vv. 26-33). The first and second subunits begin with the disjunctive particle "however" (the NRSV does not reflect the second instance), and the initial predicate echoes the root word of the subject ("a firstling . . . which as a firstling," v. 26; a "devoted thing" that has "been devoted,"

vv. 28 and 29). The third subunit carries a corresponding pair of introductory phrases to mark it off from what precedes ("All tithes," vv. 30 and 32). There is a consistent use of the third-person impersonal verb forms throughout the chapter.

Exegetical Analysis

Votive Offerings of Living Things (27:2-13)

There are several examples in the Old Testament of individuals pledging persons or objects "to the LORD" (also in the New Testament; Acts 18:18; 21:23). The most infamous is the case of Jephthah and his daughter (Judg 11:29-40); the vow of Hannah has a happier ending (1 Sam 1). A vow to the Lord is conditional, usually dependent on the Lord's positive response to an individual's request for divine help. Some vows are paid to the Lord in the form of a sacrifice; others are given to the priests, to help them fulfill their official responsibilities.

This text deals with two overlapping issues: determining the true "value" of a nonmonetary vow, and allowing for substitutions. Vows are often made at stressful times, so someone might wish to alter one's pledge after the distress has passed; but the nature of a vow (it is made to the Lord) makes the payment incumbent. Some assume that the vowing of persons originally implied human sacrifice, pointing to ancient Near Eastern examples and the case of Jephthah as proof. Jephthah's vow is very specific, though; he identifies in the vow the mode by which he will give to the Lord the one who greets him. The example of Hannah and Samuel is probably more typical (1 Sam 1:9-11, 21-28).

The first laws allow for monetary substitutions for persons so pledged. Persons are "assessed" according to age and gender. (The terms "equivalent," "assessment," and "assess" in this chapter derive from the same Hebrew root.) The fact that someone might be unable to afford the "equivalent" (v. 8) shows that monetary substitution was assumed. Some commentators contend that the price is high to discourage such vows, but others believe that these amounts reflect the "going price" for a human life (2 Kgs 15:20). Some propose that the difference between the valuations for male and female betrays an urban orientation, and there is some merit to that. The Levites did not receive a tribal allotment, but the Lord designated cities and their surrounding pasturelands for them instead (Num 35:1-8; Josh 21:1-42). This chapter places houses before fields (vv. 14-25), in contrast to the instructions for redemption (25:18-34). Perhaps these commandments speak more directly from a Levite's social orientation than previous chapters.

The instructions regarding animals assume the passage of time between the pledging of the vow and the payment of the vow. A change of heart (or fortunes) might prompt someone to bring an animal of lesser value. These instructions remind the people of the seriousness of their words. Any attempt to substitute for a sacrificial animal will result in the payment of both animals (v. 10; cf. v. 33). Some interpret the "unclean animal" designation in verse 11 as a reference to an animal that the priest declares to be blemished upon delivery. This does not conform to the distinctions set up earlier, though. Animals that are blemished can be eaten but not sacrificed (22:17-30), but "unclean" animals are species that cannot be used in sacrifice (chap. 11). Priests could still include such animals among their possessions and use them for nonsacrificial purposes (v. 27). Those bringing these animals could redeem them. Perhaps their economic situation has changed, or perhaps they expected a higher valuation for the animal (and a greater "value" in the eyes of the Lord for their gesture). In any case, if those bringing the animal decide now to redeem it, they must pay the full price for the animal plus 20 percent. These laws ascribe this "penalty" consistently for any vow that the individual decides to redeem (vv. 13, 15, 19, 31).

Offerings of Real Property (27:14-25)

It was possible to "consecrate" a house or a field. The same term can mean "sanctify," but it is clear that those consecrating the property are not in a position to sanctify; instead, they are designating something for sacred or priestly use. The text does not indicate how the priests would make use of these houses. They might inhabit them, or they might sell them and devote the funds to the sanctuary treasury. It is possible that this law applies only to houses inside a city (25:29-34).

The text differentiates between a field that is an "inherited land-holding" and a field that has been "bought." Some question whether the priests actually own the fields or just enjoy the income from them. The situation for inherited fields is not clarified until the Year of Jubilee, when the field becomes the property of the priests. The bought field reverts to its previous owner, for whom it was part of the family inheritance. The distinction arises because the latter individual did not choose to forfeit the inheritance rights when the property was sold. The text mentions an unredeemed inherited field that "has been sold to someone else" between the time it was consecrated and the Jubilee year (v. 20). What is unclear is who sold the field. If it is the priest, this exposes a loophole that the priests could use to their advantage. If it is the one who gave the land, there is no explanation of how someone has rights over land consecrated to the Lord. Some question whether the seed "assessment" refers to seed that will be planted or seed that will be harvested (v. 16), but the growing consensus seems to be the former. The valuation is a reflection of the cost of the investment, not an estimate of any profits the land might provide. A more practical question concerns who would work such a field. The priests are not allotted fields, but pasturelands; it is possible that they would not be expected to work these fields. Perhaps the donor provided workers, and the sanctuary enjoyed the produce; or perhaps this was a way for priests to come into possession of land.

Exceptions (27:26-33)

It is difficult to know how to correlate these exceptions with other passages on the same subjects. The first exception concerns "firstlings." It assumes that the firstborn of many (all?) animals carried this special designation, whether clean or unclean. The primary law on firstborn animals envisions only livestock and humans in this group, and humans and donkeys are to be redeemed (Exod 13:11-16; 34:19-20; cf. Deut 12:6, 17; 14:23). This law prohibits redemption of sacrificial animals (see vv. 9-10), but it does not explain why they are to identify the firstborn of unclean animals (Num 18:15-17).

Similar questions arise regarding persons and things "devoted to destruction." The laws refer only to the imposition of bans imposed during war (Deut 20:16-18; Josh 6:17-18) or as a result of covenant infidelity (Exod 22:20; Deut 7:26; 13:12-18; Ezra 10:8). This passage speaks of persons, livestock, and ancestral landholdings that are devoted to destruction, but it does not explain how they came to have this designation. Perhaps the devoted things have been acquired in war, and the possessor is now trying to find a way to keep them. If so, the message is that the Lord cannot be bribed to compromise.

The final law concerns tithes, where there are significant inconsistencies with parallel laws. This law calls for tithing of grain, fruit, and livestock. This is the only law that mentions the tithing of herds. It implies that the tithes are given voluntarily and that they will go to the priests alone. Numbers 18:21-32 is similar, but it does not mention animals and it gives other details. Deuteronomy 14:22-26 gives a different picture. There, tithing is mandatory and annual for harvested goods, and the persons who bring the tithes are to consume them at the sanctuary. Other instructions order that tithes be set aside in storehouses every third year for feeding the Levites, aliens, orphans, and widows (Deut 14:27-29; 26:12-15). The few historical references to tithing in the Old Testament are only suggestive. Two passages in Nehemiah mention grain tithes that are stored in the Temple (Neh 10:35-37; 13:10-13). The Chronicler provides information regarding tithes during a time of rededication to the Lord under Hezekiah. The text records that the people from the nation gave tithes from their fields, but there is also a note about tithes of cattle and sheep coming from those living in the cities (2 Chr 31:4-10). Perhaps this is another clue that Lev 27 speaks from an urban perspective.

Theological and Ethical Analysis

One can read this chapter from two perspectives. One perspective sees in this a call to provide for those who serve and minister on the Lord's behalf. Israel's priests live in a society that is based on agriculture. Those with land have financial security, and those without land are at risk. In this environment it is significant that the Lord allots no land to the priests. They are dependent on others to provide their financial security. These commandments implicitly encourage the people to fulfill their obligations to provide this security. If they do not do so, then nothing that has been prescribed before in the book can be accomplished. Modern priests and ministers often face similar risks. It is important that others provide them with the necessary means to be secure.

From another perspective, this chapter is a call to genuine worship. The laws concern voluntary offerings. The people bring them out of the goodness of their hearts. They should fulfill these voluntary obligations with the utmost integrity. The laws assume that the people might try to maximize the benefit of worship while minimizing the cost. These laws call them to wholehearted worship, to fulfill the spirit of the law and not just the letter of the law. If they make this their attitude with voluntary commitments, then they will be more likely to adopt the same attitude with mandatory obligations. This will spur them on to be truly holy as the Lord their God is holy.

ANNOTATED BIBLIOGRAPHY

Balentine, Samuel E. 2002. *Leviticus*. Interpretation. Louisville: John Knox. —Balentine writes his commentary primarily with Christian preachers and teachers in mind, with more emphasis than most on the ethical and theological dimensions of the text.

Brichto, Herbert C. 1976. "On Slaughter and Sacrifice, Blood and Atonement." *Hebrew Union College Annual* 47:19–56. —Brichto addresses two questions: the meaning of "atone," and the sequencing of biblical strata concerning centralization of the cult. He argues that "atone" implies the payment of "composition," not giving a ransom. The major literary strata (P, H, and D) probably emerged and developed simultaneously, rather than sequentially.

Budd, Philip J. 1996. *Leviticus*. The New Century Bible Commentary. Grand Rapids: Eerdmans. —Budd's historical-critical commentary emphasizes an inherent ambiguity in the laws of Leviticus, reflecting the complexities of life.

Douglas, Mary. 1999. *Leviticus as Literature*. New York: Oxford University Press. —Douglas proposes that Leviticus is constructed symbolically in imitation of the Tabernacle. The ritual laws point to the compassion and justice of the Lord.

Gane, Roy. 2005. *Cult and Character: Purification Offerings, Day of Atonement, and Theodicy*. Winona Lake, Ind.: Eisenbrauns. —Gane provides extensive argumentation to substantiate Milgrom's thesis regarding the Day of Atonement ritual. It is the second phase of a two-part process involving purgation and forgiveness of the offender, and then purgation of the sanctuary and cleansing of the people.

Gerstenberger, Erhard S. 1996. *Leviticus*. Translated by Douglas W. Stott. Old Testament Library. Louisville: Westminster John Knox. —Gerstenberger supplies a thoroughgoing historical-critical analysis, proceeding from the assumption that the book is the work of a post-exilic priestly school.

Gilders, William K. 2004. *Blood Ritual in the Hebrew Bible: Meaning and Power*. Baltimore: Johns Hopkins University Press. —Gilders approaches the issue of blood manipulation in Old Testament sacrifice from the perspective of ritual studies. He argues that this act "indexes" worship participants, indicating their relative status according to who handles sacrificial blood, where they handle it, and how they handle it.

Gorman, Frank H., Jr. 1990. *The Ideology of Ritual: Space, Time and Status in the Priestly Theology*. Journal for the Study of the Old Testament Supplement Series 91. Sheffield: Sheffield Academic. —Gorman lays out the Priestly understanding of the world as a well-ordered structure. He describes the Priestly theology in terms of a tripartite worldview (cosmos, society, cult), rituals for establishing and maintaining a system of opposing categories (e.g., holy/profane, life/death), and conceptualizations of these in terms of space, time, and status.

Harrison, R. K. 1980. *Leviticus: An Introduction and Commentary*. Downers Grove, Ill.: InterVarsity. —Harrison interprets the laws of Leviticus in terms of how they provide spiritual foundations for understanding Christian doctrine.

Hartley, John E. 1992. *Leviticus*. Word Biblical Commentary. Dallas: Word. —Hartley gives a careful and detailed analysis of the text from a conservative scholarly point of view.

Hayes, John H. Atonement in the Book of Leviticus. *Interpretation* 52 (1998): 5-15. —Hayes understands sin as a force that damages relationships and contaminates the sanctuary. The atoning sacrifices in Leviticus are the final stage in a fourfold process that restores right relationships between the offender and victim and between the offender and God, and—on the Day of Purgation—that purges the sanctuary of uncleanness.

Hertz, J. H. 1936. *Leviticus*. The Pentateuch and Haftorahs. London: Oxford University Press. —Hertz provides his commentary primarily for a modern Jewish audience, but he draws on Jewish and non-Jewish resources to inform his comments.

Houston, Walter. 1993. *Purity and Monotheism: Clean and Unclean Animals in Biblical Law*. Journal for the Study of the Old Testament Supplement Series 140. Sheffield: Sheffield Academic. —Houston analyzes Lev 11 and Deut 14 with a social scientific approach, arguing that the absolutizing of Old Testament dietary laws parallels a shift from monolatry to monotheism in Israelite thought.

Jenson, Philip Peter. 1992. *Graded Holiness: A Key to the Priestly Conception of the World.* Journal for the Study of the Old Testament Supplement Series 106. Sheffield: Sheffield Academic. —Jenson utilizes a "conceptual approach" to Priestly texts concerning cultic matters. This reveals an ordering of the world according to graduated levels of (un)holiness, which he sees as being developed along four dimensions: space, persons, ritual, and time.

Joosten, Jan. 1996. *People and Land in the Holiness Code: An Exegetical Study of the Ideational Framework of the Law in Leviticus 17–26.* Supplements to Vetus Tetamentum 67. Leiden: Brill. —Joosten focuses attention on references to "people" and "land" in Lev 17–26. He concludes that this paraenetic block confronts a pre-exilic audience with religious and social obligations, based primarily on the covenant relationship established by the Lord with the people of Israel in the exodus from Egypt.

Kiuchi, N. 1987. *The Purification Offering in the Priestly Literature: Its Meaning and Function.* Journal for the Study of the Old Testament Supplement Series 56. Sheffield: Sheffield Academic. —Kiuchi confirms the understanding of "purification offering" (rather than "sin offering") for the *hattat* rituals prescribed (primarily) in Leviticus 4–5. A major challenge is to explain the need for purification of the sanctuary (Lev 16).

Klawans, Jonathan. 2000. *Impurity and Sin in Ancient Judaism.* New York: Oxford University Press. —Klawans argues that biblical laws in Leviticus assume a clear separation between ritual impurity (temporary contagion caused by contact, usually natural and unavoidable) and moral impurity (long-term contagion caused by sinful activity). He then traces out conceptual developments in regard to impurity in Second Temple Judaism and early Christianity.

Knohl, Israel. 1995. *The Sanctuary of Silence: The Priestly Torah and the Holiness School.* Minneapolis: Fortress. —Knohl reverses the usual theories about the literary growth of the legal material in the Tetrateuch. A "Priestly Torah" emerged in the centuries between the construction of Solomon's Temple and Assyrian incursions (8th century), and the "Holiness School" expanded and redacted this during the period of Assyrian hegemony.

Levine, Baruch A. 1989. *Leviticus.* JPS Torah Commentary. Philadelphia: The Jewish Publication Society. —Levine adopts the mainstream scholarly view of the complicated literary development of

Leviticus, yet he presents its contents as a realistic reflection of priestly practices and beliefs at the time of the composition of its various sources and redactions.

McCarthy, Dennis J. 1969. "The Symbolism of Blood and Sacrifice." *Journal of Biblical Literature* 88:166–76. —McCarthy examines ancient Near Eastern evidence concerning sacrifice and concludes that the Israelite emphasis on blood is unusual in that culture.

Milgrom, Jacob. 1991. *Leviticus 1–16*. Anchor Bible 3. New York: Doubleday. —Milgrom's massive three-volume commentary (see Milgrom 2000a and 2000b) provides the results of a long career of study on the book of Leviticus. Its 2,700 pages of translation, commentary, excursi (including responses in later volumes to criticisms of the first volume), bibliographies, and indexes offer a wealth of information for students of all levels.

_____. 2000a. *Leviticus 17–22*. Anchor Bible 3A. New York: Doubleday. —See Milgrom 1991.

_____. 2000b. *Leviticus 23–27*. Anchor Bible 3B. New York: Doubleday. —See Milgrom 1991.

Noth, Martin. 1965. *Leviticus, a Commentary*. Translated by J. E. Anderson. Old Testament Library. Philadelphia: Westminster. —Noth utilizes his skills in source-redaction and tradition history to reconstruct the development of the book, composed of late pre-exilic priestly legislation that has been redacted together and placed within a post-exilic Priestly narrative.

Rendtorff, Rolf, and Robert A. Kugler, eds. 2003. *The Book of Leviticus: Composition and Reception*. Supplements to Vetus Testamentum 93. Leiden: Brill. —This constitutes a collection of twenty-two essays addressing the "prehistory, contents, and themes" of Leviticus.

Sawyer, John F. A. 1996. *Reading Leviticus: A Conversation with Mary Douglas*. Journal for the Study of the Old Testament Supplement Series 227. Sheffield: Sheffield Academic. —These colloquium essays reflect a renewed appreciation for the teachings of Leviticus among scholars of the Hebrew Bible, Second Temple Judaism, and the New Testament, as that appreciation has been generated by the ideas of Mary Douglas.

Schearing, Linda S. 2003. Double Time . . . Double Trouble? Gender, Sin, and Leviticus 12. Pages 429-50 in *The Book of Leviticus: Composition and Reception*. Edited by Rolf Rendtorff and Robert A. Kugler. —Supplements to Vetus Testamentum 93. Leiden: Brill.

Schearing provides a brief historical overview of interpretations of the law on impurity and childbirth (Lev 12).

Wenham, Gordon J. 1979. *The Book of Leviticus*. New International Commentary on the Old Testament. Grand Rapids: Eerdmans. —Wenham's commentary brings together comparisons of Israelite ritual and law with those of other ancient Near Eastern peoples, the insights of social anthropologists, and "new literary criticism" to interpret the book. He presents all of this with the modern Christian pastor/minister in mind, searching for the more abiding theological meaning underlying these instructions.

Wright, David P. 1987. *The Disposal of Impurity: Elimination Rites in the Bible and in Hittite and Mesopotamian Literature*. Society of Biblical Literature Dissertation Series 101. Atlanta: Scholars Press. —Wright turns to Akkadian and Hittite texts to illuminate the distinctive characteristics of biblical laws and rituals concerning (im)purity and purification.